THE CYCLE OF LIFE

A FIFTEEN-YEAR COAST-TO-COAST JOURNEY -
ONE-ON-ONE TIME AND SHARING STORIES

GREG SCOTT

"Apparently there is nothing that cannot happen today."
– Mark Twain

For all the thoughtful draft reviews by some wonderful people - thanks Cindy, Brad, Marg, Pam, Lana, Wendell, Karen, Mark, Mike, Cori, Hali.

The Cycle Of Life
Copyright © 2024 by Greg Scott

All rights reserved. No part of this publication may be reproduced, distributed, or transmitted in any form or by any means, including photocopying, recording, or other electronic or mechanical methods, without the prior written permission of the author, except in the case of brief quotations embodied in critical reviews and certain other non-commercial uses permitted by copyright law.

Tidbits of Change Foundation
www.tidbitsofchange.org

Cover Illustration by Mick Scott
Designed by Alberto Bastasa

Tellwell Talent
www.tellwell.ca

ISBN
978-0-2288-4692-5 (Hardcover)
978-0-2288-4691-8 (Paperback)
978-0-2288-4693-2 (eBook)

To every parent who has thought about doing something one-on-one with their kids ... don't wait.
To my family and friends over the years who I have ridden a ski lift with, sat beside around a campfire, or shared a laugh with in a hockey locker room - thanks for all the stories and phenomenal tidbits in life.

And to Buddy ... already looking forward to what we're doing together next year.

IT'S HOW FAR TO NEWFOUNDLAND?

Time can fly by as a parent. The milestone of my son Buddy turning ten years old caught me off-guard in a "whoa, when did that happen?" kind-of-way. A week prior to his birthday, I was daydreaming on a drive home from work on a scorching summer day. My mind's eye had me cruising in a sports car with the windows down, tunes blaring, and completely carefree about where I was headed. I was in a minivan. I remember it as the first time wrestling with how speedy a decade can sneak past.

Buddy is my son's nickname. I've called him that since he gazed up with his big probing blue eyes at me and my wife Pam in the delivery room, and I whispered, "Hey there Buddy." A never-before-felt surge of joy engulfed me when I held him for the first time. The rest of the world seemed to rotate around us.

Why was Buddy's tenth birthday such a gulp moment for me? I had been cherishing my dad time with him and his younger sister Hali, but that birthday got me antsy about how much more I wanted to do as a parent. It prompted realization that our kids would no doubt be finding more *why-in-the-world-would-we-want-our-parents-involved* interests. I took it as a reminder to not get so caught up in the endless web of routine parenting details that I simply missed opportunities that were in plain sight right in front of me.

In my younger years, I felt I had a knack for being ready for adventure. It led to some amazing—sometimes crazy—experiences. But after ten years in the parenting game, I wondered if I had lost any of my free-wheeling spirit. I hoped I hadn't become susceptible to parent-zombie walking right past potential moments or falling into a trap of seeking out experiences only in the safest of places.

With Buddy turning ten years old and me being forty, I didn't want to blink to see another decade gone by and staring into a rear-view mirror at a pile of lost opportunities. One of my son's birthday cards hit home with a quote from Mark Twain.

> *Twenty years from now you will be more disappointed by the things you didn't do than by the ones you did do. So throw off the bowlines. Sail away from the safe harbor. Catch the trade winds in your sails. Explore. Dream. Discover.*

Twain's words stuck in my head. They poured life into an idea I had been toying with about finding something unique I could do, one-on-one, with each of my kids. Some spirited adventure where I could give each of them my undivided attention and maybe something they could embrace as their own personal time with their dad, me.

I figured I had a little more time to come up with something for my daughter. She was only five. But Buddy was now sporting double digits. I didn't want to waste time or fall victim to that all-too-common predicament of getting lost in ideas and not acting on any. I set myself a deadline to have a fully baked plan for no later than to be a gift on his eleventh birthday.

I filtered through all sorts of potential adventures. We could explore little discovered parts of the world! We could solve unsolvable mysteries! Maybe we could learn something new together.

It sounded good, right? But it proved tougher than I thought to pin down just the right idea.

Then one night, I was out with my life-long buddy Wendell and we were reminiscing about some of our favourite adventures (and mischief) that we had revelled in (and survived). We were laughing about an event-filled bicycle trip we had in rural Cuba and a one-of-a-kind bike journey we took through the mountains from the Okanagan Valley to Vancouver for World Expo, when a light bulb popped on for me.

I wanted to bike with Buddy across Canada, from coast to coast.

The idea immediately checked off a bunch of boxes. It was big, adventurous, challenging. It also raised daunting questions. How old would Buddy have to be to tackle such a huge trip? Could we handle a seven-plus-thousand-kilometre slog? How would we work around his school? How much time would I need to take off work? If I waited until he was older, would we both be able to arrange a few months at the same time? How old would I be then? The unknowns mounted, but I was adamant to not let them dispirit me. I kept returning to a desire to get going on something before my boy wasn't a boy anymore.

It took a few months of mulling over possibilities, but then came my eureka moment—I would make it an annual dad-and-son adventure. We would start on the west coast and cycle east for as many days as my young son could manage. Wherever we ended up stopping would become our starting point for the subsequent year. Each annual trip serving as a benchmark, kind of like what a birthday does, and together, bit by bit, we would make our way across the continent.

Everything about the concept felt incredibly right. The yearly one-on-one time had me fired up. The coast-to-coast aspect seemed such a Canadian thing to do too.

For a surprise on the morning of Buddy's eleventh birthday, he and I jumped on our bikes for a short ride to a café. We ordered hot chocolates and found a small table in the corner with two high-backed chairs. Buddy thought the bike ride for drinks was his special treat. I leaned in and laid out my big idea about cycling to Newfoundland. He sat up and looked at me like I had suggested we bike to the moon. Then he started to squirm around in his chair with excitement as I laid out how we would tackle it in sections each year. I explained how we would start by dipping our bike tires in the Pacific Ocean—ride through ten provinces together—then dip our tires again in the Atlantic Ocean. Buddy asked how long it would take. I answered him as truthfully as I could. I had no idea. My plan looked something like this:

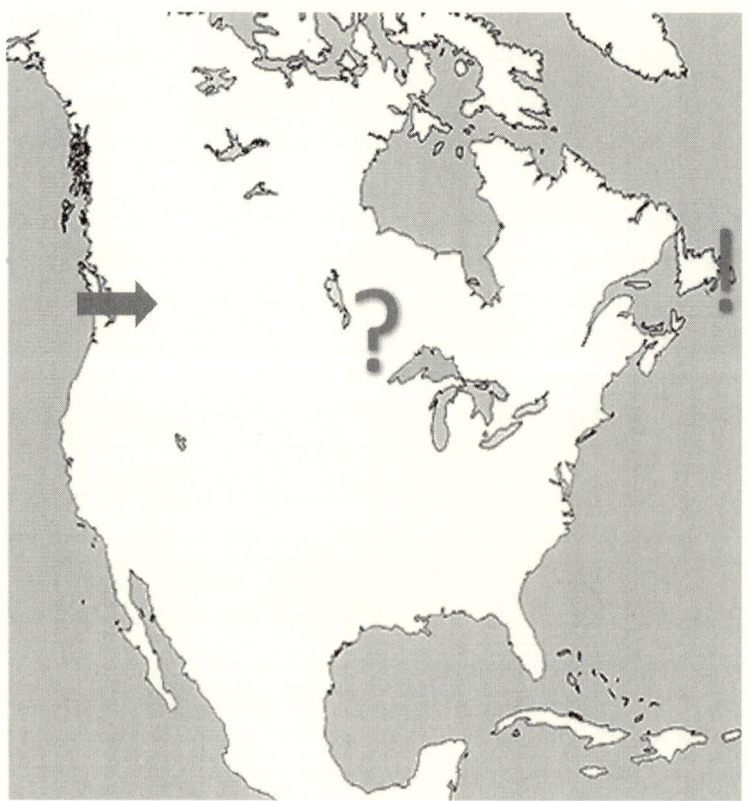

Buddy was unfazed by my lack of detail. He was hooked and as excited as I was.

I took out two journal notebooks from my backpack and gave one to him. I suggested it might be cool if we both kept track of all the moments we experienced together. Things like crossing five and a half time zones, riding over mountain ranges and across the prairies, passing through small towns and big cities. I figured we would find out some amazing things and lesser-known details about our country. But what would we learn about each other? About ourselves?

"Hey, Buddy," I said, talking fast, "maybe we could swap our journals when we get to the Atlantic?"

I admit that I found the thought of me keeping a journal somewhat amusing. I had barely kept notes at school or university. Nonetheless, I was determined to give it my best. I was convinced there would be plenty worth capturing as we rode across Canada. It also crossed my mind that I would have found it fascinating to have known a little bit about what was going through my own parents' minds when I was younger. So, wouldn't it be good if I could do that for Buddy?

The easy part was done: telling my son what we were going to do. Now I had to make it happen.

What if we didn't make it all the way or didn't like it? If life got in the way? Or if Buddy got tired of biking with his dad? Or just plain tired of me in general? One thing I was sure was that we wouldn't find out anything if we didn't start. As Wayne Gretzky professed, "You miss 100% of the shots you don't take."

And so it began—a dad and son adventure that we affectionately dubbed *The Cycle of Life*.

YEAR ONE –
Buddy 11 Years Old

A TINY BIKE AND A PANNIER FULL OF QUESTIONS

Starting out from the docks of the glorious Inner Harbour in Victoria, B.C. As our trip neared, my mind flooded with questions. How would Buddy handle the trip? How would I? How far could Buddy's little legs pedal this first year? How would we deal with traffic? Was I crazy for starting this adventure when Buddy was only eleven? I mean, I could still pick him up under one arm.

But apart from the questions, and more importantly, I was beyond excited.

Our family had recently moved to Hornby Island on the inland side of Vancouver Island. It had a full-time population of about a thousand, which soared to ten thousand in the summer. Prior to making that family lifestyle decision we had lived in Calgary for an eight-year stretch while I had been President of the Alberta Alpine Ski Association and doing business and sponsorship development for Alpine Canada Alpin and the National Ski Team.

From Hornby Island, we had two ferries and a two-and-a-half-hour drive to get to Victoria on the southern tip of Vancouver Island. We had decided to start our cycling journey there, in the capital of B.C., home to Mile Zero of the Trans Canada Highway.

That morning, Buddy jumped up like a rabbit into the back of our pick-up truck and I passed our bikes up to him. Then all of us, my wife Pam and our daughter Hali included, loaded into the vehicle for our drive south. They were coming along to see us off safely and start us off right.

We began our father and son cross-country biking adventure on a radiant July summer day, with crystal clear skies and tiny diamonds of sunshine dancing across Victoria's Inner Harbour. We rolled our bikes along the boardwalk in front of the iconic, ivy-covered Empress Hotel and the oxidized green-copper domes of the majestic provincial legislative buildings. Morning water taxis, cruise ships, yachts, ferries, and kayaks all scurried about. And float planes too. With more than a hundred take-offs and landings per day, the Inner Harbour of Victoria had become one of the busiest water airports anywhere in the world.

Buddy pulled on a sweatshirt and giggled when his head got stuck in the arm hole. I safety pinned a reflective ribbon on his shirt-back and he wrapped a few more around his arms and legs. We both put on our helmets, bike gloves, and sunglasses. I slipped on a bright safety vest and then hung my pannier saddle bags on the back wheel of my Trek mountain bike. I was carrying a few days of clothing for us both, basic bike repair tools, a water-proof sleeve for my phone and wallet, sandwiches, six granola bars, two apples, and a huge bag of trail mix with oodles of chocolate chips. I always said that a trail with chocolate chips sounded better than one without, right? Attached to the frame of my bike was a red Nalgene water bottle and my old bike pump to fix flat tires, which we hoped we would not get. We didn't pack a tent as we were keeping things simple our first year and planning to stay in motels and maybe even one night with our friends in Burnaby, just outside of Vancouver.

Buddy was adamant about sharing our load. So, on the back of his red and black flamed Specialized Hotrock BMX, which only came halfway up my thigh, was one of those small racks that suspend straight out from the seat post. He strapped on a black day pack filled with a few snacks, a map, a bike wrench, a spare ball cap, and sunscreen. He was particularly keen on carrying a wrench so that *he* could fix our bikes in case they broke down.

"Where you guys headed?" a fellow getting off his boat asked.

Buddy and I looked at each other and smiled. "Newfoundland!"

The guy did a double take at Buddy's bike and looked at us as if we were off our rockers. I wondered if maybe he was right considering the bike looked like it was meant for riding around a neighbourhood, not the set of wheels to be starting a cross-continent bike trip with.

Then together, side-by-side, father and son, we walked our bikes onto one of the docks in the harbour. Our tires strummed over the wood planks and gaps and sounded like a slow-moving train at the beginning of a journey. Pam and Hali were close on our heels, snapping pictures and encouraging us with moral support. Hali, five years Buddy's junior, had been crawling over us all morning and was hilariously just as pumped up as we were. At the dock's end, Buddy and I bumped fists with gusto. We held our bikes over the edge and carefully dipped our front tires into the clear, dark blue Pacific Ocean. Pam had to hold herself back from helping Buddy with his bike from her fear of him toppling over and plunking himself and his bike in the harbour.

With our tires ceremoniously christened, we were ready to roll. I smiled at Buddy and will never forget him taking off his sunglasses and beaming back at me, his eyes wide with sparkles of anticipation. Until that day, the farthest he had ever biked was around our home neighbourhoods. I'm sure he had no idea of what to expect on our ride. And I was right there with him with that thought.

After a few last hugs and good luck kisses from our send-off duo, Buddy and I jumped on our bikes and started kilometre one of our journey to Newfoundland.

Together, we proudly rode out of the harbour, glancing over our shoulders to see Pam and Hali wildly waving and shouting out cheers. "It is going to be fun dipping our tires in the Atlantic," Buddy said before they were out of view.

To stay off major roads and city streets as much as possible, Buddy and I crossed over the Johnson Street Bridge, then followed the Galloping Goose bike trail out of Victoria. Sun shimmered through the trees and lined our path. Buddy was amped up and pedalling fast, his little legs going up and down like jack hammers. Like eleven-year-olds do, he would pump furiously for a minute or so, then coast to nearly a standstill, and then pedal like mad all over again.

I followed behind, avoiding rocks and cracks in the pavement while Buddy bunny-hopped obstacles or steered directly over them. For a moment I thought to warn him about puncturing a tire, but he was having too much fun.

"Just go with it," I whispered instead.

We weren't out to set any speed records. I mean, what did I expect? He was eleven. Sticks, stones, garbage—anything he could run over—was a potential target. Flattened pop cans were big bonus items. If Buddy missed one, he sometimes circled back to hit it with both tires. *Thwack, thwack.*

"Got it!" he would yell.

To compound the fact that he had to pedal twice as much as I did with his smaller wheels, he was travelling twice the distance as I was with all his little detours and circle backs.

Setting out from Victoria meant we were getting our journey underway from below the 49th parallel. It was hard to imagine that the southern portion of Vancouver Island had almost been negotiated to be part of the United States. In 1846, when the Oregon Treaty established the 49th parallel as the southern border of western Canada, Vancouver Island in its entirety was singled out as the exception. Dealings between Britain and the United States nearly set the border along the Columbia River, which would have put most of what eventually became the state of Washington in Canada. Instead, the British put priority on keeping Vancouver Island intact rather than trading away its southern portion to the United States. Big-time trades like that often have ripple effects. Turned out that in players to be named later in that deal, Canada lost out on Seattle-born Jimi Hendrix, but we picked up southern Vancouver Island's Pamela Anderson, one of Canada's 'Centennial Babies', born exactly on the nation's 100th birthday in 1967.

Buddy and I rode for over three hours to get to Swartz Bay, outside of Sidney, where we were to catch a ferry across the Strait of Georgia to mainland B.C. I was feeling good about our pace overall, but still had a lingering question about whether we would be able to keep this up year after year. Had I promised more than I could keep? It's strange how doubt and fear have a way of creeping into your thoughts sometimes. Jim Carrey once said, "Don't ever let fear turn you against your playful heart." Good words. I told myself that I did not have room to carry fear on my bike anyway; my panniers were full.

At the ferry terminal, we were greeted with a summer message that people living in British Columbia are all too familiar with, a two-sailing wait. About twenty-two million passengers and eight million vehicles are transported on BC Ferries every year, so it shouldn't be surprising they sometimes get backed up. But grumbling about the ferries is something that has woven its way into the coastal fabric. The sentiment goes all the way back to the late 1950s when strikes at Canadian Pacific Ferries completely stranded Vancouver Island. It prompted the Victoria Chamber of Commerce to push for a series of tunnels and bridges to be built between the Island and Anacortes, Washington, for a proposed sum of $25 million. The provincial government stepped in and created BC Ferries in 1960. Then followed that up by taking over five ships, seven terminals & land, and American Black Ball Ferries routes between the Canadian mainland and Vancouver Island for a grand total of $6.7 million. Turned out to be a heckuva deal; it would involve a few more zeroes to get the deal done today.

Fortunately, being on bikes, we didn't have to wait out the two-sail wait. Buddy was strutting tall when he pushed his little bike to the front of the long lines of cars and then walked up the ramp before them all to board the ferry.

I was looking forward to the hour and a half crossing as it gave us a nice stint off our bikes.

"Keep your eyes peeled for *Beachcombers*," I said as our ship left the dock. "Bruno Gerussi and Relic might be out there somewhere."

"Who?" said Buddy. Sadly, from a Canadian point of view, he had no idea who I was talking about.

"Ok, maybe we'll spot the *SS Minnow* of *Gilligan's Island* fame," I tried again and pointing out that the actual three-hour tour ship used on the TV series had been relocated and now called Canada home at its berth in Vancouver Island's Nanoose Bay.

Perhaps more sadly, from a Canadian point of view, Buddy did know who Gilligan was.

B.C. has an incredible 27,000 kilometres of spectacular coastline. Our cruise across the Strait of Georgia, through narrow channels around the southern Gulf Islands, gave us a beautiful sampling. No *Beachcombers* to be seen, but Buddy spotted three sleek orca whales popping in and out of the water. I don't know where he learned it, but he informed me that they are among the most widely distributed mammals on the planet and exist in every ocean in the world. The kid knew a lot of stuff at eleven years old. Pam and I have always known we needed to be on our toes with Buddy. We clued in when he was only two years old and was inquiring about the possibility of the government cancelling bedtime.

Our ferry pulled into Tsawwassen, 35 kilometres south of Vancouver, in the late afternoon. We pushed our bikes off the ramp and onto mainland B.C. It started to sprinkle rain, which wasn't a shocker considering Vancouver gets 192 rainy days on average a year.

The Tsawwassen Ferry Terminal is huge, the largest in North America. It sits on an artificial island that is almost 57 acres. We had to bike a three-kilometre-long causeway before if felt like we had reached the actual mainland. I tailed Buddy and by the time we got off the causeway, I could tell we were ready to wrap up our adrenaline-packed day. I called ahead to the Tsawwassen Inn to book a room for the night. I thought it would be fun to have something special to mark the completion of our first day, so I asked about ordering a congratulatory dessert in advance through room service. The front desk clerk kindly told me that her husband was picking up a fresh blueberry pie from nearby Richlea Bakery and suggested I order one too. She convinced me it would be one of the best pies we would ever eat.

We rolled into the motel feeling accomplished. We had tallied 43 kilometres and our journey had begun. We checked in and our pie was waiting. We pulled our bikes right into our room, sat on our beds, and polished off the entire pie while we recapped our day.

"This pie is so, so, so yummy," Buddy mumbled, his mouth half-stuffed and his lips tinged blue.

I didn't know if it was due to extra robust appetites from cycling or all the excitement of getting our journey underway, but we were both wowed from the first bite. Buddy thought the bakery deserved a provincial award. We fell back on our beds and decided that pie was indeed a good thing.

I pulled my journal out of a dry bag with the idea of capturing the unabated joy I was feeling. Words seemed too clumsy to do that though.

I had to admit that I had started to enjoy the journaling process. Prior to our trip, I even went as far as jotting down a few stories about my past with ambitions to share them with Buddy along our way while we biked. I thought of my own parents and how little I really knew about them. I knew the generic - where they grew up, where they met, what they did for work information. But the really good stuff? Like their screw ups? Dreams? Fears? What really made them tick? I wish I knew more of those things. Maybe as parents we don't think to tell stories about ourselves to our kids because they don't ask. And as kids we don't think to ask our parents to tell us stories until sometimes it's too late. I thought of myself open with my kids, but also wondered if had only been sharing my resume material too. Revealing more meaningful stories had to be worthwhile, didn't it? I decided to take the initiative to do that with Buddy during our adventure. At the very least, I reckoned that telling him about some of my own gaffes growing up could create some valuable learning moments, or at least a shared laugh.

That first night on the trip, the timing seemed right to give it a go. As Buddy curled up under his covers eagerly anticipating my tale, I did my best to impress him about a time I took a dangerous expedition to a mysterious fortress.

Fatherly Advice On Surviving Torture

It was when I was five years old.
Buddy giggled.
I told him how, leading up to Grade One, I had imagined school to be a mystical place where kids gathered and magical things happened all day long. I had been under the impression that as soon as I got to school, my astronaut training would officially be underway. I suspected something awry on my first morning when I had not escaped gravity, not once. But the day was not a complete loss because I met a kid named Gordon who was literally twice my height. We confirmed it by having Gordon lay down in the courtyard. I drew a chalk outline of his body and I fit in it exactly twice when I lay down. We both considered that magical—maybe not quite anti-gravity chamber level stuff, but remarkable nonetheless. The chalk experiment ended up looking like a crime scene investigation, but it proved our theory that I was indeed a very short kid and Gordon was pretty darn tall.

My first year of school life took a fantastic turn on a cold Alberta prairie Monday morning in mid-January. An incredible marvel of architecture had appeared in the school field over the weekend—a magnificent snow fort. Our minds were bursting all morning, daydreaming about what might lie behind the igloo-like entrance.

As recess loomed, Gordon the Giant and I carefully devised our plan to beat every other kid to be the first inside. Gordon blocked the school exit with his massive wingspan, while I utilized my small stature to squirm through the doors before anyone else. I darted across the field and did a headfirst dive into the small opening of the snow fortress, but my feet stuck out.

"Get in there!" Gordon yelled.

He gave me a big shove and scrambled in behind. We were in. And there was no room for anyone else, which might put a little perspective on what a grand fortress looks like to a kid in grade one.

Every other kid tried to squeeze a peek inside, even Stephanie, the self-appointed teacher's pet. Gordon and I were in kid heaven, like someone had served us chocolate cake for breakfast. No one could enter our snow lair and we were not about to come out.

The end of recess bell rang. Gordon and I grinned at each other.

"Don't tell them where we are!" we yelled from the opening at the boots running by.

"You guys are gonna get it," scolded Stephanie.

We basked in the glow of our accomplishment for five triumphant minutes until Mrs. Keeley trudged towards our fort with twenty kids hollering out the class windows, "They're going to stay in there forever!"

When Mrs. Keeley arrived she seemed moody, which was disappointing in that we considered her to be our first official guest. Her attitude emboldened us though. We bunkered down.

Try as she might, Mrs. Keeley could not reach in far enough to get a hold of us. We cherished the structural engineer who had built our magical, impenetrable kingdom. We were defeating the establishment and convinced that we could stay in there forever.

And then came Mr. Lynn, the school principal.

Unfortunately, this occurred before *the strap* was abolished from schools. The stories of Mr. Lynn's strap were legendary. They echoed down the halls of our school with his every step.

By the time Mr. Lynn reached our fortress, our resolve had started to dwindle. He arrived looking like J. Jonah Jamieson, Peter Parker's boss from Spiderman, with puffs of steam escaping out the neck of his sharply starched white shirt and grey suit. By the time his foot came through the wall of our snow fortress (also bringing into question the actual structural integrity of our fort that we had earlier heralded), the fear of *the strap* replaced every jovial thought we had entertained regarding the never-ending recess. By the time we were planted on the bench outside Mr. Lynn's office, after being grabbed by the scruffs of our winter jackets like disobedient puppies and hauled across the school yard, my palm felt like it was already swelling up from the mere thought of our impending torture. My hopes of becoming an astronaut seemed lost.

My five-year-old pain threshold maxed out that day.

Removed from Mr. Lynn's torture chamber, Gordon and I with our tear-streaked faces were unceremoniously deposited back into our classroom. There were no cheers upon our return. No accolades about our revolution or defiance—just a bunch of shocked kids silently staring at our red puffy eyes, and Stephanie with an *I told you so* Cheshire Cat grin.

The incident raised profound concerns for me on the Canadian penal system, but as a hardened criminal I bit my tongue and lay low for a full two weeks. Then came a day when a couple of junior high kids from the neighbouring school recruited an army of us elementary school kids to roll a giant snowball onto the street beside our school. My swollen hand was a distant memory.

To our delight, the snowball was big enough to block a school bus. A snowplow had to be summoned. What could be more magical to our young eyes than being ringside for a tank-like vehicle crushing a mammoth snow boulder? We could hardly contain ourselves.

The only thing that snapped us back to reality were cries of "Mr. Lynn! Mr. Lynn!" echoing across the field. I felt a dull phantom ache in my hand. We scattered quickly—torture averted and a victory for the little guys. I felt a new level of satisfaction in grade one and thought maybe this whole school thing wasn't so bad after all, even without an anti-gravity chamber.

Buddy sat up on his motel bed and laughed his little eleven-year-old butt off, especially when I got to the part about refusing to come out of our snow fort. I think it helped him feel justified in his own defiance of the school system, questioning that there must be a zillion ways to use his time more effectively. I didn't think he was all wrong. I had wanted to tell him that story to let him know that he wasn't alone in how he might be feeling. He had lived through some trouble with the principal at that same age too. He could spell a lot of words by the time he got to kindergarten, which turned out to be a decent resource for when a couple of friends inveigled him to write out a few unmentionable words that were subsequently discovered by his teacher, as those kinds of things have tendencies to do. The teacher immediately knew it was Buddy because of his spelling savvy. It led to a few meetings with the principal. I put on a serious face, but I'm sure a tinge of my pride shined through that the reason Buddy got singled out was spelling acumen. At least there was no strap involved. Buddy was a little shocked to hear the repercussions of my brush with the elementary school authorities in my younger years. No more than I was though, I thought to myself.

Buddy gave me a great big hug, like only a kid can do, and went to sleep still giggling.

I wrote in my journal that night, "A dad's cloud nine."

My spirit soared with how special the evening had been. It brought about another thought. What if I turned the story telling into an annual event as well? It could turn into a part of our yearly adventures—me revealing an on-topic tale for each leg of our journey. If I chose the right stories, I saw it as an opportunity to share with my son how my own curiosities had steered me to some incredibly unique places and unforgettable times. Some events in particular that literally changed my life; a number that involved tight squeezes; and a few occasions that still comically remind me of how dumb-ass lucky I had been.

Buddy and I slept soundly after all our biking. I woke up still smiling from the night before and relieved that I had no strap nightmares.

We headed out early on our second day, skirting around Boundary Bay. We rode past the filming locale where a teenaged Ryan Reynolds from Vancouver got one of his early breaks in the *X-Files*—just a couple of episodes prior to the appearance of another local Vancouver guy, a young Michael Bublé, who ended up getting fired from the set for sneaking a hot dog off the craft services table. Needless to say, Bublé rebounded pretty well from that incident and probably isn't planning too many wiener heists these days.

The Dyke Trail around the bay was flat and elevated a couple metres. It served as a berm to separate the ocean from a lot of low-lying land and houses. For us it made for good views across the bay to Washington State.

"What happens if the water gets higher than this mound?" Buddy asked.

I told him I hoped that didn't happen in his lifetime, but the reality was that biking along that berm gave us a first-hand look at some of the impending challenges of global temperatures rising.

There was a nature-educational sign on the trail that explained how over one million birds pass annually through that area, on a back-and-forth migratory path referred to as the Pacific Flyway, stretching as far to the south as Patagonia for some. That number stuck in my head when we soon after skirted past the Peace Arch, one of the busiest border crossings between the U.S. and

Canada, where two million cars pass annually, on a back-and-forth migratory path referred to as Cross Border Shopping, stretching as far to the south as Seattle for some.

"Should we be concerned that it is two cars to every bird?" I asked Buddy and then muttered that I hoped that they had built that berm high enough.

Buddy and I turned directly east in front of the Peace Arch and proceeded to ride along 0 (zero) Avenue for the rest of our day. We biked straight down the 49th parallel with the U.S. over our right shoulder and the whole of Canada on our left. Most of 0 Avenue is separated from the U.S. by only a ditch. Except for the odd clue like U.S. flags on the houses on the other side, we would have been hard pressed to know there was even a border there. The simplicity tributes both countries and their long-standing ability to boast the longest unprotected border in the world. I mentioned to Buddy how fortunate we were to be living in such a peaceful part of the world.

"Yup," he agreed.

I pointed to a kid playing outside a house on our right.

"You could have a friend living over there, throw a ball back and forth from each other's front yards, but live in different countries."

"So weird," Buddy said.

We rode past a house on the Canadian side that infamously came under suspicion a year earlier when border patrol agents saw truckloads of lumber disappearing into a Quonset hut. *Something fishy is going on here* radars went off and led officers to discover a 360-foot tunnel—right under the road that Buddy and I were biking on—that rose up into the living room of a house on the U.S. side. The U.S. had dealt with multiple tunnels on their southern border, but this was the only known tunnel under the unprotected border to their north. The end result of the Canadian discovery? Two 50-kilogram bags of B.C. bud were confiscated while being smuggled into Washington State. How's it goin', eh?

At five o'clock Buddy and I had got as far east as Campbell Valley Regional Park, and we were ready to call it a day. We locked up our bikes against a fence outside the Albatross Veterinary Clinic. Pam had driven 50 kilometres or so from Burnaby to get us. The arrangement worked well for Pam to ease her mind that her boys were not worn out, but it was mostly awesome for us as we got a chauffeured visit to stay for the night with family friends, their three fun-loving kids, and of course Pam and Hali. I didn't even have time to get my seatbelt off in our truck before Buddy and all the kids were already in their backyard pool. When you're eleven years old, switching gears is fast and easy. B.C.'s Daniel Powter's recent billboard number one song, *Bad Day*, was playing poolside, but it couldn't have been further from the truth for that day. Great Day was more like it! From cruising along atop a bike seat to pool cannonballs with the kids, another grand day for a dad to remember.

Buddy and I woke bright and early the next morning, and Pam kindly drove us back out to our locked-up bikes. Buddy slept the entire way.

We set out for on our third day of biking with Koma Kulshan, aka Mount Baker, jutting up ahead of us, a 3286-metre-high glacier-capped volcano—one of 20 major volcanoes and 4000 volcanic vents that make up an area referred to as the Cascade Arc, spanning from B.C. to Northern California. Riding past a volcano was not something that had come to mind for our Canadian journey. I was absolutely shocked later to find out that there had been a volcano eruption less than 250 years ago in northwest B.C., the Tseax Cone, which killed 2000 people in the Nisga'a Nation. That was as many fatalities as Pompeii! How in the world had we learned at school about the Italian event and not one in our own backyard?

Buddy and I didn't think too much about Mount Baker blowing, but if we were going to worry about anything it probably would have been that we had become aware that we were riding through the Cascadia Subduction Zone, a massive 350,000 square kilometre area where one major tectonic plate, the Juan de Fuca plate, is slowly colliding and sliding under the North American plate. The more famous San Andreas fault in California is quite the lightweight in comparison to the Cascadia Subduction Zone.

Happily, no one had pissed off Mother Nature and left her in any sort of earth-shaking mood that morning and our biking remained peaceful through the lush farmlands of the extensive valley. In the early evening, we rolled into the Fraser Valley city of Abbotsford, only to find all motels fully booked. There was a big volleyball tournament in town. We eventually found one room at an inn on our way out of town, along North Parallel Road, where the desk clerk informed me, "It's the honeymoon suite, so there are no children allowed."

"You do realize I need a room for me *and* my son, right?" I said.

"I'm not sure what we can do about that," he said. "You could stay in it, but don't think it's going to work having your son in there."

I thought he was joking at first but was bewildered to find out he was serious. I imagined Pam might have had something to say if I was sleeping in a cushy heart shaped bed while our son hit the curb in the parking lot.

The desk clerk was convinced he was doing the right thing and stood his ground, stating, "Those are the rules."

He had no other suggestions for us.

"You've got to be $%#&@*$ kidding me," I said.

Buddy's eyes opened wide. There was a good chance he learned a few new words in my subsequent exchange with the guy.

It was getting late, and we were running out of options. After I told the desk guy ~~where he could shove his suggestions~~ that I had some concerns about his customer service, I called around and by good luck the Abbotsford Super 8 had just had a last-minute cancellation. It was a room that allowed smoking, which was not optimal, but more importantly they allowed Buddys, which was really the most integral accommodation option I had been looking for. It wasn't the freshest of rooms, but Buddy still found joy in that it had an ice machine at the end of our hall. He was on the verge of reaching an age when he might not be interested in running down a motel hallway to get buckets of free ice, but he wasn't there yet. I thought how nice it would be if as adults we could all be pleased so easily.

After three big days of biking for a little guy, I wondered if he was getting tired. Nope. That was clearly not the case. That evening, Buddy was like an Energizer bunny bouncing around our room. In an effort to spend as little time as possible in the smoking room, I said, "Wanna go to a movie?"

"Like in a movie theatre?" Buddy said.

"Not *like* a movie theatre, in an actual movie theatre."

Buddy jumped up. "Let's go!"

"This might be a funny question, but wanna bike to the theatre?" I said.

Not surprisingly, Buddy thought that would be cool.

We laughed together as we rode. We were taking a break from riding our bikes all day long, by going for another bike ride, proving to me yet again how the simplest of moments can be the ones that build lasting memories.

With a big tub of popcorn on the chair arm between us, we kicked back and watched Spider-Man spin a web and *catch a few thieves, just like flies.*

Back at our motel, we plugged our noses, got a big night's sleep, and were back on our bikes early the next morning. We headed out in shorts and t-shirts as we were treated to another cloudless, bright blue sky.

We skirted alongside the Vedder Canal, which we affectionately referred to as the Pearl Jam Canal, and passed scads of dairy farms that lined the Fraser Valley. Cows never seemed fazed by vehicles roaring by, but our bikes and occasional mooing sounds could send them into a comical frenzy.

It was flat riding. The whole area had once been underwater, a huge inland lake before being converted to farmland. By the time Buddy and I rode into the Boston Pizza parking lot in Chilliwack, we had travelled 176 kilometres since leaving the Inner Harbour in Victoria. Can you imagine biking that far on a little kid's bike? Buddy was a champion. Pam and Hali were there waiting for us, waving as we rode up, and had a Great White North pizza, with pineapple per Buddy, at the ready.

A good deal of relief eased out of Pam's body as she hugged her son. Hali lovingly jumped up onto my shoulders.

Buddy couldn't wait to show off his chainring tattoo, a grease mark on the inside of his right leg from rubbing against his bike chain. It was a badge of honour for an eleven-year-old.

I had started the year with absolutely no expectations on the distance we might travel and was ecstatic to end up getting as far as we did. Every day, someone had asked us how many years it was going to take us to get to the east coast. I still didn't have a clue and never once bothered to guess. Buddy and I chuckled that we were only two per cent of our way to Newfoundland, but I was giddy thinking about how much I was looking forward to all the years that would take us farther east.

It seemed to me that Buddy had grown up a smidge, right before my eyes on our four-day ride. Even Pam made a comment about him seeming older. Any reservations I had about the trip, or how Buddy would hold up, had been firmly cast aside. At eleven years old, he was cruising. As a dad, I was absolutely digging all of this.

Buddy was glowing. He told me we had started something special. I couldn't have agreed more. He told me that before we got going that the whole 'all the way across the country thing' had sounded a bit overwhelming. But he wasn't worried anymore. I realized that through all of my own apprehensions before we got started that I hadn't checked in with him nearly enough. Crazy, right? A good learning moment for me. Now with one year under his belt, he was raring to continue and already talking about the second year. And I was right there with him.

I wondered how far we would get in our second year?

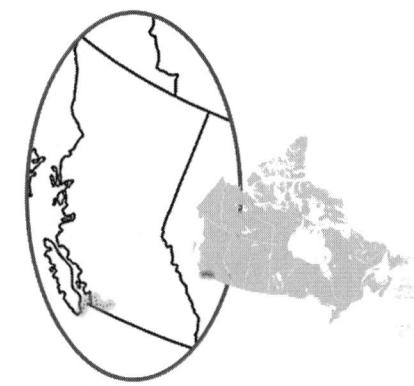

Year One Completed

Kms 0 to 179
Days 1 to 4

Victoria to Chilliwack

YEAR TWO - Buddy 12 Years Old

BIKING THROUGH THE SNOW

Into the rugged mountains of the Coquihalla we go. Frequently through the year, Buddy and I chatted about the next leg of our bike trip. We were thrilled to have gotten as far as we did in our inaugural year.

One morning when we were sitting on the couch together, Buddy still in his pajamas and his hair all tousled, we got laughing about which day of our first trip seemed the most challenging on the butt meter. We concurred that it was the third morning when we had to do the most coaxing to get our rear ends back on our bike seats. Buddy said, "We're both going to be way faster out there this year." My soul did a little jig. He was looking forward to our adventure as much as I was. I suspected our trips were already putting more bond to the strong relationship we had.

Leading up to year two of our trip, however, I almost made a colossal mistake that could have derailed it all. I was challenged to find a window for us to get back out there. I was beginning a new restaurant venture, and our summer opening date was proving problematic to schedule around. I've been known to get immersed in projects and could have let this become a convenient reason to skip a year of our bike trip. But I was determined to not let work take precedence over something so important to me – to us. It would have been ridiculous for me not to find a few days to do the trip, no matter how busy life seemed. Would our entire journey have fizzled out if I had let ourselves miss our second year? To this day, I am forever glad I stayed true to our adventure.

Pam and Hali were keen to help us get underway again. They drove Buddy and me, and our bikes, to Chilliwack where we had left off in year one. They then continued on to Harrison Hot Springs for their own mini getaway. Buddy and I planned to meet up and stay with them after our first day of biking. It was a dad bonus: the luxury of a soft bed for one more night.

We loaded our gear onto our bikes and prepared ourselves for a different kind of ride than the previous year. We had to get over the Coquihalla Pass, and to do that would mean climbing 1235 metres (over 4000 feet). How would Buddy do? He was still on his little Specialized BMX. The elevation gains would be a new challenge after gaining a mere 20 metres over sea level to get to Chilliwack in year one.

Weather-wise, it was as if we hadn't missed a beat. Skies were bright, clear blue. We started biking alongside the mighty Fraser River, the longest river in B.C. at 1399 kilometres. It was a milky colour from all the silt it carries out of the mountains – discharging about 20 million tonnes of sediment each year into the Pacific Ocean south of Vancouver. It would be like dumping an amount of sand equivalent to over three million elephants into the ocean every year. On our ferry ride to the mainland the prior year, we had noticed the defined colour change the Fraser makes in the water over a vast area around the Tsawwassen terminal.

Buddy and I rode at a gentle pace in the opposite direction of the fast-flowing grey water. The scene was like a painting. The shores dotted with pale beaches, lined with deep green trees, in front of mountains reaching up into endless blue. There was so much more to take in on a bike versus travelling by car. It unveiled a few ugly things, too. The natural beauty was contrasted with the odd abandoned appliance and pile of garbage along the river's edge. "I guess people don't see that from their cars," Buddy said. He was a bit disgusted.

In the late afternoon, Buddy and I wheeled into the scenic mountain town of Hope. It got its name from Fort Hope, built in 1848, a couple of years after the Oregon Treaty was signed, when the British 'hoped' to find a *Canadian* route through the mountains that did not force them to dip below the 49th parallel.

We stopped at the Blue Moose Coffee House where our two beautiful chauffeurs, Hali and Pam, were waiting to take us to our hotel for the night. But not before Buddy devoured a giant slice of banana cream pie. "We might have to keep this pie thing going as part of all our trips," I said.

Buddy beamed. With his mouth stuffed with pie, he mumbled, "I'd be down for that." I took it as a challenge and noted another potential tradition to add to our journey.

After a family night of swimming and hanging out on Harrison Lake, Buddy and I were back at it early the following morning. We set out from Hope up the Nicola Valley Trail. We saw why people could feel claustrophobic around Hope, with the narrowing valley and mountains jutting up all around. We figured that was exactly why they picked it as the location for the first *Rambo* movie, *First Blood*, with Sylvester Stallone and Bruce Greenwood. The lush mountainsides created the perfect setting for *Rambo* to hide in and sew up a gash in his arm, a haunting movie scene that we had no interest in re-enacting.

As expected, elevation gains started to factor in east of Hope. We worked our way up the westernmost section of the old Coquihalla Subdivision of the now defunct Kettle Valley Railroad system. The abandoned railroad gave us an approachable way to climb into the mountains on our bikes. Since the rail routes are no longer in train use, cyclists have been left with terrific places to ride on gentle railway grades that were built only as steep as the trains could handle going up and down the mountains.

The Coquihalla Subdivision was the most expensive railway per mile in the world when completed in 1916 and is still an engineering marvel today. It was referred to as McCulloch's Wonder, named after the lead construction engineer, Andrew McCulloch. An avid Shakespeare fan, he named all the stations and infrastructures after the playwright's characters, such as *Romeo, Juliet, Jessica, Lear, Portia, Shylock*. We biked past roads and signs with Shakespearean names. Being Harry Potter fans, Buddy and I kidded that if McCulloch had built it today those places might have ended up being called *Potter, Dumbledore, Hermione, Longbottom, Weasley, Hagrid*.

The gorgeous and densely forested trail led us all the way into Coquihalla Canyon Provincial Park. Well, almost all the way. We came across a locked eight-foot-high fence that blocked our way into the public area of the Othello Train Tunnels.

"What's with the fence?" I said. "I sure don't want to have to double back and go around to the highway."

We could see people up ahead, inside the park, and deduced the fence was there to keep them from venturing down the railway trail and not vice versa. After a brief deliberation, we made the choice to clamber over the fence, bikes and all.

Getting a twelve-year-old to climb over a fence, even a high one, was not the difficult part. "Jump up there and climb over," I said. In a flash, Buddy monkeyed himself over and was standing on the other side.

The more challenging part of our plan was hauling the bikes and packs over the fence. For a moment I debated what I was teaching Buddy about disregarding locked enclosures and wondered if we were going to get in trouble for scaling the barricade. I figured one way or another, it was going to turn into a memorable tidbit of our journey.

I climbed up with the panniers and gear and dropped them down to Buddy on the other side.

"Now for the hard part," Buddy said, chuckling at me.

I struggled up the fence, fighting with each bike one by one, especially mine. From the top, I would heave them over and lower them, as slowly as I could, down to Buddy on the other side. Our 'break-in' turned out well worth the effort as it saved us from a significant amount of backtracking and having to retackle the elevation gains we had already made. Besides, on the other side, our suspicion seemed confirmed that the fence had been put in place to deter park visitors from venturing down the trail that we had taken.

"How cool is this!" Buddy said, instantly preoccupied with the tunnels and bridges up ahead.

Plenty of engineers had concluded it would be impossible to build a railway through the area where the Othello Tunnels now sit. It was not difficult to see why. The tunnels, supported by elaborate wooden and steel supports, were carved into the granite mountainside of a mesmerizing gorge with a sheer drop to the roaring Coquihalla River below. As we walked our bikes through, we could see soot from the trains still streaked on the jagged rock walls. Going over a trestle between the tunnels, I was tempted to check over my shoulder to make sure a train wasn't coming.

As we continued east, the only route that was available to us was out on the Coquihalla Highway. We had a short distance to go until we could join another part of the railway trail again. From the highway, I was surprised at how simple the access was to the Othello Tunnels. I had driven that route countless times but had never been inclined to stop. A good reminder of how easy it can be to miss special things, even ones in plain view.

The highway portion, at a far higher grade, turned into a steep, onerous ride. I'm sure it would have felt even more difficult, if it wasn't for Buddy distracting us by listing off his favourite

Hayao Miyazaki films - *Spirited Away, Kiki's Delivery Service, Porco Rosso...* Buddy loved the storylines and style of animation. I mentioned how his taste in entertainment was more sophisticated than mine at his age as I reminisced about *The Flintstones* and *Bugs Bunny.*

"Any others?" Buddy asked, challenging me for ones that might be more obscure.

"*Rocket Robin Hood* was cool," I recalled. "Being a Canadian creation and 'saving the far-off galaxy in the outstanding year 3000'." I knew he would check it out, although I also knew he wouldn't be nearly as interested in the animation as he was with Miyazaki's work.

Our bike ride chat branched into a comparison of favourite superheroes. We both had *Batman* at the top of our respective lists.

"I have to tell you though," I confessed, "I'm a little sentimental for the old *Batman*, with Adam West as the original Caped Crusader."

"He wore baby blue tights!" Buddy said. "You do know that's not how Batman was meant to be? He is supposed to be the Dark Knight."

"Yeah, but West had that never-ending-bag-of-tricks-utility-belt and a grapple hook," I said. "And he could climb down a rope ladder below the Bat Copter, punch a shark in the nose and spray it with shark repellent. Pure cinematic gold. Classic!"

"More like *Jurassic*," said Buddy. The kid was too sharp for me sometimes.

Regardless, after 60 plus years, it was evident that *Batman* had stood the test of time and impacted both our generations, perhaps for different reasons. The flaws and darker side to Buddy's *Dark Knight Batman* added realism into the character and I think Buddy could relate to his intelligence. Whereas the unrealistic and campy part of my *Batman* was what likely attracted me.

Biking with my twelve-year-old son on the side of a mountain, chatting about cartoons and superheroes. "I love this," I said to

Buddy. "By the way, it sure would have been helpful to have a grapple hook for when we were scrambling with our bikes over the fence."

"I think maybe you could have used *Spider-Man*," Buddy said.

The whole conversation made our arduous climb far more enjoyable. It's funny when something like that makes a tough task so much easier to tackle.

Later that evening, I was ecstatic to find Buddy had been looking forward to another story from my past. I tried to tell myself it was all the sage fatherly advice I divulged with my grade one story, but I am not sure if an example of what *not* to do at recess could be considered sage.

I was prepared though, with a story in waiting. My mom passed away when I was twelve years old, something that I am sure subconsciously contributed to my desire to create one-on-one moments with my kids. I was sad that they never had the chance to grow up with her around. That evening seemed timely to relay one of my favourite stories of my mom to Buddy. Perhaps not as mystical as a snow fortress, this one involved an outhouse.

How to Win a Race

I didn't have many things to complain about growing up. Although I do remember being mightily pissed off that some head honcho in television programming made an awful decision to water down the *Bugs Bunny Show* by splitting the bill into the *Bugs Bunny/Road Runner Show*. It's not like we had alternatives with other Canadian weekend television options of *Hymn Sing, Singalong Jubilee,* and *Question Period*. Another major injustice I remember involved family races, where being the youngest of three kids didn't have a way of working out to my liking. It seemed I was always last. I was like *Wile E. Coyote* pointlessly chasing around the *Roadrunner*.

Our family had a little cabin on a spectacular lake nestled among spruce, poplar, and birch trees in the toe of the foothills of Alberta. The winter when I was six years old had an incredulous amount of snow. Drifts were so high that we could jump off shed roofs into snowbanks, perfecting our *Captain Kirk* shoulder rolls each time. Races though, remained highly problematic. Whether on foot, snowshoes, or sleds, I was always the last one back to the cabin.

Our family had two Ski-Doos. Our dad was in his winter glory on his black T'NT 440 Everest, about as mean a machine as you could get back in its day. Our mom cruised with her classic yellow Bombardier Olympique 335. If we were out on longer trips, it was most often the case that I would be solo on the back of my mom's Ski-Doo, and my brother and sister would be huddled together on the back of my dad's seat. Most of the time I had absolutely no issue with this arrangement as I wouldn't trade my Ski-Doo memories with my mom for anything. However, I wasn't so approving of the arrangement when it came to speed. It always resulted in my older brother and sister out in front. It was infuriating. Just once, I wanted to win a race.

One crisp winter morning with sunshine glittering off a skiff of fresh snow, my mom made a plan. During breakfast, she casually delivered a *maybe we should race across the lake this morning* challenge. Each member of our family knew that before any snowmobile adventure we were duly bound to clean up the kitchen, stoke the fires, bundle up in our snow gear, and then one by one file out to the outhouse to avoid the inevitable stop(s) that often happened minutes after we were out on the snowmobiles. The stops for someone to take off umpteen layers of gear so they could pee in a snowbank while others waited around freezing.

That glorious morning, my mom pointed out it was my brother's and sister's turn to do the dishes and we seized that favourable circumstance. Mom and I silently slipped on our snowsuits, boots, mittens, and toques and scattered everyone else's gear. We even tied the legs of my siblings' snowsuits into giant knots. Then, in a flurry, my mom and I burst out the door yelling, "Race is on!" with screams of objections ringing from the kitchen.

I scampered to the outhouse while Mom started her snowmobile, and not Dad's, and swept off the snow that had accumulated on her Olympique overnight. We high-fived each other as I ran back from the outhouse and Mom headed for her turn. Panicked ramblings came from inside the cabin as my brother and sister scrambled to find and pull on all their gear. I almost had to pee again when I heard my brother's furious roar, trying to get his legs into his snowsuit.

Everything was going perfectly. I could taste victory. We were finally going to beat them across the lake - one of the most prized races of all. They were still in the cabin, their un-started Ski-Doo covered in snow, and pending bathroom visits loomed. There didn't seem any conceivable way they could catch us.

I was perched on my mom's Ski-Doo seat, imagining myself as *Mario Andretti*, while my mom finished up in the outhouse with the door wide open so she could see me. Her mitts hung off each end of the handlebars as I daydreamed about cruising to victory in the final lap of the Indy 500. That was when all hell broke loose.

I did not think I pulled the silver throttle lever on the Ski-Doo handle, not even a little bit, but evidence suggested otherwise. The Olympique 335 shot across the yard. My eyes bugged out to fill my goggles and I did what made sense to a six-year-old in that situation—I hung on for dear life. This resulted in the throttle lever being pressed even harder, which was intrinsically linked to the volume of my screaming.

The Cycle Of Life

The scene unfolded like this:

First, my sister and brother fell out of the cabin—confused and half-dressed—to see a yellow blur racing over the snow and heading towards the frozen, snow-covered lake, and my deafening shrieks of distress trailing through the air.

Second, there I was, bundled from head to toe in an oversized snowsuit, squeezing the handlebars of a rocketing Ski-Doo so tightly that the knuckles of my mitts were turning white, while the yellow blur I was on was narrowly missing trees and careening off banks of fresh snow towards the lake.

Third, my mom bolted from the outhouse going nearly as fast as the Ski-Doo in an ungraceful, full out, loping run-gallop-hop combination with her one-piece snowsuit hanging down around her knees.

Last, my dad burst out the cabin door just in time to see my mom's bare bum sprinting down the fresh tracks of a Ski-Doo.

"Just let go!" they all screamed at the top of their lungs. "Idiot!" my brother added, unnecessarily.

And then I did what I still maintain any six-year-old would do in those circumstances with everyone yelling, "Let go!" I let go. I released every muscle in my body and flew off the back of the Ski-Doo, flipping through the air as if I was in *Cirque du Soleil*. I face-planted into the snow—disappointingly—considering the lost opportunity to show off my mastery of the *Captain Kirk* shoulder roll. Of course, as soon as I performed my Hollywood worthy stunt, and let go of the throttle in the process, the Ski-Doo unceremoniously came to an immediate stop, in a manner that was not congruent in any way with the preceding chaos. Death defying scrapes with trees, blood curdling screams, and a half-naked woman streaking across the snow with a roll of unravelling toilet paper streaming behind her.

I will never forget what happened next. My mom—my hero—did not miss a beat. By the time she caught up to me and the Ski-Doo, she had managed to get her snow suit almost all the way back on. She scooped me up and plunked me on the back of the machine while grabbing her dangling mitts that were amazingly still hanging off the ends of the handlebars. There was no *what the hell were you thinking* tirade, which could have been entirely appropriate under the circumstances. Mom just boldy stated, "Let's win this thing!" And we roared the Ski-Doo back into action.

Back on the porch, my siblings were frozen in disbelief as if they had been hit by *Kirk* with phasors on stun. By the time they resumed action, it was far too late. The race had a forgone conclusion. I hugged on tight to my mom and guessed that Mario Andretti never had a victory as sweet. No matter how many times we would arrive second from that day on, I could cite the glory of that fateful morning. A little justice had been restored, something that I did not hesitate to repeatedly remind my brother and sister over the rest of that winter, like only the youngest sibling can do.

When I finished the story, Buddy and I happily agreed that moms were the bomb. My mom had inspired me all the time, as Pam does with Buddy and Hali. There are times when moms have a way of showcasing a beautiful extra care gene in just the right moments.

I could have used some special mom intuition when we got back on our bikes the next day. Buddy and I faced an important route decision, with two significantly different possible options to take over the Coquihalla Pass.

The highway, built in the 1980s, cuts directly through the mountains for a much faster and highly travelled route into the interior of British Columbia. When heading northeast up the pass, the highway is a steep 8.5% grade and busy with traffic. It sees over 27,000 vehicles cross its summit on peak days.

There was a rugged back-country alternative for us to consider. It utilized another section of the old Coquihalla Subdivision rail line that had been abandoned in 1961 after numerous washouts. It was a far rougher trail than anything we had been on around the Othello tunnels. The climbing grade was more reasonable, but the route involved a tough combination of single-track trails, some completely washed-out railway sections, and some steep forestry roads. It would be full on mountain terrain and a whole day of remote biking, on the far side of Needle Peak, until we could merge onto the highway near the Coquihalla summit.

After our night talking about moms, Pam's voice was in my mind while we contemplated the two options. I knew she would be nervous about the remoteness of the rail route, but she also would like the idea of us avoiding the busy highway as much as possible. The choice was further complicated by an extremely late spring thaw that increased the chances of snow to be remaining in the backcountry. Still, Buddy and I both chose the remote adventurous route. Considering all the recent hot weather in the area, we figured if any snow remained it would be melting fast. It would be a great adventure for Buddy and he was fully up to the challenge.

It was the last week of June with a higher-than-normal temperature on the morning we started our ride into the Coquihalla backcountry. We were already in our bike shorts and t-shirts, right from our start. As expected, the railway grade provided us with a steady climb as we made our way around the backside of Needle Peak. The ledge of the trail upon which we were biking dropped sharply off our right side towards the raging creek that snaked its way through the valley below. Bright snow-capped peaks loomed high up all around us. Buddy was working his little pedals as hard as he could. It was a long way to the top of the Pass, and I was hoping that his twelve-year-old legs would hold out.

For our lunch break, we rested on an old forestry bridge that crossed Needle Creek. We were at our farthest point from the highway in either direction. Other than the roar of surging water from the spring runoff, it was incredibly serene. Buddy grabbed a few sticks and tossed them into the gushing water. I had a big dad smile planted on my face.

We pushed on after we crossed the bridge and made our way up a tree-lined forestry service road along the bottom of the valley. Our progress was slow but steady while we continued to climb.

We could make out remnants of the old railway line, with numerous washed-out rail trestles, hanging off the mountain side above us.

Soon after, we started to see patches of snow on the sides of the road. The higher we got up the Pass, the larger and more frequent the patches, until we came to a point where snow skiffed over the road in front of us. We still had a fair distance to reach the summit, but held out hope that further ahead, when our route crossed back over the creek again, that our path might be more in direct sun and there would be a way for us to sneak our way to the top of the Pass.

But the snow got deeper.

"I don't know, Buddy," I said. "This doesn't look promising." It was a difficult thing for me to admit.

"I think we can make it," Buddy said back.

I did not want to turn back either, but as we tried to continue we were forced to half carry half push our bikes through the snow as it got too deep to ride.

When we finally got to our targeted bridge crossing, near what used to be Iago Station on the old rail line, a foot of snow lined both sides of the deep pale grey rushing waters. From there we still had a daunting twelve kilometres to go to get to the summit. The sun was warm, the trees were green, we were in shorts and t-shirts, but the ground was completely white. If anything, the snow on the other side of the creek was even deeper. It was becoming more apparent that we weren't going to make it through.

I knew Buddy wanted to push on carrying our bikes, but I also knew that twelve kilometres was a long way. And I was concerned about the amount of daylight we had left. It created a conflicting dad moment, between my adventurer desire to push on and a parental voice about keeping Buddy safe. In the end, we yielded to Mother Nature and made the decision to turn around and ride back out. We were not aware of it at the time, but that choice turned out to be astute. We found out later that the forestry road, the one we would have continued on up to the summit, had experienced a mini-avalanche earlier that day and had been completely blocked a short distance further from where we turned around. Had there somehow been a mom's intuition in play?

We marked the Iago Bridge on our map. It would be the starting point from where we would need to find a way to continue the following year. We carried our bikes back down over the fresh tracks we had made coming up - through the snow to the point where our route was clear enough for us to start riding again. This time, however, we were descending. It was the first time of our entire trip that we were riding downhill for any sustained length. It was a welcome relief after working so hard carrying our bikes through the snow. The route that had taken us hours to climb took us a fraction of the time to descend. It had seemed like a gentle ride up, but by travelling back down on the same path, it gave perspective as to how steep it had been.

Buddy and I were disappointed we had been forced to turn back because of the snow, but we chatted about how sometimes turning back can be the right decision. "I probably didn't fully grasp that notion until you came along and I became a dad," I admitted to Buddy. I still don't always get it right. If I had been on my own, I likely would have pushed on further, only turning back when I got to the mini-avalanche. Decision-making as a parent, however, is an entirely different task. Turning back was the right call. Was it a better learning moment for me or my son?

When we looked at the day as a whole, we both took pride in how cool of an adventure we'd had, and how far we had got by putting in such a valiant effort, despite the snow.

I could see Buddy's youthful imagination churning though. "I wonder how deep it got," he still questioned.

We promised to each other that next year we would conquer that summit and have a different tale to tell. We fist bumped to that.

I had some planning to do first. What would be our best way to get back to our starting point?

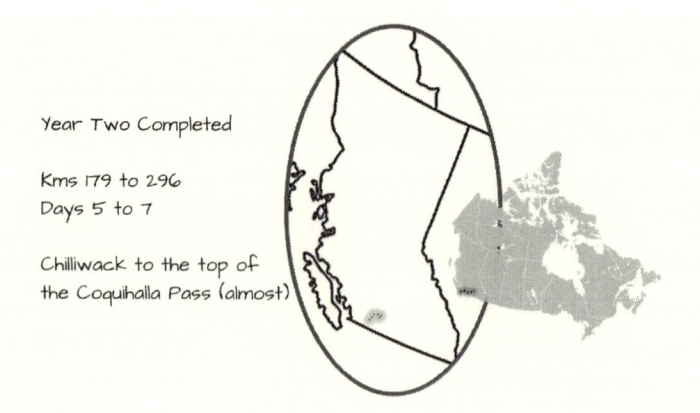

Year Two Completed

Kms 179 to 296
Days 5 to 7

Chilliwack to the top of the Coquihalla Pass (almost)

YEAR THREE – Buddy 13 Years Old

CHASING BEARS AND DODGING GHOSTS

From the top of the Coquihalla Pass (almost). Second-guessing can easily creep into a parent's routine, but it had no part in our Cycle of Life. From the moment Buddy and I got off our bikes, we were itching to get back out for another year. Despite the snowed-out setback, we shared a happiness that we had decided to take the more adventurous route. I was thrilled those types of experiences were becoming part of our journey.

    A month prior to starting year three of our trip, I came across a swanky second-hand, copper-coloured, Kona mountain bike for my newly minted teenage biking partner. It was a mid-size bike that I thought would last Buddy at least a year or two before he outgrew it. I tried to play it cool, but it was tough to hide my smile watching Buddy on his larger ride. He was more confident and powerful with every pedal. It also meant that he could carry panniers. My legs smiled too.

    The Saturday afternoon before we left, Buddy and I sipped on hot chocolates and laid out a topographic map on our kitchen counter to determine how best to get back to our starting point. We decided to ride our bikes twelve kilometres downhill from Coquihalla Lakes, from the summit of Coquihalla Pass. It was a counter-productive move back toward the west coast, but it seemed the easiest way to get back to the exact spot where we had been snowed out.

We headed out on the same calendar week of June as the previous year, but this time there were no lingering traces of snow. The trail was clear and completely dry.

Within our first few minutes of descending into the wilderness on the other side of Needle Peak, it began to feel remote. There was no one else around. We were surrounded by slate grey rock faces, deep green Pacific Silver Firs, pale blue alpine waters, and pure white peaks. I pointed out to Buddy how lucky we were in Canada to have backcountry areas like this that are still fairly accessible. Almost two-thirds of British Columbia is fully forested. That's equal to an area about the same size as all of France, where over 65 million people live.

We were cruising fast, downhill, back toward the old Iago Station. I was in front of Buddy and carrying a decent amount of speed. I came around a sharp bend and ended up face to face – well face to butt – with a black bear. It scared the bleep out of me as I frantically slammed on my brakes. As alarmed as I was, I might have shocked the bear even more. Separated by maybe a metre, the bear jumped straight up with all four feet off the ground, executed a weird mid-air twist like a frightened cat, and launched off like a rocket through the trees. It was astonishing to see how fast a large animal like that can move. I had been close enough to see the hair standing up on the bear's back. I was exceedingly grateful to see more of the animal's rear-end disappearing through the trees than face coming the other way.

Buddy skidded to a stop behind me just in time to see the big guy crashing off through the trees down the mountainside. "What was that? Was that a bear?" Buddy asked.

It definitely did not seem the most appropriate time to have an in-depth David Suzuki conversation about *The Nature of Things* or a *Hinterland Who's Who* discussion about the habits of the black bear in the Canadian mountains.

"Let's go!" I ordered, my eyes as wide as pancakes.

The odds of being attacked and injured by a bear in the wild are something like one in two million, but I had not heard what the odds were of being attacked and injured by a bear after riding a set of handlebars up his backside. We quickly tested how fast Bud's new bike could go. In all likelihood the bear was long gone, but I didn't think it necessary to prove that theory. My heart and dad brain were both racing as fast as they could. We did not stop again until we got all the way to our Iago Bridge destination.

We had successfully returned to our exact ending point from the previous trip, but again faced a tough decision.

"What is it with this bridge?" I chuckled to Buddy.

Our original plan had been to bike back up the same trail we had just come down – now referred to as the bear trail. Or avoid that by once again going back down the same route we had exited on last year, but then be left with a tough ride up the highway on the other side of Needle Peak to the top of the Coquihalla Pass. The latter would be a massive step backwards and involve riding in truck traffic that included a tunnel-like highway section aptly named the Great Bear Snow Shed. It didn't sound the most appealing option, but neither did riding past the Great Bear Scare Me Out Of My Bike Shorts route.

My dad brain had been rattled, but I knew logically that we had just as much chance seeing a bear no matter which way we biked. We decided to ride back the way we had just come down, but we were going to make sure we made as much noise as possible while we rode.

Nervously glancing around while I led us back up the trail, Buddy and I almost went hoarse singing at the top of our lungs, "This is the song that never ends ... it goes on and on my friend ..."

In only the first moments of our trip, we had ventured back down to our snowed-out bridge, played tag with Yogi, and then successfully completed our needed summit of the Coquihalla Pass on our bikes (on our second attempt due to snow the previous year). It was an eventful start to the third year of our adventure.

At thirteen years old Buddy still had that go-for-everything enthusiasm of a young boy, but he was also starting to think deeper about more worldly things, too. He had taken to illustrating and was producing amazing pieces that seemed beyond his years. Almost on cue, Buddy was also noticeably bigger and stronger as he began his teenage years. He was still a small guy for his age, just as I had been, but our annual bike trips made me more aware of how much he was growing. Our year-to-year journey legs were indeed acting as benchmarks.

Moving up into a larger bike, Buddy was notably faster too. Which I was happy about with our bear encounter.

Once we got to the top of the Coquihalla Pass, our plan was to take a 70-kilometre back-way yomp to eventually connect with the Crowsnest Highway to the south. Our path to get there was mostly via another remote section of the old Kettle Valley Railroad system, the Princeton Subdivision, which had also been abandoned and not in use for many years. Soon after we branched away from the Coquihalla Highway again, Buddy and I rode through a little off-the-beaten-track town called Brookmere, where remnants of a rail station water tower still stood along with some other old buildings from when it had once been a key station along the rail line. Both Buddy and I got an eerie feeling biking there, as if we were riding through a ghost-town. There were still a few residents though, which we became aware of when Buddy caught a brief glimpse of a lone guy emerging from an old building and soon disappearing again. Images from the film *Deliverance* banjo'd through my mind.

South of Brookmere is home to the isolated canyons where Billy Miner allegedly holed up in a secret cave. Billy Miner was credited with pulling off the first train robbery in Canada, shortly after escaping prison for several stagecoach robberies in the U.S.

He was known as the *Gentleman Bandit* for his politeness and reputed to have originated the phrase 'Hands Up!'

As Buddy slowly rode ahead of me on the sandy trail, I pictured how vulnerable we would be to an old-west ambush in the canyon. It seemed like a fun place for a break, so we sat on a big rock and had a snack.

"This feels like the middle of nowhere," Buddy said.

No one showed up to yell 'Hands Up!' and rob us of our gold bars, well ... golden wrapped Eat-More bars.

After quite some time, our cross-country railway path eventually linked into roads. When we got to Otter Lake, we stripped down to our underwear for a teeth-chattering swim. We followed that up with a slice of apple-and-cinnamon-best-pie-of-this-year's-trip from the Tulameen Trading Post. By the time we got back on our bikes and rolled into the little town of Coalmont, it was late afternoon and we were ready to pack it in for the day.

After checking out the historic and rumoured to be ghost-filled Coalmont Hotel, we happened upon a cool little bed and breakfast called The Mosey-On-Inn. They had three rooms to choose from – The Bank, The Saloon, and the Barbershop.

I asked Buddy, "Do you want a haircut?"

"Does the Saloon have a bar fridge?" Buddy replied.

Bob Sterne, the Innkeeper, suggested we "deposit ourselves in the Bank" and I was sure that wasn't the first time he had used that line.

We settled ourselves into our room. I oiled our bike chains while Buddy rambled around and checked out an old two-seater airplane that Bob had refurbished and wedged into the Inn's backyard. When we turned in for the night, I broke out a story for Buddy. In good theme with our bear encounter, I had some Canadian wilderness advice that I wanted to pass on to my son.

How To Find Out What The Inside Of A Beaver Lodge Looks Like

Our cabin at the lake was an incredible place for a nine-year-old to be all summer long. All of us kids roamed around on an endless string of daily adventures. We would set out after breakfast and wouldn't come back until we heard our parents ringing a big triangle of iron, the size of a home plate in baseball, kind of like what you would see hanging on Lorne Greene's rickety old porch on *Bonanza*. It was a signal for us to bee-line straight home for dinner.

One day, my brother and I were wandering through the trees and down the shoreline to a big beaver lodge. We crashed through the brush making as much noise as a herd of elephants. Stealth not the strong suit of a couple of young kids marching through the woods, especially with my brother's baby blue Radio Shack transistor pocket radio cranked to the max, distortedly belting out Bachman-Turner Overdrive's *You Ain't Seen Nothin' Yet.*

We neared a giant pitcher's mound of tangled branches that made up the beaver home. We knew the main entrance to their lodge was under the water, thanks to the National Film Board and their grainy nature films. Those films also taught us the beavers needed air holes to keep their dwelling breathable. We clambered over the rounded mass of sticks and mud searching for the illustrious vent to see if we could peer inside. My imagination was working double time. What would it be like inside that den?

And then we found a gap that looked like it might reach right down to the inner chamber, but it was dark and scary. My brother laid out an irresistible offer.

"I'll tell you what, since you found the gap, you can go first, try crawling through."

Everything was happening fast. I couldn't say for sure if it had been me or my brother who had found the opening. My nine-year-old noggin was struggling to keep up. Why exactly was I being let to go first? What would I see inside? Holy moly, would a giant fire-breathing-beaver-from-hell be waiting for me with massive front teeth bared and foaming at the mouth?

As suspicious as I was that this might be one of those times when a younger brother should be questioning an older sibling's motives, we both knew that as soon as he had offered me the chance to go first, I wouldn't be able to resist.

I turned my Edmonton Eskimos ball cap backwards, gritted my teeth, and mustered up enough moxie to say, "How cool is this going to be?!"

I worked my legs and feet down through the gap, scratching my shins on branches while Winnipeg's Terry Jacks crooned *Seasons in the Sun* over my brother's radio. It was a tight fit. I squeezed far enough into the opening that my legs were dangling in mid-air, with my entire lower half of my body hanging inside the lodge chamber. The excitement of being inside a real live beaver lodge had started to overtake any fears I had about the giant-fire-breathing-beaver thing – just before I felt an awful pain in my legs and the sudden realization that something was horribly wrong. With only my head and one arm still sticking up through the tangle of branches, I shrieked with all my might, "BEAVER!!!!! MAD BEAVER!!!!."

My brother fell backwards and nearly rolled into the lake. The only thing that stopped him from going in the water was his shirt getting caught on one of the gnawed branches sticking up through the tangles.

"AAARRRHHHHHHH!!!!!," I screamed as shooting pain ran up my legs.

My brother stared at me with utter terror etched on his face, which made me even more scared. What seemed like ten minutes to wriggle half-way down took less than a nano-second to pop back out. I shot out of the gap like a cork firing out of a champagne bottle. Shaking from head to toe, I looked down at my legs expecting to see gnawed off stumps of flesh. And that is when the reality of the situation came into focus. There had been no beaver attack. I screamed again! Louder than any dinner bell gong. "WAAAASSSSSPPPSSSS!"

To this day I have no clue if there had been any beavers in that lodge or what it even looked like on the inside, but I can categorically attest that beaver lodges make outstanding places for wasps to build extensive settlements. Wasps were pouring out of the cracks like a scene gone terribly bad from *Winnie the Pooh*. In this scene though, there was no Pooh-bear love floating in the air while he tucked his honey-covered paws into a tree full of bees. My brother and I screamed like there was no tomorrow as an angry swarm of flesh piercing bombers loomed over us like a dark cloud moving in perfect concert with every running step we took. By the time we thrashed

The Cycle Of Life

through the trees and got back to the cabin, I was sure I had been stung a million times, maybe even a billion, or a gazillion if that was a thing. Every part of me was in pain and starting to swell.

For the following two days, we were lathered in Lanocane from head to toe. I was wrapped in gauze like I had been found in an Egyptian tomb. One wasp had stung my lower lip and made me look like Mick Jagger after a failed Botox injection. My brother ended up getting stung as bad as I did. I either couldn't or wouldn't talk to him. The two of us ate soup through straws. With each sip, I glared at my bro though my bandage openings, like a cursed mummy staring down Billy Van on *The Hilarious House of Frightenstein*.

As I sat and swelled those days, I did my darnedest to blame my brother for the ordeal, but the reality was that it wouldn't be the last time my curiosity got the best of me.

Buddy visibly cringed while I was relaying the wasp stinging.

"What do you think the inside of that lodge looked like?" he puzzled over.

"On one hand, I hope you find out one day. On the other, I hope you never have to find out," I said, wincing at the memory.

I confessed to Buddy that it's funny how later in life you end up cherishing those crazy moments, and how they become some of the most memorable and special times. I clarified regarding the wasps though, definitely memorable, not sure how special.

While we fell asleep, I could have sworn I heard something buzzing in our room, but I shut my eyes and was too tired from biking to worry about it.

The next morning we started our longest riding day to date – from Coalmont to Keremeos, close to ninety kilometres. It helped that we got riding by seven o'clock. With no bears, no ghosts, no train robbers, and no wasps to deal with, we got twenty kilometres in before we even stopped for breakfast. There was no doubt Buddy was clipping along at a faster pace than past years.

Buddy may have been a small guy for his age, but his appetite was legendary. It was always amusing to watch the reactions to this cute little guy's food orders at our various diner stops. His metabolism must have been off the charts because he could put away a ton of food. Our server at the Belaire Restaurant in Princeton thought he mis-ordered and then could not believe her eyes at how much he was able to plow through. Eggs, sausages, bacon, potatoes, and a fruit cup. And a stack of pancakes! It was a total pig out and her various stages of shock kept me entertained.

Our route from the coast, through the Coquihalla, and now along southern B.C. put plenty of ecological changes on display. The trees thinned out. The hemlocks, western red cedars, yellow cedars, and sitka spruce had given way to ponderosa pines, lodgepole pines, and some rocky mountain junipers.

As we rode, Buddy and I had a chance to talk about my beaver lodge story again and he asked how long it took me to get over the wasp fiasco with my brother. I admitted that it had only taken a couple of days to get over the buzz of it all and before I was bouncing along behind him somewhere else again. I was close with both my brother and sister, and Buddy knew that. I relayed how comforting it was to know that I could always count on either of my siblings if ever needed. I also briefly alluded to how fun it was to be able to get together with my siblings and laugh over family history or think back on certain memories and secrets that only the three of us would know.

Buddy's ears perked up. "What kind of secrets?"

"Silly things, like our brother in his teens with his big '70s style Afro hair, dancing to disco music in his platform shoes and big bell bottoms, like he had *Saturday Night Fever*," I said.

"Or things about our parents only us kids could know. Like how my sister loved combing our dad's hair with a wet comb, while

The Cycle Of Life

he sat on the floor. At least until our dad realized that my sister was not tall enough to reach the bathroom sink to get the comb wet."

"That meant …" Buddy paused.

"Yup."

Before I could suggest that Buddy would not have much to say about me as a dad, he was far ahead of me. He joyfully pointed out that he and Hali already had plenty to laugh about. Fortunately, I had clued in and embraced my 'dadness' early on with my kids. I saw how simple things like wearing 'dad socks' could spark a twinkle of excitement in their eyes. They got giddy when they had a chance to point out those socks to each other. Or heaven forbid if I ever wore sandals over those socks. Or mention something as archaic as a phone book. I consoled myself that I was simply doing my part to create sibling bonding moments.

Buddy and his sister Hali were cute together … most of the time. They had their moments like only siblings can, but I am grateful they have bonded like they have. They've been close since the day Hali was born. When I took five-year-old Buddy into Pam's room at the hospital, he was glowing as we put his sister in his arms.

"I thought I was going to be a good big brother," he said, "but I didn't know I would be this good." Just an hour into big brotherhood and he surmised he had it all figured out already.

On our last night of this year's trip, Buddy and I camped in the gardens of the Old Grist Mill in the town of Keremeos, in the Similkameen Valley. We set up our tent in the shadow of the waterwheel that had first powered the mill to grind locally grown wheat (grist) into flour back in 1877. They then sold the flour to the settlers and First Nations people of the area, and the miners and travellers on the major horse trails. The estimated population of all of British Columbia back then was less than 50,000. For almost a quarter century, the mill could not produce enough to keep up with demand. All of that changed when the railroads went through and traffic patterns were forever shifted.

The mill business was completely shut down by the early 1900s. The historic building was relegated into being used for storing all sorts of stuff, briefly as an artist studio, a hay loft, and even as a chicken coop, until 1984 when it was restored to its original glory, complete with the waterwheel and an operating mill again. It is the West's last remaining pioneer flour mill with the original mill machinery intact, and most importantly for us, a super place for a couple of bikers to camp.

Snugged up side-by-side, by the light our headlamps, we checked out our maps for the next day's ride and jotted down a few journaling notes. Things about where we had rode, places we stopped to eat, mishaps we laughed about, and grocery lists for the following day. The shadows made from our lights jumped to life every time we adjusted our positions. We could hear birds cooing nearby. I loved these moments in our tent at the end of a long day of biking.

The next day, the ride from Keremeos down into the southern Okanagan Valley in central B.C. was long and fast. The trees around us became increasingly sparse. We both let out a big "Woot-Woot!" when we saw the deep blue of Osoyoos Lake spread down the middle of the valley below us. The surrounding mountain terrain was more arid. Sage and prickly pear cacti dotted the roadside hills. Desert landscapes didn't typically come to mind for either of us when picturing Canada, but the scenery was yet another example of the country's incredible diversity.

Across the other side of the lake, Buddy and I saw what lay ahead for us. We were going to have a toilsome climb to get back out of the valley. Buddy was delighted to point out that we would not have to tackle that section until the following year.

At Osoyoos Lake, some of our best friends were there to welcome us. We joined six other families for an annual camping get-together. "See ya, Dad!" Buddy yelled as he hopped off his bike and jumped into the action.

Buddy and I had now pedalled a total distance of 535 kilometres on our overall journey. It represented roughly half our way across the province of British Columbia.

So far so good. So far so great actually. So incredibly great. I would not have changed anything, even the bears and ghosts.

Year Three Completed

Kms 296 to 535
Days 8 to 11

Top of the Coquihalla Pass to Osoyoos

YEAR FOUR –
Buddy 14 Years Old

CACTUS NEEDLES & A DRAGONFLY AT ALTITUDE

Heading out from Osoyoos. I am a believer in family traditions. As simple as playing a family Thanksgiving football game, doing a Christmas puzzle, or having crepes on Sundays. Now Buddy and I were building our own traditions through our Cycle of Life. Of course there was the biking together, but also devouring pies, recounting tales from growing up, and our shared excitement when we started to get ready for another journey. Every year made me more appreciative of what we had started by embarking on this adventure together.

One of the treasured traditions our family has been a part of is an annual Canada Day camping week on Osoyoos Lake with six (sometimes more) families of our closest friends. We parents have all known each other for decades and have remained close even though none of us live in the same city anymore. The kids in our collective families have been a part of the tradition for most of their lives and have become so close they refer to each other as fuzzins, a hybrid of friends and cousins. It never disappoints as a time to create some memorable tidbits in life for all of us.

For two years in a row, the location of our camping week worked out perfectly for our father and son bike trip. The previous year we finished in Osoyoos and timed it exactly to coincide with the camping extravaganza. And then it served as the starting point of this year's leg of our journey, still giving Buddy the chance beforehand to get some fun in with all his fuzzins.

Lake Osoyoos is divided by a spit into two sections. The name came from the Syilx First Nation word sẁiẁs (*soo-yoos*) meaning narrowing of the waters. To get our journey underway again Buddy and I biked across the spit to the east side of the lake on a blistering hot day. The lake also has a second submerged spit, about a foot underwater, that is nearly possible to walk along from one shore to the other, except for a channel dredged-out for boats. The current through that channel is strong and can be dangerous. During one of our annual camping trips, our good friend Lucci, with his fast thinking and the convenient use of his daughter's Ogopogo inflatable water toy, once saved a young teenager from drowning in that channel. Timing is everything sometimes.

Over the first three years of our biking Buddy and I didn't have a single flat tire. That string of good fortune ended on our intense climb out the east side of the valley, up Anarchist Pass, purportedly named in honour of a wild Irishman who settled in the area in the late 1800s. The pass rises about 700 metres (2300 ft) out of Osoyoos and boasts lots of cactus needles scattered on the shoulder of the road – cactus needles that seemed particularly attracted to my tires. On the bright side, my first flat of our journey gave us a good rest break in the heat and the intensity of the long tough climb. The higher out of the valley we rode, the higher the temperature got in the arid air away from the lake. Any wintery reputation of Canada was at complete odds with the sweat rolling down my nose as I worked on the flat and showed Buddy how to use repair levers to get the tire off the wheel.

At the next roadside pullout, we looked back at our climb and the views of all the cherry orchards surrounding the lake. The region is one of the key producers of B.C.'s estimated annual 17 million kilograms of cherries, 90 per cent of the total grown in all of Canada. The area produces nine varieties of cherries: Rainier, Vans, Chelans, Lapins, Sweetheart, Skeena, Staccato, Christalina, and Bing.

When I picked up my second flat on that same climb *(*spits on ground*)*, Buddy's patience was tested. He didn't show much interest in the levers or my progress this second go around. We had a bag of cherries with us and he busied himself by spitting pits off the cliff beside us. When I finished the repair, we had a pit spitting contest. World cherry pit spitting champion 'Young Gun' Krause didn't need to worry about us. His 100 feet record (longer than a basketball court) was safe.

Buddy had once again moved up to a larger bike and we were now both riding Trek mountain bikes. His speed was noticeable on our first climb and throughout that whole first day. Not surprisingly, Buddy continued to step up his pace as he grew into his teens. At fourteen, he was occasionally starting to push me on our rides. He still had his boyish looks, decked out in shorts and a t-shirt, but his frame and muscles were starting to develop.

Our route took us through Greenwood, the smallest incorporated city in Canada and home to the legendary Jolly Jack's Lost Gold Mine. As Jack's last surviving daughter stated in 1967, "Many have looked for it but none have ever found the place yet." *Yet* being the hopeful key word for thousands of gold seekers since. Buddy and I didn't find any glittering gold there, but we awarded a gold star to the best pie of the year—a fresh cherry pie at the Pacific Grill, which once was temporarily branded as the San Piedro Island's Harbour Hotel for the filming of the Academy Award nominated film *Snow Falling on Cedars*. Many of the ocean themed signs from the movie still remain on the buildings in the town, despite being half a thousand kilometres from the coast.

The Cycle Of Life

On our next section heading into Grand Forks, Buddy and I nearly melted. The 35-degree Celsius heat made it feel as if our bike tires were squishing into the pavement. We were dripping with sweat when we found our oasis, the Tastie Treat Drive-In. We grabbed a patch of shade and devoured some much-needed and well-deserved ice-cold milkshakes.

"Looks like you two have travelled a long ways," greeted Evelyn, the proprietor whose family had owned the Grand Forks landmark for over 50 years.

"We heard you had really good ice cream," I offered back.

She smiled proudly.

Evelyn's restaurant was a staple during most of the summer, but apparently especially when the Grand Forks International (GFI) was in town, the largest invitational baseball tournament in Canada. Since 1975, world-class baseball players have descended on Grand Forks and the Tastie Treat Drive-In. The likes of John Olerud, Jeff Francis, Josh Beckett, two-time Cy Young winner Ted Lincecum, and the best hitter ever to come out of Canada, Larry Walker. Buddy and I weren't the only ones saved by ice cream in that town's heat.

When we got back on the road that afternoon, it was so scorching hot that I started to feel my bike pedals through the soles of my shoes. We withered along, but as we approached Christina Lake, heralded as Canada's warmest tree-lined lake, we saw a weather change forming behind us. We were slowly being chased by ominous, nasty looking clouds.

After an *as-fast-we-could-shop-because-there-is-a-big-storm-coming-and-we-are-on-bikes-pit-stop* at the Huckleberry Mountain Market, and an extra tire tube from the super friendly gang at the neighbouring Wild Ways Adventure Shop, Buddy and I scurried with our bikes up a two-kilometre, switch-backed road that wound its way up to the abandoned Columbia & Western (C&W) Rail Line. We moved as fast as we could to stay ahead of the impending storm for as long as we could. The rail path hung on the side of the mountain and gave us a clear view of the squall raging towards us over the lake. There was a sweet, pungent zing in the air that made me think the storm was going to hit hard. We bolted along, searching for a spot big enough to pitch our tent, but there were not a lot of flat options with the rail line cut across a steep mountain face. After ten minutes, we finally found an area just wide enough. We leapt off our bikes just as the skies let loose. The trees around us swayed wildly. Buddy and I did not say anything to each other as we scrambled like mad. We had never worked on setting up camp so fast. We came close to losing our tent fly in a big gust of wind that resulted in a small rip but could have been much worse. We succeeded in getting our little Marmot tent up, our bikes tucked under a big tree, and our panniers squeezed under a tent fly newly adorned with a strip of duct tape. We were soaked as we crawled inside and felt lucky to be out of the storm that had slammed down on us. We stripped off our wet clothes and cozied into our sleeping bags, amazed at the constant drumming of the torrential rain.

We had plenty of time and being bunkered down early seemed like a good cue to break out Buddy's story for the year. I had been thinking I should tell him more about how I had been short through my early teens and into high school. With Buddy approaching high school himself, and still to hit his big growth spurt, I figured he might relate to a *short* story about me. Fittingly Canadian, and given our recent tent repair, it also involved duct tape.

Timing is Everything Sometimes

I attended an exceptionally large high school in Edmonton, 2500 students, so being the shortest among that many kids meant I was really short. At the start of grade ten I was five feet even—well, almost five feet. Truth be told that to be five feet, I needed to stand on my toes and spike my hair. And I had hit an age where my height raised some concerns within on the prospect of dating.

During my first week of high school, I developed a little crush on a girl who was about five inches taller than me. Unfortunately, I had theorized an invisible sound barrier around the five-foot mark that made it difficult for those above to hear from those of us below. More unfortunately, that girl was annoyingly steady-handed and never dropped anything that would bring her ears below the barrier. I needed ingenuity if I was going to have a conversation with her, so with prescient *Red Green* creativity I duct taped together a scheme. No one should ever underestimate the lengths teenagers are willing to go to get noticed by someone they're interested in.

I convinced myself it would be a good idea to duct tape two blocks of wood to the bottom of my shoes, for a little extra height for when she walked by my locker. Utilizing unhemmed pants, I was sure no one would notice.

A note of caution: In the event you ever find yourself using duct tape to secure blocks of wood to your shoes in order to get into a conversation with someone you have a crush on, don't use too much tape because it is a bugger to get off. I found this out the hard way after she didn't end up walking by my locker that morning. In the name of love—and not wanting my homemade elevator shoes to be noticed by my friends, plus the fact that I couldn't physically remove the blocks from my shoes from all the duct tape I had used—I ended up standing beside my locker and missing the entire first class of the day.

My next chance was at the break after first class. I had a full hour to practice my stance and balance with my newfound height and confidence, neither of which ended up lasting long. The bell rang and the halls filled. It took just one subtle accidental bump from the throng of schoolmates streaming by to knock me off my stilts and squarely on my butt. It was, of course, precisely at the exact moment when she walked by. It became painfully apparent that the invisible barrier only affected sound and did nothing to impede vision. Maybe she couldn't hear me, but she could certainly see me. Sprawled out with blocks of spruce strapped to my feet. Timing is everything sometimes.

Of course there were other challenges outside of dating with being short. A few weeks into that first year of high school, a couple of guys pondered the possibility of *fitting* me inside my locker. I could have saved them a lot of time determining the outcome. As a small kid there is entertainment value in finding out on your own where your body can't and can fit. I knew I couldn't quite jam myself into my hockey bag, but I did know that I could squeeze into my locker with room for a basketball and my backpack. Not a lot of interest was shown when I offered my opinion on the matter to the two guys.

Timing is everything sometimes. And in that moment I had three things going for me:

1. Their proposed experiment coincided with Big Harry strolling by. Big Harry was the biggest kid in our entire school. One of the guys hightailed away immediately.
2. Harry liked me. Maybe it was the fact that he was the biggest guy in school and I was the smallest. In any case, Harry didn't like what he saw.
3. I still had a roll of duct tape in my locker.

Fun fact about duct tape: It turns out to be strong enough to hold the full weight of a high school student a foot off the ground against a concrete pillar.

Smugly satisfied, Harry slapped me on the shoulder and strolled off down the hall. I looked at the guy strapped to the pillar, his urgency to conduct the *me and the locker experiment* well passed. I was tempted to leave him there and walk away too, but I thought better of it. I could probably do without deepening bad feelings and making enemies, especially knowing that Harry was graduating later that same year and wouldn't be roaming the halls forever with perfect timing. I grabbed some scissors and snipped the guy out of his bonds. Funny how things turn out sometimes because he and I ended up being friends down the road. And right when I was cutting him down, the girl I had a crush on walked by and said, "Careful with the scissors, you sweet little teddy bear." It was far from getting a date with her, but sometimes you gotta take what you can get. Right? When you're 5 feet (almost) tall in Grade ten, I figured "sweet little teddy bear" was something I could work with. Timing *is* everything sometimes.

Buddy never seemed as concerned about his height, but I felt it certainly couldn't hurt for him to know more about how I was small at his age too. There can be benefits from sharing commonalities like that through stories.

"You know I'm not worried about you being short," I said to Buddy. "I just wanted you to know how good duct tape is."

We both noticed that our duct tape was holding on our tent fly as it continued to rage outside and we slowly nodded off.

The next morning as we woke in our sleeping bags, all we could hear were birds and we could tell that the storm had passed.

Outside, the early morning sun was coaxing mist off the trees all around us. We crawled out of our tent and were confronted with how much wind there had been. Our bikes were knocked over and branches were scattered all over the place.

The trail was soaked, but the sunrise lit up the entire valley in red hues all the way down to Christina Lake. The lake was so still that every tree on the other side was a perfect reflection of itself in the water. Nature's own Rorschach test.

We dried off our bikes, packed up our wet camping gear, and continued our way along the C&W Railway again. This time not at the frantic pace we'd been keeping before the storm.

The Crowsnest Highway had been climbing parallel to us, but at a faster rate of ascent and was soon much higher than our trail. It eventually crossed over top of us on a massive bridge as it continued up towards the Bonanza Pass. Our route took us under the highway and around to the secluded north side of Mt. Shields, where we had far-reaching views across Arrow Lake, part of the Columbia River waterway.

"Pretty cool not to hear or see a single vehicle," Buddy said.

The abandoned railway was filled with old wooden trestle bridges and hand drilled tunnels, each bored through the syenite of the area—rock as hard and similar to granite. It made it feel like we were biking through a scene out of *Lord of the Rings*.

When we got to the one-kilometre-long Bull Dog Tunnel, we jumped off our bikes and started walking. It got darker and darker until we got to a point of complete blackness. There was a bend in the tunnel that made it so we couldn't see light from the openings on either end. When we turned off our bike lights, we couldn't even see our hands when we held them right up to our faces.

"Helloooo!" Buddy echoed down the tunnel. "Let's see how far we can make it without lights!"

We pushed our bikes along the uneven tunnel floors slowly. Within twenty steps, I hit the side of the tunnel. We turned on our lights and Buddy burst out laughing at me standing ninety degrees and perpendicular to the soot covered train tunnel wall.

The Cycle Of Life

In a few short steps I had overcompensated for the curve so much that I was at a full right angle to the correct direction.

It was near those tunnels, in 1924, that Doukhobor leader Peter 'Lordly' Verigin and eight others were killed in a train bombing. Speculation pointed to the Sons of Freedom being responsible. The Doukhobors and the Svobodniki (also known as the Freedomites or Sons of Freedom) escaped tyranny and persecution in Russia by emigrating to Canada around 1900. They set up farms and communities in Western Canada, with the Kootenays region becoming a Doukhobors' mainstay. Their communal approach to living flourished in the Kootenays and quickly became a key part to the development of the entire region. The Sons of Freedom, splintered from the Doukhobors, exalting an extremely strict objection to materialism and property ownership. Oddly, they displayed their dissent to the government and the Doukhobors by protesting in the nude. In the 1920s and 1960s, their protests went as far as also committing arson and bombing, again in the nude. Serious tragedies resulted out of their actions, but I couldn't resist mentioning to Buddy that their chosen style of protest seemed comically strange to me.

"Prancing around buck naked and throwing around homemade explosives," I said to Buddy. "It sounded like a Wile E. Coyote accident waiting to happen."

That segued into me pointing out that the E. in Wile E. Coyote stood for Ethelbert.

"You do know a good deal of random, extremely odd pieces of perhaps useless information," Buddy said with a sigh.

I agreed. I was proud of that. I figured it was one of my important roles of being a dad.

As we completed the C&W trail and made it to Castlegar, we crossed the impressive Columbia River, just past where the Kootenay River joins it. There are fourteen dams on the main stem of the Columbia River, three of them located in Canada. We learned that the Canadian dams accounted for over 90 per cent of all electricity generated in B.C.

In the U.S., dams on the Columbia system contributed over 40 per cent of the total hydroelectric generation in the entire nation. That is some kind of powerful water. So powerful that after all those dams, it still spills out enough water into the Pacific Ocean to fill three Olympic size swimming pools every single second. Buddy and I did our own test of the flow by having a toothpick race, but instead of toothpicks we tossed two big branches into the river from atop the bridge. Buddy declared victory when his stick stayed visible for a nano-second longer than mine. Then both sticks disappeared down the rapids. We wondered if those branches made it to the next downstream dam and chuckled that perhaps they even raced side-by-side for a thousand more kilometres to eventually shoot through the Columbia Gorge and into the Pacific.

Once on the other side of our bridge crossing, we faced another killer climb and it was another incredibly hot day. Our route sent us over the Bombi Pass, 1214 m (almost 4000 ft). Buddy and I put our heads down, geared down, and crawled along on our bikes, standing on our pedals for a few stretches now and then.

About two-thirds the way up, Buddy announced, "My leg is hurting."

I asked him if it was a muscle issue? A cramp? A spasm? His knee?

"It's just really sore when I push," Buddy relayed.

We weighed our options.

"We can call it a year and ride back down to Castlegar," I said. But Buddy wanted to grit it out. His determination seemed to grow each year of our journey.

Buddy cautiously minded his leg up the pass. I sweated out about five pounds in the heat. We were both relieved to reach the top.

While we took a breather and guzzled water, a lone dragonfly hovered around the whole time as if trying to tell us a secret. Buddy's knee felt better and better, and we both started to look forward to the upcoming downhill section. We started out and the dragonfly even tried to follow us but couldn't keep up long as we rocketed down the east side of the pass.

We cruised into Salmo in the late afternoon. We could see the runs of the Salmo Ski Hill where the Huser family and volunteers have kept locals entertained in the winter for so many years. When we arrived in town, one of the first places we came upon was the Dragonfly Café. We felt it was a sign, or that we had been the unsuspecting prey of an incredibly elaborate, effective, and intensely targeted marketing campaign. Either way, we didn't have a choice to not stop there. Right? And we were glad we did. We celebrated with locally made gelato, followed by turkey and cranberry sandwiches, followed by more gelato. If it was a marketing ploy, they followed it up and delivered with great goods.

The gelato did wonders for Buddy's leg.

Finishing in Salmo, we had completed another 275 km through the mountains and were over 800 km from our start in Victoria.

"It is starting to feel like we've biked a long way," Buddy said. I whole-heartedly agreed.

We were four years in. We would soon be in another province. I wondered - would we both remain as exuberant and committed as the years rolled on?

Year Four Completed

Kms 535 to 803
Days 12 to 15

Osoyoos to the Kootenays in Salmo

YEAR FIVE –
Buddy 15 Years Old

MUPPETS AND TREE BEARS

Taking off from the Dragonfly Café. Buddy and I aimed to make it to Fernie for what would likely be our last full year of biking in B.C. Salmo to Fernie. It sounded like we were visiting the *Muppets*.

Buddy was 15 years old and had just completed his first year of high school. Suddenly, at least suddenly to me, he wasn't a little boy anymore. I was 45 but it sure didn't feel like it was thirty years ago when I was goofing around in high school. How could I wrap my head around the fact my son was finishing Grade ten? His milestone was another don't-blink reminder to enjoy the little things in life.

As suspected, Buddy was sprouting up. It was impossible for me not to notice as I oiled the chain on yet another new bike for him prior to heading out. Buddy was now on an adult-sized mountain bike. Our garage looked like a used bike shop.

In between our annual trips, life continued, and Buddy's interests gave glimpses into the person he was growing into. He was at the age when a myriad of questions were being thrown at him.

"What are you going to do after high school?"

"What do you want to do with your life?"

I think I did a reasonable job of minimizing my part in those inquiries. Buddy may have seen it differently. He was probably feeling like the chicken who dreamed of a world where they can cross a road without having their motives questioned.

Buddy was excelling at school. It was tough to find programs that challenged him. He was uncannily good at board games, too. He got adopted by a unique group of *Magic: The Gathering* game aficionados, some even ranked on the pro circuit of that massively popular card game. Buddy was considerably younger than all of them, but they offered him a spot at their once-a-week get-togethers afterhours at a small game store. I'm sure he learned a few new choice phrases hanging with a bunch of guys in their twenties and thirties, but they thoroughly enjoyed him being part of their group and his personality and level of play fit right in. If that wasn't the case, they guarded their circle and wouldn't have hesitated to bluntly show him the door.

Buddy had gravitated from hockey and lacrosse teams to more individual sports like rock climbing and Tae Kwon Do. He was enjoying the physical nature and discipline of the martial art. His instructor was a talented champion from Korea who took a shine to Buddy.

I wondered how his mid-teen years would treat me as a parent. I hoped I was giving Buddy enough space, but also enough guidance. I was navigating the delicate tight-rope of being encouraging, but not prodding. Advise, but don't preach. Respect independence, but not forget to be willing to open my wallet when needed. I was in transition from being a primary source of information for my oldest kid, to being just one of many voices, to sometimes struggling to get an opinion in there for consideration. Sure, mid-teens are confusing for kids but what about the parents?

One night leading up to our departure, I was at our kitchen table, Google-mapping potential routes which made me realize how technology had changed the way we prepared for our trips. Buddy's generation was the first to grow up with smart phones and an endless list of apps. It came with a different set of pressures at his age than I had to deal with. The world of constant information and communication added a significant edge for Millennials and Gen Z to cope with. I felt my generation had grown up with more freedom to make mistakes and learn from those mistakes, certainly compared to recent times where all is seemingly far more scrutinized and consistently under the magnifying glasses of peers and society. It made me even more glad that I had taken a see-what-comes-our-way approach to our bike trips. That outlook had already led to several occasions where we had to live with our errs and navigate our way through together. Dealing with snow, and locked fences, and bears, and crazy storms. Those moments became big parts of our adventure, and I saw value in them for Buddy's growth. So much that I oddly found myself looking forward to the next curveballs that would undoubtedly come our way.

I felt good about where Buddy was headed in life. He was deftly avoiding the pitfalls of social media that some in his generation seemed lost in. I found it admirable that he wasn't ever concerned with how many 'likes' he was garnering. I was continually impressed with his ability to focus on what he enjoyed and how he had no qualms about standing up for his own beliefs. I was proud of him. He made it a good deal easier for a dad to juggle the blend of counsellor, mentor, and friend.

Through it all, I was left with an extra bounce in my step realizing that Buddy remained excited to bike with me each year. I was incredibly grateful that we remained so close. Not every parent gets to enjoy that. I was lucky.

A few months prior to our trip, a biologist friend of mine who had heard about our bear encounter in the Coquihalla sent me a bunch of articles about bears in British Columbia. I'm not sure if he was trying to help me or scare me. I think I would have rather found out how many bears live in B.C. *after* we left the province, but there I was reading about how one out of every four Grizzlies in North America have a B.C. address. One quarter of <u>all</u> Black Bears in Canada hang out in B.C. The Spirit Bear, also known as the Kermode, is unique to B.C.

I shared the material with Buddy and we agreed it all added up to a lot of bears.

The good news; bear attacks are uncommon. There was less than one fatal Black Bear attack on people every three years in B.C., and only one fatal Grizzly attack on people every five years. The odds were in our favour, although Buddy was quick to point out that this was now five years of biking for us in B.C.

Buddy and I got in a kick out of an official looking B.C. Fish & Wildlife advisory that warned people who were going into the backcountry to not depend solely on carrying bells and pepper spray. It said to watch out for fresh signs of bear activity and to know the difference between Black Bear skat and Grizzly skat. It outlined how Black Bear poop is smaller and contains berry seeds and squirrel fur. Grizzly poop is larger and often contains little bells and smells like pepper spray.

Leading up to our departure, there had been loads of rain in southeastern B.C. where we would be biking. The forecast looked promising though.

Our first task was the Kootenay Pass. Locals refer to it as the Salmo-Creston. Buddy and I dubbed it *The Great Gonzo* for taking us from Salmo to Fernie. The pass sees its fair share of sudden drops in temperature, even in the summer that can result in temporary winter-like conditions. It boasts one of the highest mountain road passes in Canada at 1795 m (5885 ft). It has an average grade of nearly five per cent over a span of more than twenty-three kilometres. We anticipated the combination of steep and long would be, well…steep and long. Climbing mountain passes tended to be slow going by bike, but this one had the reputation of being a bear of a ride.

A short way out of Salmo, a holiday trailer pulled off onto the shoulder directly in front of us. The truck door opened. "What the heck are you guys doing here?"

It was close family friends from Alberta. Chance encounters like that make the world seem smaller and more interconnected. After hugs and high-fives, I think the coincidental meeting gave us more power in our pedals as we headed toward our climb.

As we biked along the highway, I made a comment to Buddy that since he had started high school, I had noticed that he was caring more about his appearance and the clothes he wore. He was certainly a sharper dresser than I was at his age.

"That wouldn't be for any romantic reasons, would it?" I teased him.

Buddy didn't answer the questions but jumped all over the opportunity to rib me right back. He launched into his observations on how I had completely given up on maintaining any semblance of being fashion conscious.

"You realize that you have drawers of shirts upon shirts you should have retired a long, long time ago, right?" Buddy teased me back. "You know what having a *dad's wardrobe* means? Don't you? You might want to consider having at least a few shirts that aren't older than your kids."

I had to laugh at that.

"Well, we both know I'm not going to stop wearing any of those classics."

"Classic? Dad, you realize the ski t-shirt you're wearing right now is from a race that took place more than a decade ago?" Buddy said, grinning.

He had a point, but I wasn't about to admit it.

"That race, you know, was a classic," I said.

"*Was* a classic. *Was* being the key word," Buddy said. "You're a lost cause," he giggled as he pointed to my mismatched socks.

He suggested I at least pretend to put in a minimal amount of effort.

I looked down at my socks. Also classics. I decided to pedal harder.

The highway pass was cut into the side of a steep mountain. It made for such a considerable drop beyond the road's shoulder that we were biking at the same level as the tops of the trees on our right, with their trunks well below us farther down the mountainside. Up ahead we spotted something big and black on the top of one of the trees beside the highway. By the time we realized it was a bear, we had pulled almost parallel. It was a bit alarming with the bear staring directly at us. As the crow flies, we were close. He looked like an oversized Koala as he clutched the top branch. We surmised that for the bear to make any sort of advancement towards us, he would have to go down to the base of the tree then back up to the highway. If that happened, we knew he would still be fast and we mapped out our escape to quickly turn our bikes around and hightail it back down the pass again, as fast as possible. Our recent readings about bears being able to run equally as fast uphill as down did not bolster our confidence.

The bear turned around at the top of the tree and raced down headfirst like a squirrel. His speed was unnerving, but it was immediately clear he had alternative plans as he ambled away into the forest. He wasn't in any hurry once he hit the ground, but he was headed in the right direction from our perspective.

Buddy and I resumed our way plugging up the pass, keeping a lookout for any other tree bears. I wished I had taken a picture of him in the tree, but pictures from situations like that can sometimes turn out to be a lot more bear than the photographer bargained for. Just as well keep it as a memory.

As we crossed over the summit of the pass, we were greeted with small piles of snow on the side of the road. Nothing that would turn us back around. We had made it to the 1795 m top of Salmo-Creston, aka Kootenay Pass, aka Great Gonzo.

I told Buddy that Gonzo had to be one of my favourite Muppets, along with Bert and Ernie from *Sesame Street*. How *Sesame Street* survived multiple generations was amazing, even in Canada where we almost lost the show in the '70s over a kerfuffle about the pronunciation of *zed* versus *zee*. Canadian stations started to pull the show off their programming, but Canadian kids protested. 'Bring Back Bert' picketers won the day and *Sesame Street* returned, but with content altered specifically for Canada, like a beaver named Beau and some home-grown performers like Sharon, Lois, and Bram, Fred Penner, and Mr. Dressup. Just a couple of years back, in 2008, another Canadian lit up *Sesame Street* for one of their all-time most beloved and watched moments when B.C.'s Feist performed an irresistible version of her Juno winning song, "1-2-3-4." Her stroll around *Sesame Street* garnered over three quarter billion YouTube hits.

A trucker stopped to talk to us at the top of the pass. We advised him to keep an eye out for the bear. He nonchalantly relayed how a bear had trashed a cooler from his backyard in Castlegar earlier in that month. The bear punctured every single can of a six-pack of Kokanee and left the Old Milwaukee six-pack untouched. Canadian bear, Canadian beer, Canadian content.

Our ride down the other side of the pass was a speedy one. A forty-kilometre-long joyride, as exhilarating as any roller coaster. Suffice it to say there were no vehicles passing us on our bikes, and certainly no bears, no matter how fast they could run downhill.

Our bear sighting had been exciting, but I jokingly lamented to Buddy that "we'd biked all the way around Kootenay Mountain without seeing a Sasquatch." Since first reported in 1917 in the Columbia Valley Pioneer, the legend of the Kootenays being home of the Sasquatch has playfully grown in the lore.

We spent the night camping alongside the Moyie River in Yahk, B.C., but not before Buddy convinced us to pop into a little ice cream shop called Two Scoop Steve's, located beside the Yahk Soap Company which had a bunch of goats hanging out on their rooftop. After enjoying some Bear Butt ice cream, aptly named considering our tree-top friend, Buddy I found a scenic little tent spot at the nearby provincial park. There was just enough dry ground to pitch our tent beside the swelling river from the relentless rains of the prior weeks. We were the only ones in the entire campground. "I hope we don't float away in the middle of the night," I said.

Buddy and I had gotten used to no sleeping pads, but I was happy the ground was extra soft when we rolled out our sleeping bags. Now that Buddy had a year of high school under his belt, I had a tale in mind for this year's storytelling session. The more stories I shared on our trips, the more meaningful the annual tradition had become, I think for both of us.

I looked back at high school as a time when parties entered the fray. With Buddy at that age, I thought I should take the next step with my stories and delve into that time frame in my life. I wondered as parents if we sometimes avoid telling our kids about our more free-wheeling years, or when we maybe weren't always the best example. But I figured maybe sometimes the more dubious or embarrassing stories are the ones most important to share. If I wanted Buddy to know more about me, shouldn't I be telling him about all sides of me?

How to Shake at the Lake

At the end of my high school years, I hosted a party at our cabin at the lake that turned into an annual event for the subsequent decade. It affectionately became known as the *The Shake at the Lake*. It evolved into entire weekend affairs, including a massive pig roast thanks to my great friend Dickey. We had champagne flapjack breakfasts, volleyball tourneys, music until sunrises, infamous (and often loss of pride notching) sangria races, collector

The Cycle Of Life

custom t-shirts, and the occasional fireworks display.

About a month before the party one year, my friend Jim came up with a wild idea at 2:00 a.m., just after we had realized it was the fourth of July. Ideas that arrive at 2:00 a.m. are often better not acted upon, but ten minutes later Jim and I were in his little two-seater Toyota MR2 bombing our way to Montana, racing over the 'Going-To-The-Sun Road' that had been used in the opening scene of *The Shining*. When Jim and I arrived in the small town of Whitefish, we partook in as much American Independence Day festivities that could be thrown at us in a single day, right down to some late-night snacks with locals at a 24-hour Safeway after everything else in town had shut down. Our eventful day and night ended with a strange old fella on the steps out front of the grocery store, mumbling a hex at us for being out so late in the mountains on the night of a full moon. We both thought it was a little suspicious considering it wasn't a full moon and he also asked us to buy him a bottle of Wild Turkey.

27 hours after we embarked on our adventure, we were back in Jim's car for the long-haul home. On the way out of Whitefish, we noticed a number of roadside stands with 'fire sales' who were clearing out their fireworks inventory. Immediately, we both thought about the 'Shake'. We negotiated about $1000 worth of fireworks for $150.

Toyota MR2 engines were in the back, behind the seats. It left us under the front hood for our fireworks, after a brief chat about the importance of avoiding front-end collisions with a front end full of gun powder. On the way out of the parking lot, the fireworks guy even handed us a bonus grab-bag full of firecrackers and roman candles.

When we arrived at the border, between our seats on the small console we had a bagel, two juice boxes and our little bonus paper lunch bag marked in thick black felt pen: 'ROMAN CANDLE GRAB BAG - $5'. The first thing the border custom officer said to us, "Those aren't fireworks in that bag, are they?"

We stared back blankly. Two deer caught in headlights. I suppose we could have been a little more forthcoming about our treasure we had under the hood, but technically he only asked us specifically about the little bag. We sheepishly nodded our heads and he shook his head. "No way." He gave us two options. "Either turn back around to set them off or hand them over."

With sad puppy dog eyes, we offered up the bag of firecrackers.

Two significant details worth clarifying:

1. We did truthfully answer what the border agent asked.
2. Firework laws in Alberta have subsequently changed a lot since the '80s, including allowing for the sale of fireworks in the province, so technically Jim and I could have been considered pioneers and ahead of our time.

When it was time for our pyrotechnic bonanza moment at the 'Shake', Jim and I were strutting around proudly as we *expertly* set up our questionably-imported explosives on an empty stretch of shoreline. We were on the other side of a creek from where the crowd had formed for our midnight beach bonfire. As soon as our show began, judging from the "oohs and aahs", our original 2:00 a.m. idea felt more golden by the minute. Between blasts, Jim and I smiled at each other and signalled who would light the next one. All was looking good leading up to our grand finale: the *Galaxy of Fire, a 64-shot fireworks extravaganza* and the *Burn Baby Burn, a rapidly repeating 24 shot exploding cascade that would be sure to captivate all of your senses,* according to the package. Jim lit one and I lit the other. The first blasts, from both launchers, went up together brilliantly, perfectly timed. We looked over at each other with two enthusiastic thumbs-up. From the audible collective gasp, the beach onlookers were also undoubtedly impressed.

And that was when things went sideways, literally. Maybe it was the hex the old guy laid on us in the Safeway parking lot, or negative karma from our whole 2:00 a.m.-drive-down-through-the-night-to smuggle-illegal-fireworks-back-across-the-border adventure, or simply from the lack of foresight from two guys sticking exploding tubes of dynamite into beach sand – but it all started to *backfire*. While I was looking at Jim, still with his thumb up in the air, I saw a streak of light go zooming over his head and his expression suddenly changed. He looked like Roger Rabbit after drinking a bottle of triple XXX hot sauce and his eyes-popping-right-out-of-their-sockets. Directly behind Jim, our side of the creek turned into *Apocalypse Now*. Both of us went diving for cover behind anything we could find with as many "WTFs!" flying through the air as there were explosions. The 24-shot blaster had dislodged itself from the sand and tipped on its side. The "oohs and aahs" had been replaced with other colourful superlatives.

Then, as quickly as the chaos had started, the last blast ended. Tom Cochrane's *Good Times* blared, and everyone on the beach went back to what they had previously been doing as if it had all been part of the show. Despite post-traumatic stress from our simulated war exercises, what else could Jim and I do but join in and get back to shaking at the lake.

Buddy looked incredulously at me when I finished the story. "Did you guys really do that at the border?"

I tried to reiterate that the point of the story was about starting small things that turn into bigger and more impactful events. Buddy just grinned at me. I made sure to clarify that I never condoned our border crossing or lack of safety on our fireworks show, but more than willingly conveyed how the 'Shakes' turned into a grand part of my life. There is an old adage that some people tout about how, "Nothin' good ever happens after midnight." But I admitted to Buddy that I thought maybe some good things do. Jim and I still giggle about that 2 a.m. idea to head to Montana and the exploits that followed.

Cell service had not yet made it to Yahk, so the next morning I was on the hunt for a payphone to give Pam an update. The search did not take long. In the short walk between our campsite and the ice cream shop, we found three pay phones. Those weren't the only ones in Yahk either. Payphones can be hard to find these days with more than half of them in Canada disappearing since the turn of the millennium. Not in Yahk though. And I made a note to put some extra coins in my pack for the next trip through.

There was a bulletin board beside the payphone with an advertisement for an 8-track car stereo. I had to explain to Buddy what an 8-track was while pre-emptively and defensively pointing out that 8-tracks were before *my* time, sort of. Not in Yahk though and Buddy made a note to load some extra tunes on his phone for the next trip through.

Problem solving of different generations.

Mid-morning, Buddy and I crossed into the first new time zone of our journey—going from Pacific to Mountain time. We leaned our bikes up against the sign and did a little happy dance on the side of the road. Only four and a half more time zones to go.

Before our last stretch into Fernie, we had a harrowing sprint through a short, tight-curved tunnel that was blind to oncoming traffic from both sides. We had to carefully time our dash through it amidst the constant traffic on the Crowsnest Highway. We survived and coasted into a roadside pull-out a few hundred metres to the east. While we snacked, there was a loud screech, a blaring horn and a sharp bang, all coming from

The Cycle Of Life

the blind tunnel. A moment later, a Hutterite family pulled in beside us in what looked like a brand-new Ford truck, towing a brand-new wheat swather. The implement had been side swiped on the driver's side. The family members were dazed as they got out to inspect. Then we saw a lady running towards us along the highway from the tunnel. Out of breath, she shook her fist at the Hutterite father, swore profusely at him, then turned around and ran away down the highway disappearing back into the tunnel. There had been no exchanging of insurance or contact info, just one-way profanities returned with shocked silence. The Hutterite father stood there dumfounded for a long moment with his thumbs hooked in his suspenders. He then glanced our way and said one word, "Okay." Then got back in his truck and the family drove off, swather in tow. Buddy and I were the only ones in the rest stop at the start of the whole sequence and the only ones there in the end. A crash, an onslaught of harsh words, everyone going off in their own directions, and us - a bewildered and speechless father and son holding a bag of trail mix. I was glad we hadn't been in that tunnel fifteen minutes later than we were. Timing is everything, again.

We wrapped up our biking for the year just past the turn-off to world class Fernie Ski Resort, in the Lizard Range of the Canadian Rockies. We met up with my good friend and Canadian skiing great, Felix Belczyk, who graciously offered us a ride back westward with our bikes in the back of his truck. Considering his prowess on the World Cup circuit in the 1980s, it seemed highly appropriate to be catching a lift from him after reaching the ski area used in the *Hot Tub Time Machine* movie about a group of partying skiers who are sent back in time to the 1980s. Felix had also arranged for us all to stay overnight at his childhood home in Castlegar, where he first honed his talent that made him the first Canadian ever to win a World Cup Super-G. I had met Felix's mom, author Renate Belczyk, years earlier while I was skiing in the trees in the middle of nowhere at nearby Red Mountain. She had been in her seventies at the time. She ended up skiing in the trees with us for a few runs before she needed a bigger challenge and bombed in on someone else. Felix laughed at how many times he had heard that same story from different people. And I laughed because I said I now knew the secret to Felix's skiing success.

While we recapped our biking journey to Felix, Buddy and I agreed that the hands down winner of this year's best pie went to Barb Smythe's sour cherry pie at Auntie Barb's Bakery in Cranbrook. It was so good, we figured it could bring Sasquatches out of hiding. Not in the pie category, we also gave a well-deserved nod to Shauna's cinnamon buns from the bakery in Fort Steele, worth a trip there all on their own.

It was another incredible year of biking. Buddy proudly—but not too proudly because he was 15 after all—proclaimed to his mom that we had made it into our second time zone of our journey. I stepped back while I watched him talk about our adventures, our new bear sighting, and even my socks.

Our biking would surely be a different experience the next year. We were headed into the prairies.

The Cycle Of Life

Year Five Completed

Kms 803 to 1104
Days 16 to 19

Salmo, B.C. to Fernie, B.C.

YEAR SIX -
Buddy 16 Years Old

A WINDY THREE PROVINCE JUMP

Into Wild Rose Country. After five years of hoofing it up and down the Rocky Mountains, our plan was to bike from South Eastern B.C. all the way across Southern Alberta in a single year. Buddy and I were kind of hoping to make it all the way to Saskatchewan so we could touch our bike wheels to all three of the westernmost provinces on the same leg of our journey.

For my 46th birthday earlier in the year, Buddy presented me with a drawing he had done of me on my bike, peeking back over my shoulder. I was wearing the *classic* ski t-shirt that he had given me a hard time about. I'd be lying if I said I didn't get a bit misty. Buddy had started to further explore his passion in concept art and illustration production, and he was becoming quite skilled. He didn't get his drawing talents from me. He had the goods to give it a shot if he was interested to pursue a career in the arts.

Two months before our bike trip, I tagged along with Buddy when he got an opportunity to attend Massive Black, a big concept art event in Los Angeles that featured some of the best artists in the business, like Marko Djurdjevic, Wesley Burt, Jason Chan. Buddy was on fire there, checking out firsthand all their techniques and illustrating alongside an array of great talents. I beamed as a dad to see Buddy interact in that world and see him enjoying learning so much.

Every year as we started out on another biking leg, more people found out about our journey and we increasingly got wishes of encouragement. When my good ski pal Ted Allsopp heard where our starting point was for the year, he set us up for a night at his friendly getaway in the shadows of Mount Hosmer and Ghost Rider Peak, just outside of Fernie. When the sun hits Ghost Rider Peak at just the right angle, a horse and rider mysteriously appear on its southern cliffs. Having Ted's place for a night to hang our helmets meant our trip would get underway in well-rested style.

With the Prairies ahead of us, Buddy and I finally made the switch to road bikes. I dusted off an old white 1971 Motobecane that had been a prime road bike in its day. With its high tensile steel frame and things like chrome tipped forks, the vintage touring bike is significantly heavier than modern road bikes, but it sure looked good. Earlier that spring, I picked up a sweet, blue Schwinn Traveler bike for Buddy. His bike was 12 pounds lighter than the Motobecane and put him, for the first time, on the same size wheels as me. I was determined to not yet relinquish the pacesetter role to him, but we both knew he was going to be a lot faster on his new bike, in great shape and sixteen years old.

Riding out from Ted's ski chalet, we first passed through Sparwood and stopped for a few pictures with the World's Largest Truck which was almost seven metres (23 feet) tall—the behemoth Titan Earth Mover. It made us and our bikes look like the Canadian great comedian Rick Moranis had pulled another 'Honey, I shrunk something' stunt.

Twenty kilometres further, we pulled up to the "Welcome to Alberta, Wild Rose Country" sign. Buddy and I wide-grin toasted each other with our water bottles. It was official. Our first province was in the rear-view mirror. It amazed us that there are only 30 countries in the world that are larger than B.C. The province is four times as large as the United Kingdom and twice the size of Japan. We had a long way to go, but completing all our way across B.C. felt like a major accomplishment.

Crossing the border also put us on the eastern side of the Continental Divide—the line that uniquely separates the watersheds of the Pacific and Atlantic. On the B.C. side of the border, Buddy and I biked around Summit Lake that eventually drains into the Columbia River system and out into the Pacific. Just a few kilometres further east than that, we cycled beside Crowsnest Lake on the Alberta side, where the water eventually makes its way into the Oldman River and out into Hudson Bay.

About an hour of fast biking later, with our hands down on the lower drops of our handlebars, Buddy and I rolled into Blairmore for our first night in Alberta. From the highway we could see the jagged peaks of Seven Sisters Mountain, which hosts one of the most challenging running events in the world, *The Sinister 7 Ultra*, a 161-kilometre foot race with 6,600 metres of elevation gain through treacherous terrain.

To celebrate arriving in our second province dad-and-son-style, we spent the evening visiting Blairmore's funky little movie house.

It was one of the coolest old theatres we'd ever seen. Since 1921 the Blairmore Orpheum was host to a conspicuous list of events including striking miner meetings during the Great Depression when workers weren't allowed to congregate outdoors. Buddy and I wolfed down a ton of Chinese food at Ben Wong's Café, and then went to the Orpheum to watch Charlize Theron terrorize in *Snow White and the Huntsman*. I even managed to get a couple of dad tax handfuls of popcorn out of Buddy's bucket. A great break from our biking and another memorable night.

The sun warmed our faces the next morning, pedalling east under spectacular pale blue skies that Alberta is famous for. We had a sombre stretch coming out of the Rockies as we passed through the Frank Slide area, a town that had been completely wiped out by a massive avalanche in 1903. 75 <u>million</u> tonnes of limestone broke off the overlooking Turtle Mountain and took less than a hundred seconds to bury the entire mining settlement. We quietly rode past giant boulders and endless piles of rock that still line both sides of the highway. It felt as if we were biking on a completely different planet—a vivid reminder of the fragility of life.

Southern Alberta is renown for strong winds. The gaps in the Rockies funnel strong downslope winds off the east faces of the mountains that speed up and sweep across the entire region and into the Prairies. There is so much wind in the area that in 1993 it led to one of the first commercial wind farms being installed on Cowley Ridge. Environment Canada estimates that, on average, almost one third of the region's days report winds over 40 kilometres per hour. We were hopeful that we would get some of those prevalent winds out of the west to push us along. "If we got those winds at our backs, it will be like having Donovan Bailey pushing our bikes," I said to Buddy.

Bailey actually ran faster than 40 kilometres per hour, when he set the fastest recorded speed by a human with his 1996 Olympic gold medal.

As anticipated, strong winds arrived as we approached Lethbridge. However, they were not what I had sold Buddy on. The winds were blowing hard, but directly into our faces. Buddy wished I hadn't gotten his hopes up. Jason Kwasny of Lethbridge's Headwinds Cycling Club once described it as, "Cyclists just don't have anywhere to hide. On the Prairies, there are really no trees to escape the wind when it blows." We learned quickly and painstakingly how right he was and how disheartening it can be to bike on the Prairies against the wind. By mid-morning, our arduous ride had us longing for the steep mountain climbs of B.C. instead of the relentless wind of the Prairies.

We found some relief when we ducked out of the wind for a rehydration break at the Tourist Info Centre in Lethbridge. An animated guy named Rowdy welcomed us inside. He caromed around the info booth while he talked. He let us know that blows have reached as high as 170km/hr there. But he was most interested in talking about the Calgary Stampede, which he excitedly relayed was only 13 days away and counting.

"I haven't missed the event in the last twenty years," he gushed. "Do you know they dole out over a quarter million free pancakes at the Stampede every year? If you put 'em into stacks, that would be like four CN Towers of pancakes! Do the math!"

After fighting the wind all morning, I whispered to Buddy that the only math I had in me added up to all four of Rowdy's pancake towers being blown over.

Our pace continued slow when we got back on our bikes and into the elements as we made our way through a few little southern Alberta towns. It was a wonder to us how some of the older buildings managed to stay standing in those winds.

"Maybe that's what happened to all the dinosaurs in Southern Alberta," I said. "They simply got blown off the face the earth."

It was crazy to think that scientists estimated the population of T-Rexes in the area was once so numerous that there was one of those big guys per every hundred square kilometres.

"That might have made for more stressful biking than the wind," Buddy said.

I started to laugh out loud but had to keep my mouth closed in the head-on gales.

It was nearing sunset when we eventually arrived in the town of Bow Island. Even my super-fit sixteen-year-old looked wind-whipped and maybe was exhausted as I was. We rode past the World's Largest Bean Mascot, Pinto MacBean, a statue standing five plus metres and looking suspiciously like Mr. Potato Head in a sombrero-type hat.

"Canada has some pretty weird world's largest attractions," Buddy said. He was right, and I was sure we would see more.

The gusts mercifully calmed down as evening fell. We set up our tent at the Centennial Campground and stretched out our sleeping bags. We were both drained and just lay there staring up at the roof of our tent. I had just enough energy to tell Buddy his story. Pinto MacBean's sombrero gave me a handy segue into a Mexican holiday I had with a close friend. It was just a goofy trip, but it had been my first big non-family time out of Canada and showed me how even a simple adventure can have a way of cementing lifelong friendships. I felt it was a notion worth sharing with my son.

How to Swim in the Best Pools

During our first year of university, my pal Steve and I mapped out a plan for a trip to Mexico. We ended up spending more time planning our trip than we did on a few of our classes.

We were on student budgets but our travel agent found us every deal she could. She went so far as to hook us up with discounted and ill-advised skin cancer promoting visits to the neighbouring Fabutan.

"Just so you don't burn when you get your lily-white Canadian asses down on the beaches of Mexico," she said.

Steve and I wrote our last exams for the year with our luggage packed.

We got to Puerto Vallarta and our three-star hotel turned out to be okay, at least in a shady-Mexican-joint-kind-of-way-okay. To be fair, as advertised it did have a pool. There was even towel service, if rumpled and faded yellow-lime green towels in a poolside wicker basket counted as towel service. On our first visit for a swim there was a guy lying face down on the edge of the pool. He didn't move for so long that we wondered if might be dead or simply frying his way to death in the Mexican sun after passing out from too much tequila. The situation convinced us that we owed it to ourselves to at least check out one of the fancier resorts. We gathered up our pesos for bus fare.

When we got to our chosen mega-starred resort, we strolled the grounds with our mouths gaping open as if we were Fred Flintstone and Barney Rubble discovering *Shangriladida*. The pool wasn't like anything you would find in Alberta. There were wading areas, deep ends, nooks and crannies with bridges and passageways. There were waterfalls and islands. And a curved swim up bar with submerged stools, an over-sized thatched palm-leaved cabana roof, brightly coloured tiled countertops, and beautiful people chilling out sipping tropical drinks with tiny umbrellas. Lionel Ritchie's *Celebration* welcomed us into the heavenly setting. It was as if we had landed in a beer commercial.

Steve and I dropped our towels on two of the last vacant poolside lounge chairs and headed over to the swim up bar. I pictured myself as James Bond while others swam up to have drinks beside me while I sipped on a shaken martini. Although, despite my best tanning bed efforts, I likely wasn't being mistaken for anything other than a pale Canadian student, perhaps pool trespassing, and sucking on a straw sticking out of a big ol' pineapple.

Steve and I sat at that pool bar until our feet turned to prunes.

It was when we decided to return to our loungers that we first noticed something strange. Every single lounge chair in the resort was adorned with a freshly pressed, blue and white towel. Other than a couple of rumpled and pale yellow-lime green ones draped awkwardly over two lonely empty lounge chairs, smack dab in the middle of a sea of others. They stuck out like Green Bay Packers at a Chicago Bears convention. Steve and I casually made our way over to our spot. I lay face down and nonchalantly stuffed my strikingly different towel into my beach bag under my lounger.

I was beginning to relax when I heard a deep Spanish accent. "Are you guests of the resort?"

"Oh yes," replied Steve in his most angelic tone.

"Very well and fine," said the Spanish fellow. For the briefest of moments, I was thinking - wow, that was easy. But my hope was short-lived.

"Perhaps I can assist you with getting a resort towel for you to use? What name are you registered under?" he said.

Without a glimmer of hesitation, Steve answered boldly, "Santos ... Burt Santos."

"Very well, I'll be right back with your towel, Mr. Santos, sir."

I can't imagine that my choking laughter helped Steve sell his story.

By the time I rolled over to assist Mr. Burt Santos, all I saw was the backside of a beige collarless hotel staff uniform strolling away, presumably to either return with an official resort towel for Mr. Burt Santos or hotel security to haul our lily-white Canadian asses and our pale yellow-lime green towels out of view from the beautiful people pool.

"Santos? Burt Santos??" I snickered. "Where did you get 'Santos' from?"

Steve replied with a hint of urgency, "I think from his name tag. I think *his* name is Santos."

While we didn't expect a high likelihood of our pool towel faux pas landing us any hard time in a Mexican jail, our vacation had just begun and me and Mr. Santos hightailed it out of there.

We slinked back to our own hotel where our pale yellow-lime green towels and unfortunately our budget fit in.

Ah, the Beautiful People Pool. The next day we decided it wasn't worth the risk.

Don't get me wrong. The Burt Santos incident didn't stop us from going back to the Beautiful People Pool. We just didn't think it worth the risk to bring the pale yellow-lime green towels for our second visit.

As a bonus, the weather back home was miserable the whole time we were away, which has a Canadian way of making a tropical vacation seem all the better. And we returned with much less lily-white asses too.

When I wrapped the story, Buddy asked me, "Did you get in trouble on the second visit?"

I explained how we had met some girls from the resort who set us up with the right coloured towels for our return visits. We had some good fun at that pool and our whole trip. It bonded a lifelong friendship and produced some situations that Steve and I still get kicks about to this day. Unique friendships often are an amazing result of adventures. As we chatted a while longer and it got darker, I wished to Buddy, "I hope you grab hold of opportunities that will come your way in your life too."

We woke the next morning to the hum of electric motors. Before we got up to investigate, we got our first laugh of the day. I snapped a photo of Buddy's hair that looked like he had survived a tornado. When we got around to poking our heads out of the tent, we discovered the sound we heard was from golf carts. Lots and lots of golf carts. The campground was filled with golfers, and the early rush hour traffic was for trips to and from the campground's bathroom and shower building. It gave us our second laugh of the day. Don't people walk anywhere anymore?

And then we got our third big laugh of the morning when later we found out that Bow Island got its name purely by mistake. The town wasn't even on a river or any body of water. The name had comically been mixed up with another town's name when getting registered – which the way it was told to us sounded a bit like there had been some drinking involved.

What we didn't laugh about was the forecast. The winds were going to be strong out of the east again for the entire day. While we were having breakfast at the Rolling Pin Café, two old-timers sitting at the neighbouring table, who looked eerily similar to the two old guys from the balcony in *The Muppet Show*, told us they couldn't believe how many days it had been since they had last seen winds out of the west.

"Looks like you picked the wrong year to ride your bikes through here," one of the old guys mumbled while he hooked his thumbs into his jean overalls.

"The year kind of picked us," I replied.

All part of the adventure I told myself. Although truth be told, it kind of felt like we got on the wrong end of a *trick or treat*—a phrase believed to have originated in Southern Alberta in 1927. Alberta kids have all their angles covered considering that the Prairies are the only place where Halloween'ers also yell *Halloween Apples* when they are out getting door-to-door candy. Yell *Halloween Apples* anywhere on the Prairies and everyone knows exactly what you want. East or west of the Prairies and you just get a lot of what-the-H-E-double-hockey-stick stares. Unexpectedly, our server said she felt sorry for us because of the weather and brought us cinnamon buns on the house. Her treat did the trick and took our minds off the winds for at least a little while.

Coincidentally, one of the all-time classic Halloween treats originated in Bow Island in 1982, when Tom and Emmy Droog founded Spitz. Their Cracked Black Pepper are the best sunflower seeds in the world in my opinion. From humble beginnings, Spitz grew to become the official sunflower seed of all Major League Baseball. It is funny that sunflower seeds are technically not seeds, they are achenes. But I guess that makes sense—a wildly successful misnamed treat from a small, mistakenly named town in Southern Alberta, just south of where trick or treat became a thing.

Buddy and I set in stone a 'no *Spitz* rule' while we biked into the wind. We felt that it could make it nasty for the guy in second position. It's all fun and games until someone gets hit with a Spitz at 40 kilometres an hour.

All day long we grinded it out against brutally harsh winds as we forged east towards Medicine Hat. It was hard not to get discouraged. The strong winds battered all senses and even left teeth feeling gritty. The intensity of the sound alone dampened our spirits as it ripped through all our clothing and rushed past our helmets. Buddy compared it to biking through sand, working twice as hard to go half as far.

I would try to crouch as low as I could on my bike, hunched over my handlebars, but could only ride for so long in that position. Buddy and I drafted behind each other whenever we could. The wind was relentless. There was no escape.

During one respite we took shelter behind a big highway sign.

"We need a distraction," I said to Buddy. "Remember how that superhero chat distracted us on that climb up the Coquihalla?"

"It would sure be nice to have a superpower to help us battle the winds," he said.

I reminded Buddy that I already possessed a superpower that made me pretty special. Unfortunately, my special superpower was the ability to grow skin hundreds of times faster than average people. Buddy didn't think my psoriasis was going to impress anyone on a superhero level and it wasn't going to help us much with the wind either.

Back on our bikes, we weren't able to distract ourselves with any discussion. It was too difficult to hear each other over the wind, even when we shouted. The winds got stronger and stronger, but we slowly pedalled onward.

We struggled our way around Medicine Hat, the town that was said to be *born lucky* with its wealth of natural resources. There was so much natural gas there that *Jungle Book* author Rudyard Kipling once said, "This part of the country seems to have all hell for a basement, and the only trap door appears to be in Medicine Hat."

Those words apparently had an impact on a Medicine Hat high school aged Gordie Johnson, as evidenced by his later penned lyrics, "About heaven in Alberta. Where they got all hell for a basement," for one of *Big Sugar's* biggest hits.

East of Medicine Hat, a peculiar natural feature called the Badlands Guardian had been recently discovered. A mysterious 250 square metre formation of natural rock that, when viewed from the air, bears the striking resemblance of a human head wearing a First Nations headdress. The image was so distinct that many find it unnerving when they first see it. The only thing manmade in the area are the roads leading to a lone oil well, which adds a strange touch to the landmark in that it looks like the head is wearing ear buds, the roads as the headphone wires and the oil well as an earpiece.

The rest of the way across the southeast corner of Alberta remained taxing. At points we wondered if we were being pushed backwards. When we managed to look up from the wind for brief moments, we would catch glimpses of the mystical Cypress Hills majestically jutting up over the otherwise flat prairie landscape. We would have likely visited them if not for our wind battles. The Cypress Hills are home to Canada's largest dark sky preserve, a

39,600-hectare interprovincial project between Saskatchewan and Alberta, and in conjunction with the Royal Astronomical Society of Canada.

By the time Buddy and I made it to the little hamlet of Irvine, about 20 kilometres before the Saskatchewan border, we were completely out of gas. We had planned on tenting that night but wanted a break from the wind, so we treated ourselves to The Treat Dreams B&B located above the Hamertons' General Store. All the ceilings in the building, even on the second floor, were ten-feet high and covered with stamped tin, an emblematic feature from the early 1900s. The General Store had played an important role in Irvine, especially through the height of the rail years when the town was an important stop along the Canadian Pacific Railway. To this day it serves as a central gathering spot in the quaint village nestled away from the bustle of the Trans-Canada Highway. In the corner of the store sits an old built-into-the-wall safe. During the Great Depression, a train-hopping mob broke into the place and tried to blow the safe open with dynamite. Apparently, the mob went to all that work for nothing though. As Buddy inspected the scars from the blast on the safe doors, Karen Hamerton told us how the robbers didn't realize it at the time, but the doors of the safe had in fact been open. They weren't locked at all when the dynamite was set off. The kicker was that the safe had been completely empty at the time because, like a lot of businesses on the Prairies, the General Store was just as depressed as the train hoppers.

Relaxing in big, high-backed chairs in the B&B that evening, Buddy and I rated our pies from across Alberta. We gave a nod of appreciation to a homemade savoury meat pie that we got from Premium Sausage in their replica grain elevator building in the town of Seven Persons. But on the yummy scale, Brenda at the Coaldale Bakery sweet-talked us into a mouth-watering Dutch Apple & Raisin selection on our ride out of Lethbridge and that pie hit our top spot.

Sadly, the next morning, the wind still hadn't yet died down. We had to show a lot of determination to get back onto the highway, the winds out of the east seemed even fiercer.

"It would be great if we made it into Saskatchewan," I said.

"Ya, maybe," Buddy responded. "I guess at least to the border," he continued.

"Ya, maybe," I replied.

Our excitement of being out in the wind again was palpable.

We did end up making it from Irvine to the Saskatchewan border that day, to ensure our tires touched all three western provinces on the same leg of the journey. But that's where the winds screamed at us "No Farther!" At the border, we propped our bikes up so that they wouldn't blow over and snapped a few pictures at the Welcome to Saskatchewan sign with flags flapping loudly from ever-present gusts. That welcome sign would be where we would need to pick up again next year. We then walked our bikes over the highway meridian, turned back west, and rode with the winds mercifully going with us.

When we crossed over the border back into Alberta, considering it was such wide-open space, it was hard for us to imagine that Alberta's famed Rat Patrol has been so incredibly effective keeping the province rat free. "How do they not just blow into the province with these winds?" Buddy joked.

The story goes that Norway rats made their way to the east coast of Canada in 1775 and slowly extended their territory westward at an estimated rate of about twenty-four kilometres per year. By 1930 the rats reached eastern Saskatchewan and wreaked havoc on farms and caused millions of dollars in losses. To combat the spread, Alberta stepped up to the challenge and held conferences and distributed thousands of pamphlets on rat control to the towns throughout eastern Alberta. The province went on to create an official Rat Patrol in 1950 that grew to over 250 officers within a decade and has since kept the province completely free of the rodents.

We stopped at a rest stop just inside Alberta and ran into two guys from Québec who were cycling west. The winds had been a lot kinder to them than us. When they finished their way across Canada, their plan was to bike down the west coast of the U.S. to California. Buddy and I couldn't think of any other cyclists we had come across during the first six years of our journey and concluded it was due to the fact we'd been off road a lot or on quieter highways in B.C, and that no cyclist in their right mind would have been on the same eastward trek we had just experienced through these past days of winds in Alberta. We expected to see more cyclists in the upcoming years now that we would be on the Trans-Canada Highway for long stretches.

At the rest stop, we found ourselves a ride back to Medicine Hat with our bikes in the back of a pickup truck. Then boarded a Greyhound bus for our return home.

I couldn't have asked for a better bike partner than Buddy. I told him he was fun to bike with every day of every year of our journey so far. We had just been put through demoralizing conditions, but Buddy remained fully up to the challenge. I imagined a lot of sixteen-year-olds might have complained a good portion of the time about having to put up with all those winds, but Buddy didn't voice objections. Maybe the annual nature of our adventure helped by knowing this was just one leg of our journey among many. It was after all about the whole journey. Regardless, beyond being my son and me being proud of him, Buddy was really a good guy to experience all this with.

"I love that we're on this journey together," Buddy said to me on the bus.

"Me too, my friend! Me too," I said back. (*big, big lump in throat*)

Six years in and we had crossed over our second, and then third, provincial border. The headwinds pushed against us but hadn't beat us. Maybe we picked the right year after all, thinking back to our old guy friends in the Rolling Pin Café. That said, we kept our fingers crossed that when we came back that the flags would be flapping in the opposite direction, and we still might get to enjoy those infamous prevalent Prairie winds out of the west. Just to be on the safe side, I made a note in my journal not to jinx anything by saying anything about any winds of any fashion in advance of our trip next year.

Year Six Completed

Kms 1104 to 1563
Days 20 to 24

Fernie, B.C. to the Saskatchewan border

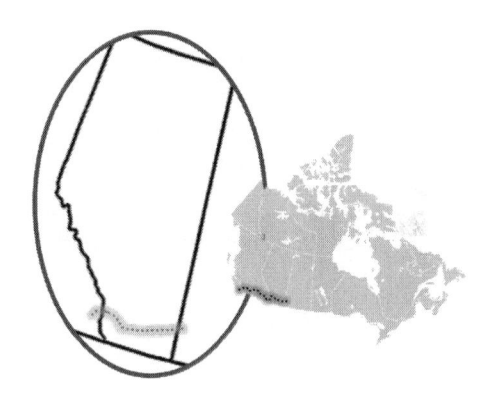

YEAR SEVEN -
Buddy 17 Years Old

ROUGHRIDER TERRITORY, COWBOY RODEOS, AND GOSPEL JAMBOREES

Into Saskatchewan. I was a very proud dad. We had big news to celebrate in our family ... Buddy graduated from high school. That notion was a bit of a *gulp* moment for me.

We started the first year of our Cycle of Life when Buddy was in elementary school and now he was a high school graduate. THAT notion was a bit of a *big gulp* moment for me.

In fact, he not only finished high school but qualified for a program that allowed him to complete his high school while attending college courses. So somehow he managed to finish off an Associate of Arts degree from college in the same year! My little boy was now a college graduate?!? NOW THAT was a bit of a *super big gulp* moment for me!

Completing both programs at the same time seemed so normal while he was going through it that we almost forgot how impressive it was. It had not been a case of school being pushed on him or being his sole focus. The truth being he was more into his extracurricular activities than anything to do with school. It just happened to be a program well suited for him. Buddy took it in stride, but it was an exceptional accomplishment, and I am super proud of him for taking it on. He's a talented guy and continues to inspire me. I'd compare him to *Doogie Howser*, but he wouldn't know who I was talking about.

I had some trepidation this year heading into our bike trip as Buddy was in better shape and getting stronger all the time. He had been biking long distances to his college every day and working to complete his black belt in Tae Kwon Do. I, on the other hand, seemed busier than ever at work and had limited my workouts to passing a kidney stone and being asked to walk backwards slowly away from eye vision charts. I could feel the Cycle of Life pacesetter torch starting to singe my fingers.

Our ride this year was going to be quintessential Canadian Prairies. We packed plenty of mosquito spray and guessed we would be sharing the road with prairie dogs (gophers). Gophers are the enemy in Saskatchewan. Apparently, a single gopher can excavate approximately a tonne of farmland in a single year.

The first pickup truck to pass us after we restarted our ride at the Saskatchewan border had a bumper sticker that read: "My other car is a John Deere." Two trucks later, "Life is short. Farm naked." A few after that, "Gophers Suck. Blue Bombers Suck More." We were definitely in Saskatchewan.

Buddy boldly announced, "I'm picking a gear and riding all the way to Regina without changing gears once." He had become interested in fixed gear bikes back home and I knew how determined he would approach his personal challenge to succeed.

The Prairies were gradually, but constantly developed over hundreds of millions of years in the area between the Pacific Shield and the Canadian Shield. Over time, the land was forced up and down, alternating between inland seas and grassland landscapes. Most people picture endless wheat fields in the Prairies, but that doesn't do justice to the striking nuances formed in certain parts of the province like grassland hills and tranquil lakes. But hey—or is that hay?—Buddy and I figured we would be seeing our fair share of wheat among those nuances, with an incredible 11.8 million acres of wheat farming in the province.

The fields that were the most striking to us from atop our bikes were mustard. Brilliant yellow stretched out on the horizon. Saskatchewan grows so much mustard that it is highly probable that the next bright yellow bottle squeezed all over a hot dog, veggie patty, or hamburger anywhere in North America is thanks to Saskatchewan farmers.

I've always considered most folks in Saskatchewan to be down to earth, community oriented, friendly, hockey-loving, and downright obsessed on the Canadian football front with eyes for no one other than the Saskatchewan Roughriders. When the Ottawa Rough Riders (that's Rough-space-Riders) folded in 1996, it mercifully put a stop to the question, "Wait ... wtf is the deal with two teams (out of nine) in the league with the same name?"

Quirkiness is part of the charm of the Canadian Football League though. Like the fact that the Parkdale Canoe Club once played for the Grey Cup 1909. But still ... with only nine teams in the league, couldn't someone come up with another name?!

In any case, with the Rough Riders gone, Saskatchewanians had sole claim to Rider Pride. And wow, did they claim it.

Rider Pride was in-your-face on our entire bike journey through Saskatchewan with flags, jerseys, and green banners all over the place. I swear I could even hear the echoes of a few *Grrrrrrrrrrrrrrrrrreeeeeeeeeeeeen Riders* cheers drifting across the fields. The entire province is fanatically mad in love with their football team.

Each little town we rode through emanated its own weirdly wonderful, down-to-earth vibe, something I think every Canadian would be lucky to experience first-hand instead of just from re-runs of *Corner Gas*. Buddy and I pegged Maple Creek to be right up there with the best of them. The prairie town aptly boasts 'Where Past is Present'. Its main street is lined with those old two-storey buildings that are mainstays in old western towns. We arrived while their Cowtown Pro Rodeo was going on at the High Chaparral Arena. The Calgary Stampede may be the high-priced pinnacle of rodeos, but the small-town events give spectators the chance to get right up close to the action with many of the same cowboys and livestock. There are over one hundred annual rodeos in Western Canada, and we figured the timing was meant to be as we attended the show in Maple Creek that night. And we learned all kinds of local things, too. We found out that hoodies in Saskatchewan are called bunnyhugs, although no one could tell us why. We were told about the importance of buying watermelons *that fit*—more on that later. And we also saw a job posting for a repair shop that was looking for a new welder that in part read: "male or female as long as you can play right wing."

After the rodeo, Buddy and I rolled our bikes to the Ghostown Blues Bed & Breakfast. They had covered chuck wagons converted into swank mini-cabins, and found a nice spot for us to pitch our tent. At breakfast the following morning, we walked into their saloon with two of the staff fittingly singing along to *The Last Saskatchewan Pirate* by The Arrogant Worms.

Prior to breakfast, our day started like many of our mornings on our trips. I would wake and mention to Buddy it was time to get up. Buddy would sleep. I'd crawl over Buddy to get out of our little two-person tent. Buddy would sleep. I would stretch and take a short stroll around. Buddy would sleep. I'd shake the tent and tell Buddy to get up. Buddy would sleep. I would put snacks together for the day and fill our water bottles. Buddy would sleep. I'd open the tent and poke Buddy and tell him to get up. Buddy would sleep. I would then take the fly off the tent, shake the dew off and hang it to dry for a bit in sun or breeze while I jotted some things in my journal. Buddy would sleep. I'd reach in and shake Buddy and tell him to get up. Buddy would sleep. I'd pull up all the tent pegs and the tent would start to collapse. Buddy would get up. We worked together like clockwork, me and my teenage son.

As we got ourselves rolling down the Trans-Canada again, we passed wide open fields and made our way to more wide open fields.

"I feel like I'm in one of those old cartoons where the landscape backdrops are on continuous loop," Buddy said. "I think I had recurring dreams about it last night."

I confided that I had a weird recurring dream back in grade two about showing up to school in my underwear.

"I hear that is common and a lot of people have had a version of that nightmare," I told him. "But if that is not the case, maybe don't go advertising my phobia of showing up to school in nothing but my ginch." Or "gotch" as we found out at the rodeo is apparently how underwear is referred to in Saskatchewanese.

Buddy and I faced gentle head winds for most of the early part of the day, but nothing compared to what we had been up against the previous year. Perhaps it was coming from the wrong direction, but we welcomed the light breeze to help keep the mosquitoes at bay. Mosquitoes can't handle winds over 10 kilometres per hour. When there was no breeze and we stopped for a break, the mosquitoes would instantly swarm us. Even biking too slow sometimes gave mosquitoes too much free access. The faster we rode, the less we had to deal with mosquitoes.

We rode fast.

The breeze also made the shimmering golden wheat fields sway back and forth all around us. It gave an ease about the Prairies, that and the slow roll of colour changes on the fields through the day. I was becoming more in tune noticing different or unusual landscapes that appeared on the horizon. Not that I needed any heightened sensory perception when it was something as surprising as the gigantic salt pile deposits near Chaplin Lake. They're not easily missed. The twenty-five-kilometre-long lake serves as an important bird sanctuary for over 30 different species in the area, and the source of one of the richest and purest, natural-forming sodium sulphate deposits in the world. A massive salt manufacturing operation in the middle of the Prairies was quite unanticipated, but there it was. The lake on its own was enough to catch us off guard. But it shouldn't have. Chaplin Lake is just one of 100,000 lakes in the province, which we guessed surprises a lot of people who only think of Saskatchewan as endless wheat fields.

Just east of Chaplin, Buddy was pedalling ahead of me when we passed a giant billboard announcing the hamlet of Parkbeg as the home to *Gainer the Gopher*. Even mascots of the Roughriders' football team were cherished and idolized in these parts.

We pushed our biking late into dusk and made it to the Besant Park Campground, an oasis of poplar trees among the farm fields surrounding it. The campground, however, was hosting the Sandy Creek Gospel Jamboree and was fully booked. Quite graciously the hosts found enough space for us to pitch our tent.

Gospel songs echoed through the park while we set up camp. Meeting the jamboree organizer got us chatting about how there are so many different possible paths in life. People find happiness in all kinds of ways. I suggested to Buddy it was good to challenge and explore different paths. He had his whole adult life ahead of him and who knew what lanes he might consider. Or what safe lanes he might choose to change out of.

As we snuggled into our sleeping bags and with singing still floating through the campground, I supposed to Buddy there were times in my life when I probably played it safe, but I for sure felt lucky to have explored some unobvious paths as well. Working abroad, being in the ski industry, starting a board game venture, even going off to some far-out places. I figured all of it played into my happiness and what I like to think was quite the bounteous life. That night in our tent I told Buddy a story about a time when I most certainly steered out of a safer lane. My aim was to illustrate what I saw to be the importance of keeping eyes open to possibilities - and maybe sometimes looking a bit outside the comfort zone.

How to Sauna Like a Scandinavian Pro

Sometimes life's tidbits pop up on the most unexpected of paths. Through a fortuitous series of events while at university, I got an opportunity to do a working internship for a steel structure exporter in Finland. I could have easily missed it and travelled a far safer route, but I am forever grateful curiosity won the day.

I went into my Scandinavian adventure embracing a *roll with the punches* approach, which came in handy right out of the gate when I ended up in the wrong port in Stockholm to catch the overnight passage across the Baltic Sea to Helsinki. It turned into a good example of how sometimes even errant turns can lead to some outstanding life tidbits. I quickly made two new friends who had made the exact same mistake, and soon after found myself racing to the correct port in a Swedish cab with two Irish girls, frantically trying not miss our ferry to Finland.

My new companions, who mischievously referred to themselves as Irish One and Irish Two (in ode to Dr. Suess's *Thing One* and *Thing Two*), had plenty of advice to share during our cab ride. Irish One told me to ready myself for an onboard party. Drinking in Scandinavia was expensive – but with tax free alcohol on the open water, many Swedes and Finns took *full* advantage on the ferries during weekend jaunts across the Baltic Sea.

Irish Two told me to be wary of Akvavit, a strong Scandinavian spirit, ambitiously named "the water of life." I was warned that, "it could knock you on your keester if you aren't careful."

A few hours into our crossing, Irish One winked an 'I told you so' look at me as she pointed to everyone in the ship's bar singing 99 *Luftballons* at the top of their lungs. Irish Two just shook her head and lamented why none of us had paid heed to her warnings of Akvavit.

I had not booked a berth on the boat and finding a place to sleep was a challenge, especially after far too much of the water of life. Through a wee bit of resourcefulness, I found a nice quiet spot for myself at the bottom of a kiddie slide, in a magical bed of coloured plastic balls.

At 7:00 a.m. I took two, fifty-pound hits directly in my midsection. I bolted up to find myself staring into the screaming faces of two frightened kids. The last thing they expected to find at the bottom of that slide was an Akvavit monster lurking in the bowels of the ball pit. My nap had genuinely been quite pleasing, but the on-board wake-up call system left more than a bit to be desired.

At the arrival port in Helsinki, I was greeted by Oikku from the Helsingin yliopisto (University of Helsinki), to welcome me to Finland and help me get on the right train to my final destination, Peräseinäjoki, about four and half hours north. Oikku wasn't surprised by my dulled condition, I hadn't been the first foreigner that he had picked up from the Baltic booze cruise they disguised as a ferry. I had a number of hours before departure time and Oikku had arranged for us to visit a Finnish sauna house as a welcome present and to help me recuperate and relax.

It took less than an hour in Finland for me to realize what my aforementioned grade two ginch (or gotch) nightmares had foreshadowed all those years ago. I found myself standing in a room full of strangers, white knuckling a towel wrapped so tight around me that it was cutting off circulation. Everyone in the sauna was in the buff. I fixated on keeping my towel tightly adhered to my torso and averted my shy Canadian eyes to not make eye contact with anyone. I quietly parked myself in an empty spot on a wooden bench. It was so hot I could hardly breathe. I stared at the wood floor between my feet with laser beam focus.

Out of the blue...WHACK! Right across my back. Someone smacked me! Panic set in. If I looked up, I might have to make eye contact with somebody. Maybe it had been a mistake. I should just ignore it. But before I could decide what to do. WHACK! AGAIN! I shot straight up and found myself standing over a large naked lady wielding a thicket of branches high above her head ready to strike again.

I momentarily considered a counter strike but was too dumbfounded and she looked like she could have probably taken me in a scrap anyhow. WHACK! Again, but wait...she hadn't even flinched and I hadn't felt anything that time. WHACK! It went off again. Someone else was getting WHACK'ed. What in the world had I walked into? I didn't know what was worrying me most: standing completely naked, with my towel now at my ankles, and making eye contact with people in my real-life grade two nightmare; or that the puzzle pieces had started to come together to reveal a tightly packed room of sweaty naked strangers who were complicitly beating each other with tree branches.

I learned two important things on my first morning in Finland.

First: North Americans (certainly me) have a lot more inhibitions than Scandinavians when it comes to being naked in public.

Second: The *gentle* whacking of birch branches with sauna neighbours is commonplace in Scandinavia, and typically people are appreciative of the act as it helps to bring your blood closer to the surface of your skin for greater sauna benefits.

Oikku, who had watched it all, laughed—I like to think with me—but it was definitely at me. I made a mental note to do more reading about what to expect while I was in Finland.

After a six-hour train journey, I arrived in Seinäjoki, settled into my apartment, then proceeded to commute out to Peräseinäjoki early the next morning to start my internship at PPTH Norden. It was a highly successful steel structure company that I had been hired to work with on sales initiatives and developing export projects. I struck a great friendship with my boss, Kari. I even agreed to leave my apartment and live with him and his family so that he could practice his English.

They lived in a beautiful house in the country. Every night Kari would fire up their classic birch sauna and pour me a Canadian Club that he had brought in specially for me to *enjoy* and remind me of home. I'm not sure I would typically recommend a glass of straight rye in a sauna to help with English lessons, but it certainly led to some colourful conversations. Thankfully Kari never hit me with any branches in his sauna.

After my wonderful three-month term was over, on my last day at PPTH, my co-workers treated me to one last grease-dripping-down-the-front-of-my-shirt grillimakkara (bar-b-qued pork and beef combo-ed sausages suspecting-ly injected with additional grease) and presented me with a farewell t-shirt. It was an-I-can't-imagine-a-more-ideal translation of a Finnish saying from the town:

"One needs not be crazy to live in Peräseinäjoki, but it's helps."

To be sure, I thought it was a good thing to be a little bit crazy no matter where in the world you lived.

It was a time in my life I had wanted to tell Buddy about, if for nothing else than to open a conversation about not getting too attached to only one initial idea of what to expect in life. The direction Buddy chose for his life was completely up to him. But I hoped for him to keep a keen eye out and be open to possibilities - and not to be afraid to branch out from the safety of going through life with blinders on. I knew that he knew I wasn't telling him stories for just the stories, but he humoured me in my approach to fatherly advice.

I immediately could tell that my sharing of my experience had an impact on him. He said to me, "I could sure go for one of those sausages right about now." I elbowed him in his sleeping bag.

Our next major stop on our bikes was Moose Jaw, Saskatchewan's fourth largest city. Putting 'Saskatchewan large city' into perspective, Moose Jaw would have to grow its population of 33,000 by 50 per cent in order to catch Dollard-Des Ormeaux in Québec and get into the top 100 populated Canadian municipalities on Statistics Canada's list.

Moose Jaw has one of those quirky Canadian city names that fascinated people from all over the world, not to mention led to a lot of stolen road signs. It made the list of oddly cool named Canadian cities – that also included Eyebrow, Stoner, Horsefly, Medicine Hat, Dead Man's Flats, Head-Smashed-In Buffalo Jump, Climax, Flin Flon, Wawa, Punkeydoodle Corners, Saint-Louis-du-Ha!-Ha!, Crapaud, Dildo, Come By Chance... and on the list goes.

The first thing Buddy and I did in Moose Jaw was gorge ourselves on Chinese food at the National Café on Main Street. It was an early lunch. We would have sought out the Modern Café, because it was the restaurant of my friend Terry's grandfather, but it had closed its doors a few years earlier after many years of supporting a number of families and university endeavours. Chinese restaurants were the staples of so many towns through the Prairies, and they became an intrinsic part of the fabric of the western provinces. Often, they were the only restaurant in town, as highlighted in Ann Hui's insightful book about the important role they played in small town Canada, *Chop Suey Nation*. It sure wasn't easy though. Canada first allowed young male Chinese immigrants into the country because they wanted the labour, but it wasn't until 1947, when the Exclusion Act was repealed, that many of their families were finally allowed to join them. Built on some of the most admiral entrepreneurial spirit, the Chinese restaurants of western Canada remain an inspiring symbol of how hard immigrants worked and sacrificed to make better lives for their children. They played an integral role in developing what I like to think it means to be Canadian.

Those restaurant pioneers also used their ingenuity to give us uniquely North American dishes like chop suey, stir-fried beef and broccoli, and deep-fried lemon chicken. I remember being surprised in my teens to learn that ginger beef originated in Calgary. Without traditional Cantonese ingredients to use, those savvy restauranteurs created whole menus of food that many Canadians grew up with, including me.

With our biking bellies refueled, we extended our break and took in Moose Jaw's Al Capone tour. Yes, that is correct, Moose Jaw has an Al Capone tour. In the prohibition era, Moose Jaw was known as Lil' Chicago and legend has it that Al Capone had a secret getaway and covert booze operation in the Saskatchewan city. He was rumoured to have travelled by train from Chicago to Moose Jaw, where he would connect with his Canadian alcohol producers in secret meetings and make behind-closed-door arrangements for rum-runners to transport his booze across the U.S. border. There are tours of the underground tunnels beneath Moose Jaw, where the likes of Al Capone and Diamond Jim Brady allegedly hung out. The tunnels are complete with speakeasy lounges and secret passageways to this day.

Once we left the mob ghosts behind, Buddy and I got back on the road by mid-afternoon, feeling energized after our long break. And then the famous Prairie winds out of the west finally made an appearance. The impact on our biking speed was incredible. I smiled as wide as I could while keeping my lips sealed, I had to be mindful of how many bugs could fly into my mouth while we rode.

Just over a third of our way between Moose Jaw and Regina, we saw more proof of how much Rider Pride there was in the province. We biked by a big highway sign that showcased Ron Lancaster and his 46,710 career passing yards record for the Roughriders, the precise same forty-two kilometre distance that the sign was from Mosaic Stadium in Regina where the team plays. It was a game day and just past that sign Buddy and I got a good chuckle as a truckload of fans drove by us, honking their horn and all sporting watermelon hats made out of half melons on their heads. Watermelons *that fit*. Now we understood. Only in Saskatchewan. It was hard not to appreciate Rider Pride.

In the early evening, we arrived at the outskirts of Regina and stopped at an understated Welcome-to-the-City information roadside pullout. Buddy got a kick out of their tourist map billboard that highlighted three specific things in the city: museums, hospitals, and liquor stores.

A guy in a Ford pick-up truck saw us with our loaded down bikes and asked where we were headed.

"Eventually to the east coast," I said.

"Seriously?"

"Yep, and we started on Vancouver Island," I said, proudly.

He took off his ball cap and rubbed his forehead. "C'mon, surely you can't be serious?"

In homage to Regina's Leslie Nielsen of *Airplane!* fame, I was tempted to answer, "We are serious and don't call me Shirley," but I refrained and instead laid out how we were tackling our biking annually.

"Seriously?" he said, again as Buddy and I pedalled off.

As we rode towards the city centre, Buddy and I made our way around Wascana Lake. When Regina's Olympic Medallist Mark McMorris was only 12 years old, he ripped around that lake on a wake board for three and a half kilometres attempting to set a Guinness World Record. Regina isn't the first place you think of for snowboarding, but all that wakeboarding time had to have been key to McMorris' success to not only go on to snowboard in the Olympics, but to also become the first person to ever land a Backside Triple Cork 1440, which sounds cool no matter what sport someone is talking about.

The name Wascana originated out of anglicizing the Cree name for the area, oskana ka-asastēki, which roughly means *where the bones are piled,* or Pile O' Bones, which the city was referred to before it became Regina. Pile O' Bones still remains its official un-official nickname.

We bunked down for the night at Pam's cousin Danny's place in Regina, who greeted us with a bar-b-qued ribs feast ready for us as soon as we arrived. A new city always feels so much friendlier when you know someone who lives there. Our whole evening epitomized the friendliness that the Prairies are famous for. We did our best to create a pile o' bones that night from all those ribs. Buddy, with bar-b-q sauce on his chin, created a graveyard's worth on his own.

We had made it halfway across Saskatchewan and were now over 1800 kilometres from our west coast origin. And of course Buddy had managed to grind his way this trip without changing gears once. I wasn't the least bit surprised. He was a determined bugger when he wanted to be. I also wasn't surprised when he singled out a classic prairie pie, apple and rhubarb, from tall Jack at Schimmel's in Swift Current, as his favourite of the year.

The farther east we got, the more it impressed upon us at just how fantastic this adventure truly was. I marked in my journal that we still had over 5000 kilometres to go though. Beside that I had a note jotted down – "Buddy's moving into a new phase of his life. Will we still find time for our bike trip?"

I was confident we would. I felt more than lucky than ever about how close Buddy and I had become. My high school/college graduate was growing up each year of our trips—right before my eyes—and becoming a greater friend all the time.

Year Seven Completed

Kms 1563 to 1989
Days 25 to 28

Alberta border to Regina

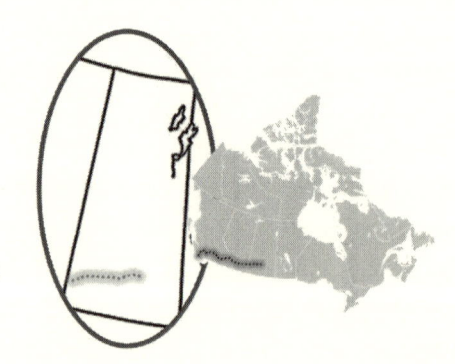

YEAR EIGHT –
Buddy 18 Years Old

THE GREAT CANADIAN BANJO BOWL DEEP FREEZE

Pedalling from the Capital of Saskatchewan. Buddy and I opted to do our trip a little later in the year for this leg – partly in hopes of seeing fewer mosquitoes and partly in hopes of avoiding summertime traffic on the TransCanada Highway. We headed back to Regina in early September. Our goal this year was to make it all the way, *Banjo Bowl* style from Regina, Saskatchewan, to Winnipeg, Manitoba.

Buddy was as active as ever, which came as no surprise being eighteen years old. His social circle was growing, as it tends to do at that age, and he added board game nights with a close group of friends into his priority mix. And I was glad to see that family activities still had a place on his calendar, too.

Also not surprising, at eighteen, Buddy was getting stronger opinions and figuring out where he stood on things that had importance to him. He was a deep thinker who didn't have any problem expressing his thoughts, whether you agreed with his stance or not. He thought people should live with a smaller footprint and he would not hesitate to tell you how and why no matter who you were. If he was interested in a topic, he'd research it extensively. He wasn't afraid to question overarching issues in society as well. Our dependence on cars, over-population, and our infatuation with acquiring more and more stuff. A live to work more, so you can buy more, so you can work more, so you can buy more ... model was definitely not for him. I could see him developing a minimalist approach to his life.

Our bike trip was still on his agenda though. Yahoo!

Following Labour Day, Buddy and I did our road trip to Regina. We drove into Saskatchewan from Alberta as weather reports emerged with warnings of a freak September snowstorm. It was hard to imagine when I looked over at Buddy's summer tan and all of Regina's patios in full swing. However, the thermometer plummeted the next morning, just as we began our ride out of the city. Buddy and I stopped into a Co-op grocery store and were prophetically offered their deal of the week by Anne at the check-out counter: little black stretchy gloves for $1.99 a pair. I bought two pairs for each of us, and they ended up being our fingers' saving grace. We ended up wearing them constantly both under and over our bike gloves. I told Anne that the gloves were going to help us a great deal for our bike trip. In true Great White North style, she nonchalantly said, "It's just flurries. It's still shorts and patio season in Saskatchewan."

Our gloved fingers were crossed that we wouldn't end up having a turn-back incident due to snow like we'd had on the Coquihalla Pass. Shortly east of Regina, the temperature dropped to zero degrees Celsius, and then freezing rains started. After biking only twenty-five kilometres, we arrived wet, cold, and tired in Balgonie. We stopped for a break at a diner, dripping all the way to our table. Balgonie is a small place, but it had a curling rink, which seemed to be a key prerequisite to putting a town on the map on the Prairies.

"It's cold," said a farmer who was filling up with gas. We had noticed. But he went on to add, "It will help with the grasshoppers."

Taking a step back for a bigger picture can provide valuable perspective sometimes. Grasshoppers may not have been on our mind while analyzing the weather, but they are a concern for farmers' crops every year. Especially since 2003 when one of the worst infestations hit the prairies and it was estimated there were more than <u>1000</u> grasshoppers per <u>square metre</u>. It sounded astonishingly creepy.

"Glad we weren't biking that year," Buddy said.

We forged on in the cold for the rest of our biking day and surprised ourselves by getting in about a hundred kilometres. Originally, we thought we'd make it further east to camp for the first night, but we packed it in at the Wolseley Motel so we could lay out everything we had to dry. Our gear was strewn over every inch of that motel room.

The following morning was as about as cold as we could handle on our bikes, considering the clothing we had. Buddy had the hood of his *bunnyhug* tucked under his bike helmet, his bike gloves sandwiched between two layers of little black stretchy gloves, two layers of sweatpants, two pairs of socks and a bunch of shirts layered under a rain poncho. We weren't going to make any fashion magazine covers or set aerodynamic records. Snow had walloped Calgary but thankfully didn't catch up to us except for the odd flurries. But the temperatures never got much above freezing for our entire day of riding and dropped down below zero at night. The wind, which was unfortunately out of the east and back in our faces, made it even colder. My rain breaker jacket zipper got moisture in it and froze stuck so that I had to pull it off like a sweater. Summer suddenly seemed a distant memory. It was a good reminder, well, at least a reminder, that we were indeed Canadian. We stopped every chance we had to warm up as best we could before pushing on again to the next stop. I began to wonder if getting to Winnipeg was realistic. Buddy was a trooper through it all. He packed on layers after layers and kept on pedalling. I think it confirmed to him how possible it was to bike through Canadian winters.

It's funny what gets remembered while biking with your young adult son through freezing cold temperature across the Canadian Prairies. I learned about *Dragon Ball Z*. Buddy helped distract us from the cold by explaining in detail how Goku and his companions went about protecting the Earth from a cast of villains and creatures. It was no *Little House on the Prairies*. I hadn't even known who Goku was, which made me an obvious minority considering *Dragon Ball Z* has had over 30 billion in worldwide viewership and is one of the most successful manga series of all time.

It wasn't until Buddy and I got to Moosomin, nearing the Manitoba border, that the sun made an attempt to break through the clouds. My friend John's mom lived there and I had mentioned the possibility of us dropping in to introduce ourselves. We didn't have the exact address, but I had been told it was a brown or beige bungalow on Main Street and that it had a 'For Sale' sign on it. We spotted it right away, but no one was home. With the sun making a brief appearance, we decided to have a snack on the front porch and see if maybe she had just gone out to run an errand and might return soon. After about 15 minutes with no one showing up, we decided we better get back to biking since the plan was to get into Manitoba that day. I took a picture of Buddy beside the elevated front porch to send to John and then we hit the road again. We later found out from John, after seeing the photo, we were at the wrong house entirely which meant we had been loitering on someone else's front porch that day. Whoops!

About 20 kilometres east of Moosomin, we passed the big blue "Welcome to Manitoba" sign. The bottom of the billboard was draped with Saskatchewan Roughrider banners, much to the chagrin of Winnipeg Blue Bomber fans I'm sure. The Riders' fanbase are a relentless bunch. Other than the sign, there wasn't much else to tip us off that had entered the fourth province of our trip. The consistency of the prairie landscape continued. We hadn't really thought about it previously, but leaving landlocked Saskatchewan made us realize that it is Canada's only province that doesn't have at least one border made from natural features – like lakes, rivers, ocean, or mountain divides. All the others have at least one.

It was still ~~freakin' cold~~ chilly, but at least the sun was peeking out occasionally and the wind had died down. We ended up completing about 115 kilometres that day and made it to Virden, Manitoba. We had started out the year thinking we would make the Regina to Winnipeg distance in five days, but we were three full days into our ride and just halfway to our destination. We were doing better than I thought in the conditions, but still wondering if we might have to add an extra day of biking. Maybe that would be mildly disappointing, but we weren't on *The Amazing Race Canada* or anything. The host of that show, Jon Montgomery, was born and raised just an hour north of where we were. I mentioned it because it was hard not to appreciate Montgomery for giving Canadians one of the most unforgettable and, well … Canadian, sport celebrations. After winning gold in Skeleton at the 2010 Olympics, a random spectator handed Montgomery a pitcher of beer that he readily accepted and immediately drank on his infamous "Whistler Beer Walk".

The forecast for the night was not encouraging—below freezing—so we opted to stay in a motel again. Virden, originally known as Gopher Creek, is a fair-sized town dubbed the Oil Capital of Manitoba. Our challenge quickly became finding a place with vacancy. To our surprise, and not in a 'Yahoo a surprise!' kind of way, everything was completely full. Between increased natural gas activity and the cold weather temporarily shutting down a lot of the late summer road construction crews—who couldn't do paving work when it was so cold out—all we found were 'No Vacancy' signs. We did get a suggestion from the desk clerk at the Virden Motel to go to Brandon as there would be lots of options there. Perhaps that could have worked for someone in a car that could travel the 100 kilometres in under an hour, but for a couple of cyclists it was as helpful as recommending a spot to eat in Prague.

Despite it dropping down to minus four degrees Celsius that night, our last resort was to break out our tent and set up for a cold sleep at the Lion's Campground. We layered up ridiculously and wrapped ourselves in every bit of clothing we had. Buddy looked like the Stay Puft Marshmallow Man by the time he squeezed into his summer weight sleeping bag. Since we were too cocooned to write in our journals or look at road maps, it was difficult to even turn our head lamps on or off, it seemed as good a time as any for the annual story. I was ready and had more to tell Buddy about stretching past comfort zones.

How To Get Out From Behind The Iron Curtain

When I was growing up, the aura of the U.S.S.R. made it a bit scary. We even needed Paul Henderson's hockey heroics with his famous Summit Series goal to thwart off the great Soviet KLM line's threat to our stranglehold on world hockey supremacy. And maybe a few other ominous red flags: the Red Army, the Cuban Missile Crisis, the Cold War, the mystique behind communism, Olympic boycotts, literally the red flag with a hammer and sickle. All of it made for the Soviet Union to seem like a very foreign place.

It was different times back then, before glasnost and perestroika and the dissolution of the U.S.S.R. The Soviet Union was quite 'closed' to the rest of the world then. It was rare for Westerners to be allowed to travel into a communist bloc country. Which made it all the more irresistible for me when I got a chance to go there during my internship in Finland when I was just twenty years old. My Finnish co-workers coached me to take brand-name t-shirts, jeans, and nylon panty hose to trade on the black market. Others told me rumours about "individuals not returning from the U.S.S.R."

There were 32 of us in total on our six-hour bus trip from Helsinki to Ленинград – a.k.a Leningrad – a.k.a St. Petersburg. Getting across the Soviet border was a harrowing experience on its own. Our vehicle got boarded by armed guards with dogs, the gas tank searched with a long wire rod, the tires deflated to ensure nothing was hidden in them, and every possible piece of literature confiscated—books, magazines, brochures—all of it. Everything suddenly seemed a great deal more serious. I remained intensely curious about how different lives were inside of communism, their freedoms or lack thereof, the economic systems, and I was fascinated in their highly active black market.

One of the locals I befriended in Leningrad was named Chevy, and he dealt on the black market. Spending time with him felt like I was in a spy novel. We would stay up late at night deep in conversation about politics, friendships, freedoms, motivation, and control. I think of those discussions often. And how they helped me form many of the political and social opinions I carry today.

When it came to trading something on the black market, Chevy would give me tips on who was safe to talk to. Once when I was trading for someone in our group who asked me if I could trade a pair of nylons for a bottle of vodka. Chevy set me up to meet a black market contact who supervised a liquor dispensary. I was instructed to knock on their large wooden back door and when I did, it creaked slightly open and a bearded face peered out. The person glanced up and down the alley then ushered me in through a massive door that was slammed shut behind me. A solid wooden four-by-four brace was then jammed into place to lock it. Again, everything suddenly seemed a great deal more serious. There I was standing on a broken concrete and dirt floor with my baseball cap perched on what I considered to be my *quite-questionably used-in-the-moment* head, and my Molson Canadian bag filled with highly-sought-after-North-American-pantyhose at my side.

A giant of a guy in a black vest who looked like a bear with a big bushy beard motioned for me to sit at a table. I slowly unzipped my bag and pulled out a pack of nylons, hoping that pulling out leggings wouldn't seem too intimidating of a move on my part. I placed my goods on the table and managed to croak out the word "Vodka??"

The Bear guy nodded to a second guy who disappeared without a word. I felt like the sweat was going to start showing through my clothes because of how much I was perspiring.

The other guy returned and nonchalantly presented me with a massive bottle of vodka that he pushed into my hands as I passed over the nylons. Holy smokes, I was thinking, was this really happening?

Then it came to a crash.

I don't know if it was the excitement of getting out of there without being given Bobby Clarke teeth, or the release of fear that had by then taken over every muscle in my body down to my fingertips, or simply that my hands were dripping in sweat. Whatever the reason, that vodka did not stay within my grasp for long.

What seemed like slow motion, I watched the big bottle hang in mid-air for a second, eluding my awkward fumbled recovery that only made things worse by sending the bottle spinning like a helicopter blade towards the corner of the room, followed by the eventual crash of broken glass and vodka spraying everywhere around us.

I felt blood drain from my entire body. I was going to be one of those *not-returning* individuals that I was warned about.

I snapped to when I heard a great roar. But it wasn't a sound of anger. The bear guy was bent over laughing his ass off. Now, I would never ever advise someone to lock themselves in a back room with a couple of giants involved in illegal black market activities in a communist county, but I believe that moment cemented a confidence within me about taking things in stride no matter how dark it can seem. Bear guy slapped me on the back and motioned for me to sit down. Another bottle of vodka was produced and drinks were poured. Suddenly there was laughter and a surprising amount of communication between people who didn't speak the same language. The more vodka, the more we seemed to understand each other. Much of the communication came in the form of charades. My hosts' favourite being a re-enactment of my grace-lacking handling of the initial vodka bottle. Each time culminating with a fairly accurate imitation of my scared-out-of-my-mind look when the bottle crashed in the corner.

"Za zdorovje!" (cheers to your health) Bear guy would yell before each drink, then re-fill our glasses.

As my confidence returned, I pulled out another pack of nylons out of my bag and asked sheepishly, "Vodka??"

I thought the rafters were going to come down with how hard Bear guy laughed. He presented me with yet another bottle, albeit not as big as the first one, and sent me on my way. He raised the wooden brace, opened the door, and gently shoved me out with my uniquely traded bottle of vodka securely in my hands.

On our last full day in Leningrad, I searched out Chevy to say goodbye. I told him what had gone down with Bear guy. Chevy told me that the guy was one of the nicest, gentlest people he knew. This was something I thought maybe he could have mentioned before I almost sweated to death in that locked room. I invited Chevy to come out with us for a going away celebration we were having before we left the Soviet Union. Our whole entourage had decided to go out in grand style and spend our last rubles - rubles that couldn't be taken out of the country. We had made arrangements to go to a 'discotheque' that was known as one of the fanciest nightclubs in Leningrad. Chevy shook his head sadly and explained that where we were going was for 'foreign officials only', and he would not be allowed. My colleague, and roommate on the trip, Roja, and I put our heads together to figure out a way to get Chevy into the club.

We ended up dressing him in a pair of my jeans, my Molson Canadian jacket, my lucky fishing hat, and my Vuarnet Wayfarer sunglasses. As our group walked through the doors for our reservation, Chevy looked more like he was going to a Boston Pizza sports lounge than a nightclub in Leningrad. But it worked and we got him in. And it was an epic night. Some music we recognized and most we didn't. Lights flashing everywhere. Fancy ruffled tablecloths. Velvet in the bathrooms. Delicate glassware. Caviar. And lots of lots of vodka and shampanskoye (Russian champagne).

At closing time, with our last remaining rubles from black market trading and all, we purchased enough bottles of champagne so that every single person in our group could head back to our hotel with their own bottle. We all congregated for our final toasts in the room Roja and I had been sharing. A photo of that moment remains one of my favourites from our trip. It was mere moments before the politsiya-militsiya banged on our door.

"Two people in room!" the lead officer shouted. "TWO PEOPLE!"

Everyone gathered up to leave and Chevy started to freak out.

"I can't have gone there tonight. I can't be inside this hotel. I can't be here. I'm in great trouble." He was pale.

We were scared too, but we weren't about to abandon him. Together—arm in arm in arm—Roja, Chevy, and I walked out the front doors of our hotel. We walked down the front steps and a black sedan screeched to a halt directly in front of us. A man in a long grey overcoat jumped out of the back seat to confront us. It was an intense moment. It felt like it could easily go from bad to worse.

We waved the guy off and walked away, down the street, with Chevy not uttering a single sound.

We zig-zagged through the streets and bridges of Leningrad, for what seemed an eternity, with the black sedan following us. Then, Chevy exhaled and declared with relief that we were okay.

"That was KGB," he said gravely. "You not want to know what they would have done."

He told us that we should take care of ourselves and head straight back to our hotel. Concerned with his choice of words to "take care of ourselves", we didn't completely yet share his relief.

The walk back was fortunately uneventful, other than us getting startled at every little noise. There was no car we could see following us and no-one waiting for us at the hotel doors.

We didn't fully relax until we were back in our room. It was only then I realized that Chevy was still wearing all my clothes and favourite sunglasses. I resigned to leave those items with him and fell face first on my bed, completely spent.

The next morning came fast as Roja and I wearily boarded the bus for the return trip back to Helsinki. Since the whole night felt like something out of a spy novel, it was reassuring to know that Roja had gone through the same experience and it all wasn't just a dream.

I was sitting on our bus when I spotted Chevy across the street. I scrambled out to meet him and he handed me a pile of clothes. My jeans and jacket were washed and pressed, and my lucky hat and sunglasses were lying on top.

"This is for you," Chevy said as he also handed me a brown cloth bag. "Last night was one of biggest of my life. I want give you something not ordinary to thank you."

In the bag was a thick, wide, black leather belt with a large brass buckle emblazoned with an anchor alongside the hammer and sickle of the Soviet Union.

"An official navy belt," he said. "I wanted give you something that you could not get anywhere else. But please don't tell you have or that you have from me."

Chevy refused to give me his address and told me that it would not be good for me to write him. That morning was the last time I saw him, but I've certainly never forgotten him.

As I finished off the story, all I could see of Buddy was his eyes staring out of his mummified sleeping arrangements. "Did you ever go back?" he asked.

I never had, but I relayed that I only ever needed a momentary glance at my Soviet navy belt souvenir, with the hammer and sickle shining bright, to remind me of how impactful that trip was. I came back from the U.S.S.R. with a far bolder attitude about what was possible in life.

I drifted off thinking how extremely fortunate I had been during those days in Leningrad. And wondering if Siberia could have been any colder than it was in our tent that night.

The next morning we could see our breath before we even got out of our sleeping bag cocoons. Frost lined the inside of our tent and fly. We packed up our gear with numb fingers and headed straight for breakfast to the Grand Central Dining Room in the old Central Hotel. "It's cold enough to bumper shine out there," said our café server.

"Bumper shine" was what Manitobans called what we referred to as "Bumpering", a Canadian pastime of grabbing on to a vehicle's back bumper and brazenly sliding behind it down an icy street. Call it what you will, her reference further convinced us that we should take our time with a lengthy, warm breakfast.

Eventually, we had to face the fact that we couldn't avoid the cold any longer. We finally braved up and returned to our chilly way among the frosted, golden Manitoba wheat fields. Thankfully, it started to warm up towards normal temperatures as we biked through the day. The winds also luckily shifted to our backs again. We figured the biking gods had seen us shivering in our tent overnight and decided to intervene.

With tailwinds and warmer weather, Buddy and I really started to move-it-on-down the highway, TransCanada style. We began to quickly catch up on the time and distance we had lost on the first three days. We kept a torrid clip through Brandon, across *The Hundredth Meridian,* on our way to leaving Gord Downie's *Great Plains* behind. We were cruising. Buddy liked our new pace.

Despite warmer daytime weather, the reports called for another chilly night. We considered a motel room when we got to Carberry but were having such a great day of biking that we wanted to push on. We felt we could survive another camping night, so we biked into the early evening and lucked out with a great tenting spot at the Shady Oaks Campground, right alongside the highway. It was still a cold night, but not nearly as freezing as the previous one. We also had the luxury of a heated bathroom with warm hand dryers that we took full advantage of. Buddy placed every item under the dryer before putting them on and heading to our tent for bedtime.

Winds remained favourably out of the west the next morning and temperatures continued to rise. It set the stage for us to get in our second 150 plus kilometre ride, two days in a row, and we made it all the way to Winnipeg before suppertime. We shared the highway with a continuous parade of Saskatchewan licence plates, green flags flapping out of windows, all heading into Winnipeg for the 'Banjo Bowl'—the annual football game between the rivalling Winnipeg Blue Bombers and the Saskatchewan Roughriders. Watermelon-headed drivers honked as they raced by. It was clear that we still hadn't out-biked Rider Pride yet.

On the outskirts of Winnipeg, some roadside castaway items caught Buddy's attention and sparked an idea about a possible Halloween costume. Knowing that we were on our last afternoon and that he wouldn't have to carry the stuff too far, he started collecting all sorts of road carnage like broken straps and tire bits for a post-apocalyptic themed costume—think *Mad Max the Road Warrior* on a whole new level. Detail was extremely important to Buddy, so he was particular with what he stopped to pick up. He was tenacious in his pursuit, finding and stuffing all sorts of dregs in whatever space he could find in his panniers, and even strapping other pieces to his bike. By the time we rode into the city limits, he sported quite the hoarder vibe.

We finished our biking at the crossroads of Canada, the intersection of Portage and Main, where Golden Jet, Bobby Hull received his famous WHA million-dollar signing bonus cheque, at the time, making him the highest paid athlete in North America.

Buddy and I had survived bitter cold on this year's journey, which we proudly thought in a bizarre way added to the overall adventure of biking across a country like Canada. Canadians can be sadistically weird that way about the cold. Winnipeggers maybe most of all. Amazingly, they have even been crowned the Slurpee Capital of the World every year since 1999 because of an oddly strange phenomenon that has gripped the entire province: Manitobans annually consume two and half times more Slurpees than the rest of Canada. Winnipeggers love that stuff when it is hot out. They love it when it is chilly out. They love it when it is freezing out. Bring Your Own Cup events are circled on calendars. People fill up anything and everything they can think of—milk jugs and rubber boots and watering cans and fish tanks and trophies and crock pots and wheelbarrows. 7-Eleven even had to create Winnipeg specific rules to discourage things like inflatables and helmets if they had any holes in them. The city's love affair with the neon-coloured ice beverage is legendary and Winnipeggers wear it as a badge of honour.

~~After freezing our butts off~~ In the somewhat inclement weather Buddy and I couldn't bring ourselves to help with the province's record-breaking streak for Slurpees, but we did not miss contributing to Manitoba pie sales. Buddy singled out a homemade apple pie from Robin's Nest in Carberry, despite my lobbying for Effie's fresh baked peach pie that we had enjoyed after a good ol' prairie perogy feast at the Garden Café in Elkhorn. When it came to pie preference, I couldn't have swayed Buddy when he was eleven at the beginning of our journey, so to have a shot at it now that he was eighteen was highly unlikely. I almost disowned him when he crazily once chose a raisin cookie over a chocolate chip.

We checked off the box for sub-zero temperatures on our cross Canada expedition. Next year, we would get to our fifth province and hopefully far warmer biking weather. We heard that the highway in Northern Ontario was tough for cyclists, but we were up for the challenge.

I couldn't wait to see Buddy's Halloween costume on him as opposed to on the side of a road. I knew it would be incredible.

Year Eight Completed

Kms 1989 to 2589
Days 29 to 33

Regina to Winnipeg

YEAR NINE -
Buddy 19 Years Old

THE CANADIAN SHIELD AND ANYTHING YOU WANT TO DRINK

Into the Eastern Half. As Buddy and I loaded up our van for our trek back to Winnipeg, it brought up speculation that this might be our last year of driving to our starting locations. Flights were looking likely to be working their way into our future logistics. The length of time it took us to drive to Manitoba made us realize how far we had already biked across Canada. It is a big country. We noted the symbolic nature of starting our annual ride in Winnipeg, at the "crossroads of Canada" and the often-cited centre of the nation.

A Winnipegger hockey pal of mine had told me that we should get a *goog* with a *fat boy* when we got back to the Peg?!? He assured me not to worry that I didn't have a clue what he was talking about, anyone from the city would know. After asking at our motel, our desk clerk grinned and told me I should plan to give my friend a *meat shoulder* for teasing us about *googs*. They apparently speak a third national language in Winnipeg. Turns out that it is a delicious language though. It led to a visit to the infamous Bridge Drive-In to devour a *goog,* a hot-fudge sundae-topped-blueberry shake combo with sliced bananas, whipped cream and peanuts.

It was double-digits warmer than the previous year. On a cloud-free, bright blue-sky morning in late August, we long-term parked the van and began our day by riding past the Royal Canadian Mint, the birthplace of Canada's money. It looked secure to us, but a worker at the Mint had recently been caught stealing $162K in gold. He set metal detectors off for 27 days, but body searches came up with nothing. They eventually determined he was sneaking out cylindrical gold discs, called pucks, by hiding them up his butt to evade searches. He had to *drop* 22 pucks in all. Talk about he shoots, he scores.

We clipped along at 20 kilometres/hour riding away from the city limits. It felt fast, but it wasn't even half the speed of Winnipeg's Cindy Klassen when she skated at over 50 kilometres/hour to break the 3000-metre speed skating world record. The Canadian Mint, in her hometown, honoured her six Olympic gold medals by putting her image on 22 million Canadian quarters.

Not far east of Winnipeg, before Dufresne, we passed a sign announcing the longitudinal centre of Canada at 96 degrees 48' 35".

"Whoo-eee!" I yelled.

"Whoo-whoo!" Buddy shouted back with his fist in the air.

It felt satisfying and a little monumental to us both to be riding our bikes past that signpost.

Moments later, I wasted no time in popping our first tire on the eastern half of Canada. After swapping tubes, we took a break at Walker's BBQ, scarfing down tantalizing slow-roasted pulled pork sandwiches in the company of their resident turtle. And soon after treated ourselves to ice cream at a popular highway stop, Geppetto's, while we sat on handcrafted, wood carved, swinging chairs. In a throwback salute to my favourite flavour as a kid, I had Tiger-Tiger. Buddy went with strawberry. I asked him if it smelled funny and as he put his face close to the dessert, I tapped the back of his head to get his nose right into the ice cream. He might be getting faster, but as I looked at him with a blob of ice cream on his nose, it was good to know that I could still get ahead of my son once in a while.

After a strong 145 kilometres of biking on our first day, we pedalled into the beach-lined Falcon Lake Campground for what would be our last night in friendly Manitoba. The lake marked the eastern edge of the Prairies and the western start to the Canadian Shield. We set up our tent, picked me up an extra tire tube at an impressive Lumber One Hardware, and then strolled the boardwalks and beach while the last rays of sunshine cast an orange hue across the water and sands.

A strange incident at Falcon Lake in 1967 remains one of the world's most infamous and reported UFO encounters. It came complete with people being treated at the hospital with mysterious chest burns, multiple witness accounts of detailed descriptions and sketches of what they saw, and radioactive metal fragments found in the cracks of the Precambrian rock around the supposed flying saucer crash or landing site. Buddy and I figured if the area was good enough for an intergalactic vessel, it was good enough for our tent.

Out on our bikes early the next day we moved into the Canadian Shield, the famous rocky middle part of Canada. Soon after we entered our fifth province, Ontario. Just as we crossed the border, I failed to miss a pot-hole and my water bottle jumped out of its holder and the top cracked when it hit the pavement. I had to laugh that maybe it was a wake-up call. We had been warned about poorer highway conditions for cycling and severe lack of shoulders in Northern Ontario. I had a second bottle that I would need to make efforts to fill up more often until I could pick-up a replacement.

The rocky out-croppings all around us presented a welcome change of scenery after the Prairies. The range of vistas across our journey continued to amaze.

We also started to notice an increased frequency of moose crossing highway signs. They depicted a spookier looking moose with a more aggressive stance and fiercer eyes than what we had been familiar with seeing on the signs in Western Canada. We deduced that there must be a lot of angry moose in Northern Ontario.

"Maybe all the black flies have driven the moose so crazy that they've turned into the moose-zombie-like creatures depicted on the road signs," Buddy said.

Over the course of our bike trips Buddy and I had all kinds of cool chats on an eclectic mix of topics. Wide ranging things like the best Dairy Queen Blizzard ingredients, the funniest horror movies, and the potential positive aspects of benevolent dictators. There were also times when we focused on our own biking. Sometimes we lost ourselves in all the new sights and sounds of the journey. Occasionally, the cracks in the highway or the rumble strips on the road shoulders grabbed our attention. And then there were stretches that offered moments of reflection while we rode in silence.

On that particular morning, I pedalled along lost in my own thoughts, reminiscing about my mom. It had dawned on me that at 49 I was the exact age as her when she had passed away after an incredibly tough battle with leukemia. I had been twelve at the time and remember clearly how hard it had hit me as a kid. My mom and I were super close. I still miss her. I often wonder how different my life would have been if I'd had more time with her. I wish she could have been around for my kids too. I think Buddy and Hali would have learned a great deal from her. She would have adored them, and they would have loved her. Because I was so young when my mom died, a lot of my thoughts at the time centered on the unfairness of my loss. Now, through my current lens as a parent, it became difficult for me to fathom how formidable and distressing it must have been for her to have fallen ill at such a young age while having the overwhelming worry of leaving children behind added to the equation. Time provides perspective. As I had grown older, I also came to understand more how hard everything had been on my dad as well, and how much I came to appreciate him getting our family through those difficult times. I also had, and still have, a huge appreciation for my older sister who took me under her wing. In a blink of an eye a whole family can shift direction.

I think being midway through my Cycle of Life journey with Buddy put additional weight on all of those thoughts. The trips were serving as a strong reminder to grab onto every single moment I had with my son. With all my family and friends, for that matter. Life can change quickly. Bloom where you're planted.

I didn't talk to my kids too much about the feelings I had when my mom died. It struck me as kind of strange for someone who had strong desires to share stories with his kids. I guess I still found it a tough subject to broach. I wondered if my journaling might help me capture some of those things and be an indirect avenue for me to share more. It wasn't lost on me that having my time cut short with my mom was likely one of the driving forces behind my wish to create special one-on-one moments with both Buddy and Hali.

At midday, when Buddy and I were almost all the way to Kenora, on Lake-of-the-Woods, I realized a lot of distance had snuck by while I had been riding along in my own little world. Buddy had been just as silent and obviously thinking about his own things. It was nice that we were comfortable with each other to be able to do that sometimes.

I was just about to ask Buddy how he was doing when he suddenly yelled out from behind me. "Oww! What was that? Pull over! Something bit me!" Buddy said while peeling off his bike vest.

A wasp or some nasty thing had got trapped under Buddy's bike shirt and stung him. It left a clear little bull's eye almost dead centre on his chest. He instantly had a slight reaction to it and we took a long break in Kenora to monitor the wound. We considered finding a medi-centre to have it checked out, but the stung area slowly started to fade. Buddy wanted to bike on, but we weren't in a rush so we took it easy for a while longer and moseyed around the downtown waterfront. Kenora's summer festival, Harbourfest. happened to be in full swing. We briefly considered staying the night and checking out a concert that featured Canadian legends Loverboy, but the lure of continuing our ride through the incredible array of lakes in Northern Ontario eventually won over the aging, but still awesome, vocals of Mike Reno. We decided to push on as *we were lovin' every minute of it*. Willard Lake was our targeted destination for the night. We had heard that the resort there had burned down a few years prior but that there still was a restaurant on the highway and good options for places to camp. In a precautionary move before we left the many food options of Kenora, we called ahead and got confirmation that the restaurant would be open when we got there.

However, when Buddy and I arrived in Willard Lake in the early evening, we were shocked to find the restaurant had closed early. The front doors were locked but we could see a couple of guys still sitting inside. Peering through the windows we could also see the rear door wide open so we walked our bikes around to the back to see if we could at least talk our way into some take-out. The restaurant owner and a friend were sitting inside. It was immediately obvious as to why the restaurant had closed early. Drinks were in full flow and the two of them were three sheets to the wind. We were greeted extremely enthusiastically, offered anything we wanted to drink from the bar, and told animatedly that there was no chance for food. The owner relayed that the likelihood of the place serving breakfast the next day was even getting less likely by the second. Again, we were offered anything we wanted from the bar.

"On the house, anything at all!"

Not too interested in anything from the bar, anything at all, we said good-bye but by that time I think they had forgotten we were even there. The scene seemed like it was right out of a comedy. We were going to have to rely on our reserves of trail mix and fruit to get us through the night.

On the opposite side of the highway, we slowly pushed our bikes down a steep gravel road that was too rough to ride. At the bottom was Pleasant Point Hunting and Fishing Camp nestled on the shores of tranquil Willard Lake. Upon hearing about our unsuccessful endeavours out on the highway, Randy Montgomery, the campground owner, set us up with not only a dandy spot for our tent directly on the water's edge, but also kindly baked a couple of frozen pizzas for us in his RV.

Most of the camp was filled with RVs on permanent pads with porches and decks. Being a good distance off the highway on a sketchy road, our arrival on bikes stirred up plenty of curiosity. News about us not getting anything to eat at the restaurant filtered its way to our neighbouring campers and they sent their kids over with hot dogs and cans of pop to help us out. What looked like it was going to be an evening of slim pickings turned into generous moments and quite the bounty of food. We happily chowed down on everything and saved our snacks for the next morning.

Before we crashed for the night, Buddy went for a hot shower and I took a refreshing swim in the glassy calm lake. The only ripples on the surface were the ones I made. I floated on my back as still as I could and calmly reflected on our day.

Crawling into our tent, I glanced over at Buddy while he settled into in his sleeping bag. My stirring up of memories about my mom had brought forward thoughts within me of how fortunate I was that Buddy and I had started and continued to embark on these annual father and son forays. I was verklempt as Ontario *SNL* alum Mike Myers would say.

Buddy turned off his headlamp and got me giggling though about the guy offering us drinks, but no food.

"I thought he was going to fall through the table when he tried to get up the third time to offer us a drink," Buddy said.

"I wouldn't want to be him in the morning," I said.

As we lay there chuckling in our sleeping bags, and gazing up at the inside of our tent, I briefly considered talking to Buddy about what I had been thinking all day about my mom but felt it might be too heavy of a topic in that moment. I later wrote in my journal that I ~~chickened out~~ figured I'd try to keep us in giggling mode. I ~~copped out~~ instead bravely launched into a story about a lawn chair mishap.

How to Build Chairs That Float

For seven glorious summers when we were in our twenties, our group of friends went house-boating to B.C.'s Shuswap Lake—the world capital of house-boating with five connected arms on a single body of water and 400 kilometres of shoreline.

Our trips were filled with diving and dancing contests, boat-to-boat water balloon tosses, tray surfing, marshmallow stuffing challenges, campfire singing until sunrises, broken down speed boats, impromptu haircuts, garbage pails of yucca flux, century club marathons, food fights, flotillas, air guitar championships, deck-to-deck hurdling, and an everlasting curse laid upon our lawn chairs. Chairs met various demises: beach-fire accidents; sunken while being water skied on; bent from dance catastrophes; and sensational sport fails. Once we pondered how many pebbles could be placed on a person sleeping in a lawn chair before the legs would give out. Turns out to be a lot, but there is indeed a breaking point.

It may sound like we brought on our own lawn chair problems, but we suspected that our *Shuswap Lawn Chair Curse* stemmed from an event during our first year of house-boating.

We had organized a convoy of vehicles to head to the Shuswaps. My buddy Mike picked me up in his Firebird and the seats of his car were jammed as far forward as they could possibly go with just enough room for me and my backpack to squeeze in. The entire hatchback was filled with four giant pontoons and boxes of metal parts. Mike had visited Canadian Tire the night before and had found "two amazing-kick-ass-floating-lawn-chairs."

"Don't pop the hatch, we'll never get it shut again," warned Mike.

He pointed at some of the food I'd brought.

"You're going to have to leave some of that stuff behind," he said. "We can buy that junk there, but these bad boys are imperative - ultra deluxe lawn chairs complete with built in coolers and drink holders, and they float!"

When it was time to board our houseboat, Mike was like a dog with a bone as he turned his full attention towards putting those chairs together. The rest of us couldn't believe how fast he built the chairs.

"Get some drinks and sandwiches," he said to me. "All your pain from our jammed car ride is soon going to be worth it."

The first five minutes in the chairs were grand. Mike beamed, opened the coolers, grabbed some chips and dip, and popped a couple beers for us. Our friends took a few pictures before slowly motoring off and disappearing down the lake, agreeing to return an hour later to pick us up.

We didn't relax for long.

In Mike's defence as to what happened next, the descriptions on the box made them out to be 'floating lawn chairs' – but a more accurate description would have been 'lawn chairs on floating pontoons'. An important distinction when combined with why it had taken Mike such a short period of time to assemble those *floating* lawn chairs. His running commentary during his somewhat flawed building process should have given us clues:

"Ahh, these fit together snug enough," he said. "It will be easier to take the chairs apart later if I don't use all the bolts."

The sight of our floating lawn chairs rapidly sinking to the bottom of the lake, put into question the *floating* aspect of the product. On a positive note, the importance of the bolts had become much clearer to Mike.

It took one simple wave from a passing speedboat to give just enough lateral movement to loosen up those "Ahh these are snug enough" pontoons. When the floating parts popped off, the lawn chair parts seemed to almost freeze in midair for a second, like a Saturday morning cartoon, before dropping and sinking to the bottom of the lake. The water there is renown for being extremely clear, which gave us unhindered views of the chairs disappearing into the depths. We maintain that it was that moment that pissed off the lawn chair gods for years to come.

For the next hour, Mike and I precariously hung on to our pontoons as they proved to be the only actual floating part of Mike's floating lawn chairs. Other houseboaters cruised past. A few asked the strangest questions with apparently no concern as to the well-being of two guys hanging onto pontoons drifting around in the middle of a lake:

"What the hell you guys doing out here?"

A loaded question to which the answer was a tad bit embarrassing for us.

"Are you guys lost?"

Which would have only seemed possible if we had bizarrely decided to leg kick a couple of pontoons out to the middle of a lake and then suddenly decided that we didn't know where we were.

"Do you guys know if there is a liquor store on the lake?"

Which is actually something you could reasonably expect to be known by a couple of guys floating on pontoons in the middle of a lake.

Generally, people must have thought we knew what we were doing (they were clearly wrong) as most sailed past happily waving like they were perched atop a parade float.

We stubbornly held on to our pride (and the pontoons) and waited it out until our friends came back in a ski boat to find us. Bon Jovi's *Wanted, Dead or Alive* playing as they pulled up. It's probably not hard to imagine the amount of sympathy (none) that two guys (by that time I had been lumped into the equation), who had proclaimed to have revolutionized lawn chairs on Shuswap (we clearly didn't), were going to get while being rescued by the buddies who were supposedly going to be awed by the chairs in the first place.

It would be nice to be able to provide a disclaimer that 'no lawn chairs were harmed in the making of this story', but admittedly that was not the case.

Unfortunately, sometimes life involves sacrifice (in this case lawn chairs) and you just have to figure how to stay afloat (lawn chairs definitely don't). Even in times of sinking feelings, life is always better when you have great friends around.

Those houseboat trips were amazingly fun, but they could have been anywhere. It was the friendships that made them special. That was the message I was hoping to get across with sharing the story. I hoped for Buddy to be lucky enough to enjoy his own silly moments with great friends like that. I as well didn't think it could hurt to further emphasize the notion about it being ok to make mistakes. It's wonderful how goof-ups have a way of being a lot more entertaining when good friends are involved.

I went to sleep thinking at some point I would talk with Buddy more about my mom. But that night I ~~ignored that even after all this time I still cope by choosing to chicken out~~ was comfortable with leaving it for another time.

It was sprinkling rain when we woke. It only made it tougher to leave the comfort of our sleeping bags and our cushy spot on the lake's edge. The rain cleared quickly though and we had sunglasses on to contend with the beams of sunshine coming through the tall Black Spruce trees for our early bike push up the gravel road.

Phssssst!

My bike got a flat on the walk out to start our day. After a quick tire fix Buddy and I had a short, gentle ride to a nice little rest stop on Dixie Lake for our breakfast of trail mix and fruit. Buddy was sleepy and didn't say much. He gave us a good chuckle though with his hair that looked like he had slept on a brick.

The conditions on the highway through that section of Canada were the poorest we had experienced so far, with scads of fast-moving truck traffic, intense driving, and virtually no shoulders. Yet here's the thing: the jaw dropping scenery of the Canadian Shield made up for the subpar road circumstances. Lengthy stretches of tall green trees, bluffs of rock, and picturesque lakes all around.

We biked for an extensive period without seeing any buildings at all so were taken aback when we suddenly came across a big ominous plant facility. After travelling so long in what seemed like the middle of nowhere, the structure struck us as completely out of place. There wasn't a soul to be seen in or around any of the buildings or the fenced-in grounds around the plant, giving it an eerie, abandoned aura.

"It looks deserted," Buddy said. "Kind of creepy being so remote."

"Maybe it's a front for a secret underground facility for all sorts of Northern Ontario 'Area 51' type experimental activities," I said while taking a pee break by the fence. "Falcon Lake saucers and zombie moose kind of stuff."

"Smile and wave then," Buddy said. "You probably have secret lab people on high tech security monitors watching you pee on their fence."

The Cycle Of Life

The conspiracy theories lost lustre when we remembered that it was a long weekend holiday, so the plant was likely only temporarily vacated. Our bubble fully burst when we biked a little further down the highway and arrived in the town of Vermillion Bay. We laughed at how close the plant would seem travelling in the other direction. We stopped at Busters' Barbeque where Buddy enthusiastically gave two thumbs up to a big rack of ribs. The blueberry flavoured bar-b-que sauce that was dripping down his chin had been featured on The Food Network. Our whole morning suddenly seemed a lot less remote.

It turned out fortuitous that we had that big feed as it was slim pickings until we were able to next stop at the Oxdrift Country Store. Even there we didn't have much luck. A survey of the aisles exemplified some of the challenges of eating well on a cross-country bike trip. As was often the case at little stores along the highway, we only found things that catered more to four-wheeled travellers—plenty of microwave options, frozen offerings, packaged goods, junk food, all in big packages. To eat well with pannier friendly items we frequently needed to be creative. Sometimes we were successful, and sometimes, like in Oxdrift, maybe not so much.

We had far more grocery success when we pedalled into Dryden. We also hit Canadian Tire Store #188 to pick me up a new water bottle. I mentioned to Buddy that it would have been surprising for us to cross all of Canada and not find a reason to visit at least one of the 550 Canadian Tire stores sprinkled across the entire country.

With our panniers full and water replenished, we felt confidently restocked as we skirted around Wabigoon Lake and finished up our day at Aaron Provincial Park on Thunder Lake. We set up camp while Erin at the site next to us sat on her picnic table playing Barenaked Ladies tunes on her guitar and wondering what she would do *if she had a million dollars.*

Buddy and I both slept for ten whole glorious hours that night.

Our fourth day began under dreary, steel grey, overcast skies. We biked past plenty of old Trans-Canada businesses that had given up over the years and were boarded up, some of the buildings more dilapidated than others.

Just before noon, my tire found a finishing nail that spiked a tiny leak between my clincher and the rim. We superhero'd the repair in record time on a decidedly tough part of the highway with no shoulder to speak of, a big ditch, and crazy amounts of truck traffic. Our heroic efforts were a precursor to a short distance later when we got to Ignace and there was a random, quirky collection of superhero statues lined up along the road.

Riding away from Ignace, there was such a big boom of thunder that my handlebars shook. It convinced us to pull into a former roadside campground spot to see what our chances were for camping. Even though it had shut-down as an official campground, the house owners allowed us to set up our tent and they even kindly gave us a large yogurt container of fresh wild blueberries from their recent picking excursion. The berries were mouth-wateringly good and Buddy and I devoured them while lightning flashed across the sky.

On average, about nine deaths in Canada are attributed to lightning strikes each year, and 22 per cent of those deaths are associated to camping.

"You know that 22 percent of nine is roughly two," I said, pointing to the two of us as we got into our tent and the skies lit up all around us.

We survived and didn't contribute to any stats.

We spent a good deal of the next day trying to dry out again, one of our continual challenges of tenting while biking in inclement weather. Wet tent and clothes. With everything tightly packed into panniers and loaded onto the back of a bike, there was never much in the way of breathing space for wet things. When we stopped for breaks, if it wasn't raining, we would try to spread things out as best we could on large rocks, fences, or trees. We used

The Cycle Of Life

an old swing set out back of the Old Country Kitchen in Upsala. Our tent and clothes flapped around in the wind while we filled up on clubhouse sandwiches. Another time we used some posts outside the Black Spruce Restaurant while Buddy took care of a slice of their homemade coconut cream pie.

With our gear semi-dry, we later found a super spot to tent for the night, right on the edge of the Savanne River that flows into Lac des Mille Lacs. The grass was lush and soft. I think we both fell asleep before we wriggled all the way into our sleeping bags.

I woke early the next morning and snuck out of our tent just as the horizon was starting to glow red. The entire riverbed billowed with an early morning fog. It was breathlessly still and quiet. I sat down at a picnic table and took it all in. The mists gradually faded to reveal the river that had been under the fog. A white-tailed deer sauntered between me and our tent as Buddy continued to sleep. How lucky are we to call Canada our playground?

When I decided to wait no longer and wake up my son, I put the blame on the white-tailed deer for pulling up the tent pegs and collapsing it on Buddy. Buddy shook his sleepy head.

The sun came out to be our companion for the entire next day of riding. Along the way we crossed 90-degree longitude west, moving into the Eastern Time Zone. Buddy was ahead of me cruising fast and did not stop as we entered our fourth time zone of our journey. No time zone dance for that sign.

Up until the Dawson Highway was built in 1871, it was canoes in the rivers and waterways that played a key role for travel through this part of Canada. Buddy and I took some time to explore the rugged forty-metre high Kakabeka Falls on the Kaministiquia River. Legend has it that *Princess Green Mantle* tricked canoeing Sioux warriors over those falls in her effort to save the Ojibway Tribe.

Later that afternoon, Buddy and I wheeled our way into Thunder Bay and got our first glimpse of the Great Lakes, just as a massive flock of Canada Geese flew overhead.

"Is it a flock of geese or a gaggle of geese?" I wondered out loud.

"When they're flying tight like that, I think it is a plump of geese," Buddy said.

"Plump of geese, doesn't that sound weird?"

"It may sound weird, but that's what it is, a plump of geese," confirmed Buddy.

We must have been tired and getting giddy, the rest of our riding conversation went like this:

"Well don't get your gander up about it," I said to Buddy.

"You're just being too loosey goosey with your language."

"I think it's you who is going on a wild goose chase."

"I'm right, so don't go killing the goose that laid the golden egg."

"What's good for the goose is good for the gander."

"No matter how many corny puns you come up with, it won't change the score. Plump one and Dad a goose egg. Plump wins."

He had a point. I surrendered.

"Mother Goose, now she was a plump goose."

"Shhhhh! You're spoiling this Canadian moment with the beautiful $#%$# Canadian Geese," I complained.

"Pretty sure it is beautiful plump of Canadian Geese, not beautiful $#%$# Canadian Geese. Did you know that *Ryan Gosling* is Canadian?" continued Buddy.

I lowered my hands down on the drops and biked as fast as I possible could. Turned out Buddy was right. It was of course a plump of geese. Knowing that was right still didn't make it sound any more right as the ~~flock~~ plump flew overhead. Anyhow, the plump of Canada Geese marked the completion of a significant leg of our journey. We had biked 728 kilometres, our longest yearly trek so far.

We had several hours to kill before the Greyhound bus was scheduled to take us and our bikes back to Winnipeg. The Canadian Lakehead Exhibition was in town, but we were more tempted by comfortable fullback movie chairs at that point, so we chilled out and took in a *Mission: Impossible* movie. Mission Possible, was more like it. We had made it to Lake Superior and the Great Lakes.

The Silver City Theatre was located smack dab in the middle of the fair grounds so we had to get permission to walk our bikes through the rides and carnival area to get to the building. The theatre also doubled as the Exhibition's First Aid Station, so we considered it one of the safest movies we had ever watched. If the zombie moose of Northern Ontario suddenly roamed into town we were in a good spot. After watching *Tom Cruise* complete the impossible mission (sorry for the spoiler if that somehow comes as a surprise), we turned on our bike lights and made our way to the Greyhound station. We popped our pedals off the cranks, removed the wheels, and packed up our bikes into big cardboard boxes for the long haul back to Winnipeg to pick-up our van for the longer drive home.

Buddy asked me if I was cold and if I perhaps needed a Canada Goose jacket. I swatted him.

Ontario was crazy big to bike across. How many years was it going to take us?

Back home when my hockey season started, my Winnipegger pal got a good chuckle when he skated on to the ice and found a couple cold cuts of ham on his shoulder.

Year Nine Completed

Kms 2589 to 3317
Days 34 to 38

Winnipeg to Thunder Bay

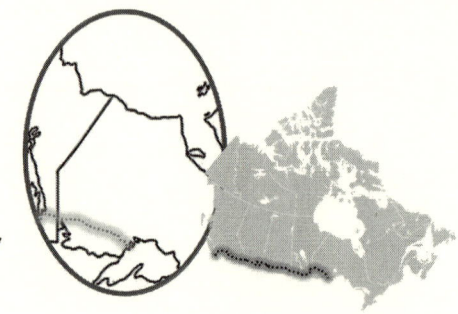

YEAR TEN -
Buddy 20 Years Old

WHERE DID ALL THESE HILLS COME FROM?

All along Lake Superior. Buddy and I had reached the Great Lakes, a big milestone for us from our journey's origin on the shores of the Pacific Ocean. We had a long way to go, but I was thinking about how I didn't want our annual journeys to end, even after we got to Newfoundland.

Embarrassingly, I had not been on my bike since we finished our ride last year in Thunder Bay. Certainly not by design, I simply hadn't found any time for biking. Although I knew full well that being too busy was just an excuse and I could have, and should have, made time. I wondered how my fifty-year-old knees would handle it.

Buddy was the opposite; he rode almost every day. He made a deliberate choice to avoid car travel whenever possible, which was often because he was such strong cyclist and rode everywhere. With a long and hilly route ahead of us around Lake Superior, I was past mulling over when the pace-setter torch might be passed and was more concerned about my chances of just keeping up.

Buddy was still my boy, but I wasn't biking with a boy anymore. He was a strapping twenty-year-old. For a portion of the past year he had lived in Victoria with his girlfriend who was going to university there. Long gone were the days when many of his decisions revolved around his mom and dad. He was out there in the world supporting himself and finding his own path. It had been ten years since his 10th birthday when I warned myself not to blink and be disappointed about a decade of lost opportunities. I felt I hadn't blinked. My soul had happy feet knowing that Buddy and I were as close as we were. We both still looked forward to our one-on-one time on our yearly adventures. I had to imagine that our bike trips over the years played into our strong relationship. I had wondered when Buddy moved away from home if he might lose some spark or interest in our journey or get too busy with other things. They were questions I had also asked a decade ago before we got underway. I was thrilled that Buddy was raring to continue our excursion.

The two of us packed up our bikes in their big cardboard boxes once again, this time for plane transport, as we flew into Thunder Bay to continue our trip. When we landed at the airport, we assembled our bikes back together and stashed our flattened down boxes behind an advertising display in the airport in hopes the boxes might somehow still be there when we returned a week later for our return flight home. But we mostly expected the airport cleaning crew would clear them out and we would need to track down new ones.

Leaving the airport, we found a bike trail that led us past Confederation College and Lakehead University. It helped us to avoid car traffic through the city and we didn't have to navigate the crazy street name changes that exist in Thunder Bay. When they amalgamated Fort William and Port Arthur into one single city, Thunder Bay, they strangely decided not to merge the street names. Instead taking a compromising Canadian approach that left street names suddenly changing along stretches of the same road. It made for a lot of confusion. One local dude even gave us directions by referring to a *Whatever Street* and *West Whatever Street*. To add further challenge, the even and odd addresses sometimes flipped from one side of the street to the other. There had to be a lot of finger-crossing when getting a pizza delivered.

On the eastern outskirts of the city, Buddy and I worked our way up to the Terry Fox monument on a lookout over Lake Superior. Terry Fox was surely one of Canada's greatest heroes and an inspiration to the world for his trailblazing perseverance. Being in the middle of our cross-Canada journey, his physical feats took on new meaning when we considered how long it had been taking us to bike distances that Fox conquered each day on only one leg, while running essentially 143 straight days of marathons. He captivated the entire country until he succumbed to the cancer that ended his *Marathon of Hope* in Thunder Bay. Buddy knew his accomplishments as well as I did, and it was pridefully Canadian to see Terry Fox's legacy survive generation after generation. I considered that Terry Fox had indirectly been another influence on why we found ourselves on a cross-Canada journey for our father and son adventure.

After the monument, we smartly avoided the highway for a good distance by dropping down onto Lakeshore Drive and riding directly alongside Lake Superior. It made for a peaceful ride to our first night's destination, the Mirror Lake Campground. Peaceful until the final half hour of the day when it dumped buckets of rain. I followed Buddy and a steady arc of water streaming off his back wheel. The campground owner let us hang out inside the funky lodge camp office for awhile and invited us to watch *A Fistful of Dollars* starring Clint Eastwood with him. We mostly focused on trying to dry and organize ourselves, until the rain let up a bit and we were able to set up for our camping.

I went to sleep that night feeling the day's biking in my legs. I assumed I was paying the price of being out of bike shape. Buddy on the other hand seemed unfazed. It led me to internally question if I was going to start holding us back? How far would we be able to get this year?

The rain continued on and off the next morning as we headed out in full rain ponchos in a futile attempt to stay dry while we biked. We pedalled hard through the wet weather until lunch in Nipigon - loaded burgers courtesy of Germaine at the Edgeview restaurant on Railway Street. When we looked over our map, we saw that we were on our last section of riding above the 49th parallel – the line that divided much of Canada and the United States. From this point forward we would be biking south of the 49th parallel all the way to our final destination.

Later that afternoon, the clouds lifted and we ditched the ponchos.

I started to realize that we had underestimated the hills we had to climb on this leg of the trip. The big red rock bluffs in the area provided stunning views of Lake Superior, but they were a grind on a bike. I was struggling to keep up to Buddy and again started to think how not doing any pre-trip biking and getting older was catching up to me. It wasn't until we got to the Pays Plat Reservation General Store that we made a crucial discovery - I had put my rear wheel on askew when we put our bikes together in the Thunder Bay Airport. If I had been biking more often the past year, or even a few times before our trip, I would have been more in tune and been able to figure out that my tire was binding. Instead, I had blindly assumed it was my fitness level without considering other reasons.

"I can't believe you didn't notice it earlier," Buddy said.

"You can't believe it?" I said. "Think about me. I've been feeling like I was dragging a rickshaw."

"How far has it been?" Buddy continued.

It had been about 180 kilometres since the airport, with me fighting friction that whole time. On one hand I was relieved and on the other I was feeling mighty silly for not clueing in 179 kilometres earlier.

It was a weight off my shoulders riding out of Pays Plat. With my wheel aligned properly, I shed a whole bunch of doubts as I cruised at a far greater and easier pace. I told Buddy how the whole incident was a good example of how easy it can be to fall victim to blind spots and create internal doubt. I saw it as an opportunity to share some fatherly advice with my twenty-year old son. Buddy, a far more straight-forward thinker, simply thought I should be more careful and saw it as an opportunity for me to gain some advice <u>from</u> my twenty-year-old son.

We had only a ten-kilometre ride left to Rossport, but it included a big climb and we were losing daylight fast. I was cruising again, but with all of our stuff completely soaked and it getting late, I called ahead to book us a spot at the Rossport Inn.

There were a lot of tiny bugs flying around so we put on sunglasses to protect our eyes. I pointed out that we had to wear our "sunglasses at night", referencing Canadian musician Corey Hart. "Did you know that Corey Hart was once considered by Steven Spielberg for the role of Marty McFly in *Back to the Future* before fellow Canadian Michael J. Fox landed the part?" I asked Buddy.

"Again, the randomness of some of the things you know," Buddy said with a sigh.

It was quite dark by the time we got to Rossport and we had our bike lights on. Knowing we were on bikes, the owner of the Inn, Ned, had grown concerned with how late it was. He had driven out to the highway to watch for us and to make sure we didn't miss the turn-off. Fantastic guy. Fantastic place.

The Rossport Inn sits above a protected harbour and an extensive archipelago of islands along the north shore of Lake Superior. The Inn itself once was a Canadian Pacific Railroad Hotel, along the tracks around the Great Lakes. Buddy and I rented one of their quaint little cabins and proceeded to take everything out of our packs and panniers and spread the stuff all over room to dry overnight. We had things hanging from lights, doors, windows, dressers, chairs, and shower rods. Buddy had his socks drying on the stove door handle. We had it looking like quite the shanty.

Ned kindly gave us some fresh laid eggs to fry up in the morning, which fueled a brisk 17-kilometre ride to the Hungry Moose Restaurant for a full breakfast. The joint was packed and the owner was run off his feet so one of their regular customers jumped up and took our order and served us. That's Canada, eh!

I was feeling so much more confident with my wheel properly aligned. The sun came out from behind the clouds for us on our way into Terrace Bay at high noon. We re-stocked groceries and I stair-chased Buddy up to the top of their lighthouse for a panoramic view of the Slate Islands and the endless expanse of Lake Superior.

Enormous doesn't properly capture the size of Lake Superior, the largest of the Great Lakes. We learned there are over 70 lighthouses dotted around its shores. From our view, it appeared more as an inland sea. It contains significantly more water than all the other Great Lakes combined. Three quadrillion gallons worth. That is enough to fill over four and a half billion Olympic size

The Cycle Of Life

swimming pools. Enough for every single Canadian to have 120 personalized Olympic size swimming pools of their own.

More than a few of the town locals warned us to watch out for bears while we biked. They had recently been active in the area, even breaking into the Station Two restaurant in town and raising havoc—the bears, not the locals—although we did meet a few Terrace Bay locals who we could see raising havoc as well.

The hills we faced continued to surprise. We had been told in advance that the climbs between Thunder Bay and Sault Ste Marie would challenge us as much as the ones through the mountains in British Columbia, but we didn't fully buy into that until we were biking through the area. It was demanding biking when you're loaded down with gear. I was so glad we had figured out my wheel issue.

The carved rock, windswept trees, and spectacular lake views made for incredible biking. The National Post listed motorcycling the North Shore of Lake Superior as one of the "100 things to do in Canada before you die" which made us think that pedalling could only be higher on the list.

We settled in for the night at Neys Campground after we chased away about a dozen rabbits from our tent spot. They were a very friendly bunch.

"I think the entire campground is filled with bear hunters," Buddy noted.

"I wonder if that's why the campground manager is wearing a bright coloured safety vest," I suggested.

The guys in the site next to us had shot a bear that same day near Mink Creek, not too far away from where we were.

Buddy said, "I think I might wear my brightest bike clothes tomorrow."

Our early morning riding the next day was cool and tranquil. The road was quiet. We silently cruised along mystical lakes with mist and fog lifting off the surface, which seemed serenely Canadian.

Then we crossed over Mink Creek. It didn't seem quite as serene for some reason, and I noticed we were pedalling a bit faster for awhile.

Our route passed the top of the abandoned Marathon Ski Hill and a beautiful little ski lodge that overlooked the valley below. The lodge had been transformed into a tourist info building after the ski hill closed. It featured massive log piles from the old docks of the Marathon pulp mill. The long reaching views from the top of the old lift station put on display how much up and down riding we had been doing. However, the view Buddy ultimately wanted in that moment was of a menu. When we found both highway restaurants in Marathon permanently closed, it forced us to head down a long, steep approach into town so that we could get Buddy his Hungry Man breakfast at the Midtown Café. The talk of the town was about a bear who had spent considerable time the night before on the roof of the nearby Wok with Chow Restaurant. Their entirely squashed bear-proof garbage can didn't come across to us as all that bear-proof.

Further east of Marathon, we rode alongside the massive Barrick Gold Mine near Hemlo, a mining area that has operated continuously for 30 years and produced more than 21 million ounces of gold. At current gold prices, that was somewhere in the neighbourhood of $27 billion in gold.

"I'd operate for 30 years for that too," I suggested to Buddy.

We kept our eyes peeled but didn't luck out finding any gold-bricks-falling-off-the-back-of-a-truck kicking around the side of the road. We had to settle with striking it rich with ice cream just a little further east at the Naturenut Café. Coincidentally, Lynn the owner was preparing to do the Terry Fox Run the following week. We made sure to sponsor her efforts.

At the end of our biking day, we arrived at White River, the birthplace of *Winnie-the-Pooh*. The real life bear that inspired A.A. Milne was a former resident. The little cub had been orphaned and took to a soldier who named him after his hometown of Winnipeg. The soldier eventually took the bear with him to England, where he ended up leaving Winnie at the London Zoo where Milne often visited with his son, Christopher Robin. Subsequently, that little Canadian bear captivated the world with his *100 Acre Wood* adventures.

Everything kept turning up bears for us. Bears seemed to be a recurring topic for the year, if not our entire journey. Appropriately, we stayed at the Paws Northern Cabins that night in White River.

Buddy's knee was bugging him, so he took a long hot bath to recuperate while I organized our stuff for the following day. When we stretched out on our beds, we got into a chat about Buddy's experiences earlier in the year of moving out and living away from home for the first time. We all learn a lot about ourselves when we move out for the first time. Some things had gone well for him, and some not the way he expected. Namely, his relationship with his girlfriend, which was really difficult as they had been close friends and important to each other for a long time.

Matters of the heart are so big in life. I felt for them to have gone through that tough period. As a parent those moments carry a different kind of hurt. So much effort goes into protecting your kids as they grow that when they reach stages in life when they are figuring out massive things such as relationships, you sometimes wish you could have a magic wand to fix it all. Of course the flip side is respecting that each individual has to experience things of that nature in their life, and ultimately find their own way through them, in order to hopefully get to a place where they find happiness - and can fully appreciate that happiness *because* of the experiences they have gone through. I felt incredibly lucky that Buddy felt comfortable and safe to chat about this stuff with me.

However, realizing that I did not know what exactly to say further about relationships and sensing that Buddy could use a slight shift on the focus of our conversation, I turned to talking about moving away from home in general. I saw it as good timing to share some of what I had gone through when I moved away to Chicago at a similar age to what Buddy was now.

How to Remain Humble When You're Signing Autographs

When I graduated from university, I got an opportunity to work in Chicago. I was sure that I would return to Western Canada, but it seemed the right challenge to spread my wings at the right time of my life. My introduction to the Windy City, however, didn't get off to the smoothest of starts.

My drive from Edmonton went well and got me to Chicago on the evening before I was scheduled to arrive, only to find several off ramps into the city flooded by recent torrential rains. I unintentionally ended up detouring on the edge of Cabrini-Green, a neighbourhood that had recently been covered on a CBS News Special about the problems and gun violence in the projects of Chicago. That was precisely where my Volkswagen Bug broke down. I nervously had to stuff all my things into a taxi for the final stretch to my pre-arranged apartment with two roommates I had yet to meet.

Despite all the complaints from the driver about my baggage, he inadvertently saved my Canadian bacon. He fortuitously, in error, approached my apartment from the back alley and started unloading my stuff out of his car. It was very late by then and if I had arrived in the front, the doors leading into the walk-up apartments would have been locked and I would have resigned myself to sitting on the sidewalk until dawn with all my boxes and belongings beside me. As luck would have it, the back door of the apartment, up a flight of fire-escape steps, was unlocked. I hauled all my boxes and gear up and into the empty apartment. I piled my bags and clothes together into a makeshift mattress and fell asleep on it completely exhausted and overwhelmed.

How did the first morning in my new city go? I was jolted awake by a woman's scarily angry face hovering over my head screaming at me.

I leaped up in my underwear menacingly waving a clothes hanger. "Who the hell are you?"

"Property manager! Who the hell are you??? And what the freaking holy hallelujah are you doing in here?!!!!"

In hindsight, I was a shocking sight. A frazzled reprobate, lying on a pile of boxes in an apartment that was supposed to be completely empty. However, understand this from my perspective, it seemed far more likely I was being attacked by a gang member who had followed me home from the most dangerous part of Chicago.

After a lengthy explanation (which I was never fully sure she bought) and the arrival of my much more put together roommates (who I'm sure were equally wondering what the hell they had gotten themselves into with me as a roommate), our landlady reluctantly left us the keys and left the apartment giving me the stink eye.

Welcome to Chicago.

I remember thinking if I could survive all of that in my first night and not turn back for home, I could handle whatever Chicago had to throw at me. I made a promise to myself in the uncertainty of the moment that I was not going to back down from anything the city could throw at me. The experience of that first night emboldened my whole outlook. I sought out and enjoyed so many amazing things in that city. From non-descript little Jazz clubs to world renown architecture, Otis Clay at B.L.U.E.S to an unforgettable impromptu late night bar jam session featuring Eric Clapton-Buddy Guy-Phil Collins-Robert

Cray, gala evenings at the Chicago Symphony to 2am batting cage practice at Slugger's Bar, famous late night hot dog sass from the crew at Wieners Circle to John Belushi style shots and *cheeseborgers* (but no fries) at the Billy Goat Tavern, an introduction to grits with a friend's family Christmas dinner on the south side of Chicago to tux and gowns on the 96th floor of the John Hancock building. In just over a year, at the expense of sleep, I can't think of many big city things I didn't experience while living there. I felt I had my fair share of *Ferris Bueller* days. For a small city Canadian prairie boy, I felt incredibly lucky to be presented with such a lustrous menu of big city activities. Not knowing anyone there when I arrived, it would have been easy to have stayed within my shell and not take any of it in, but I would have missed some incredible times.

Chicago was also the ultimate sports mecca. I lapped up opportunities to see the Mike Ditka and the Bears, Ryne Sandberg and the Cubs, Michael Jordan and the Bulls, Joey Meyer and the Blue Demons, Denis Savard and the Blackhawks, Lou Henson and the Fighting Illini, Lou Holtz and the Fighting Irish, Carlton Fisk and the White Sox, and even 'key jingling' football kickoffs of the then never-winning Northwestern Wildcats.

I had been in Chicago for a few months when the New Jersey Devils came to town to play the Blackhawks. A friend from Edmonton, Ken Daneyko, had been the first round NHL draft selection of the Devils a couple of years earlier. I had played hockey against Ken on a couple of occasions when we were younger and we knew a lot of the same people. I headed to the game early to catch the warmups. Ken saw me and we had a brief chat. We arranged to grab a beer together after the game.

The old Chicago stadium had dressing rooms downstairs under the ice level, from where players had to emerge up a flight of stairs to get to the ice surface. Ken had alerted the security guard to usher me through. We caught up for a bit while Ken was getting ready and before we headed to a bar called Mother's (which had taken on a bit of notoriety earlier that same year for being the hangout for Rob Lowe, Demi Moore, and Jim Belushi in the movie *About Last Night*).

Ken and I walked up the stairs together out of the dressing room area. Ken was in a suit jacket, and I was still wearing my suit and overcoat from my workday. When we hit the top of the stairs there was a throng of kids waiting for autographs. A group formed around Ken and he started signing a few pages when suddenly a souvenir mini hockey stick was thrust in front of me.

"Oh, you've got the wrong guy," I said and laughed a little.

The little kid had his felt pen held out trembling in front of him, his big eyes about to burst into tears. Over his head was his red-faced dad, glaring at me with his arms crossed.

Two thoughts crossed my mind. First, I couldn't believe I was about to make the kid cry, potentially making him think that hockey players are jerks who won't even sign autographs. And second, I had seen enough mafia movies to convince myself there was a high likelihood that the red faced, Al Capone doppelganger dad was very likely *connected* (if you know what I mean) and had already had his boys *fitting me for a pair of lead shoes for a visit to the bottom of Lake Michigan.*

I glanced over at Ken who shrugged his shoulders. What did I do? I grabbed the kid's mini-stick and signed away. I was glad to see how happy I made that kid and relieved to have avoided the wrath of his sure to be mobster dad. But as soon as I signed, a few other kids started thrusting books and sticks and programs toward me. Try as I might, they would not believe I wasn't a player. So what did I do? I kept on signing. While I 'autographed' a program for the second kid, he asked me what number I was. At that point I was in way over my head so I just decided to go with it and before I knew it, I was signing all kinds of souvenir things followed by my number from my minor hockey league days, #16.

People who got Ken's autograph scored a pretty cool memento from a player who would go on to play 1283 games, become known as Mr. Devil, and who arguably was the best ever to be taken in the 18th selection position of the draft. Those who got mine, not so much. I'm sure to this day there are people in Chicago still wondering, "What clown screwed up my souvenir?" Or "Was Pat Verbeek (who wore #16 with the Devils at the time) half-asleep when he scrawled some crappy name on my game program?"

Me? Perhaps with scar tissue still lingering from my first morning experience in Chicago, I was just giddy to wake up the next day without a horse head in my bed.

Also, I reminded myself, I had made that promise to embrace everything the city had to throw at me. If that meant a few autographs thrown into the mix, I figured sign away.

I've always believed that the approach I took to living in Chicago inspired a lot of happy times that influenced many other aspects of my life. It was certainly a message I wanted to share with Buddy, especially at this juncture of our journey. He was just likely relieved that the conversation had moved on from relationship talk with his dad.

The next morning, when we got ready to get back on the road, Buddy and I were both relieved that his knee was feeling better. I left him to do some stretches and went to the checkout to sign us out of the cabin. I got a little laugh by writing a #16 by my name.

Later that morning Buddy and I passed the 1000 km road marker for Ontario. We had gone a long way in the province, but we had that and more still to go. Wow, it was an enormous province to bike across.

There weren't a lot of places to grab groceries between White River and Wawa, but we scored a can of beans at the Halfway Lodge, exactly halfway between the two centres. The owner Wayne kindly offered to heat up the beans for us in his microwave.

When we rode past the world's largest Canada goose in Wawa, I made sure to point out to Buddy that the goose looked quite plump to me, despite being only one.

East of Wawa we headed to Kinniwabi Pines. We had been looking forward to stopping there ever since a Park Supervisor alerted us to it. He said it was the best restaurant of the entire 2000-kilometre circle tour route of Lake Superior. We had their signature Trinidad curry and it made us happy that we had held our appetites in check before getting there.

Back on the road though, a heavy dark purple and grey sky opened up and sheets upon sheets of rain poured down on us. Water streamed down our legs and filled our socks and shoes. The flash flood reminded me of a rainstorm a long time ago that I got caught in biking with my own dad. I remember it because it came down so hard that it washed the orange dye out of my dad's t-shirt and down his arms. Perhaps that bike ride all those years ago was a harbinger of things to come. Buddy and I didn't stop biking through the deluge.

Thankfully, after about an hour, the storm blew over and the skies lightened. By the time we reached Old Woman Bay, with high cliffs resembling the face of an old woman overlooking Lake Superior, the weather was lovely again, sunny blue skies and light winds. We rode a bit further and pitched our tent at Rabbit Blanket Lake campground. Maybe it was because we had got so wet, but Buddy and I were slaphappy that evening, giggling over the smallest things. It was always a special feeling when my son got me laughing.

We even laughed over their outhouses and bathrooms being called comfort stations, though I had to admit that they did provide a lot of comforting. Especially with their hand dryers that we put into heavy use in efforts to dry out our things before bed.

Mid-morning the next day, following a 27-kilometre downhill ride to Katherine Cove under clear blue skies, we set up for a poor-bikers-picnic on an elegant white sand beach. We had stockpiled a sizeable inventory of little packets of peanut butter and jam from restaurant stops and we dipped into our stash to make PB&J sandwiches. The change in weather also set us up for our first swim in the Great Lakes.

As I watched Buddy go down to the shoreline, I had a flashback to before he could walk. Every time we put him down on a beach he would covertly crawl straight to the water where we had to scoop him up and place him back in the sand from where he would begin his quest all over again and again. I hung back on the beach and took in the moment. I smiled as Buddy swam out to some rocks. I got photos of him doing goofy poses out on a stone pedestal sticking out of the water. I amused myself by wondering if maybe that same outcropping was in one of the sought-after paintings of the famous Group of Seven, minus the person 'dabbing' from atop the rocks.

We had two major hill climbs to tackle that afternoon. Smack dab between the two climbs was the expansive and often photographed Agawa Bay. It got its name from the Indigenous word for sacred place. There was a mystique to the area. And the way that the shallowing colours of blue waters blended into the tall surrounding evergreens and rock bluffs gave it a revivifying vibe.

The two climbs around Agawa Bay ended up taking a toll on Buddy's knee, which had started to feel strained again. I let Buddy set the pace to see how his leg held up. The injury didn't seem to slow him down much as he continued to keep us cruising along at a steady clip.

The Cycle Of Life

Our friend Ned from the Rossport Inn had tipped us off to stop for fries at the Twilight Resort in Montreal River Harbour on the shores of Lake Superior. Our mid-afternoon timing made it a perfect place for lunch. It was a nifty spot with camping sites on the water's edge and a yummy little hamburger stand. We filled up on burgers off their flat top grill and their heavily endorsed fries and hid under a big shelter just as the skies let loose with yet another intense downpour. The rain was so loud that I shot a video on my phone to capture the intensity of the noise. It sounded like an ovation at a rock concert.

Our goal that day had been to bike to Batchawana Bay, which would set us up for a final day of riding into Sault Ste Marie. We waited out the storm for as long as we could, dug out our rain ponchos yet again and ventured back out for one last uphill section for the day. This time Buddy's knee really started to get to him as we worked our way up the incline. The cool damp weather didn't help. By the time we got to the top of the climb, Buddy's knee seized up. It had moved from sore and annoying to painful, to a point where we were wondering if he should bike any further. Dejected, he sat down in the gravel on the side of the road.

"We're done with the big climbs. Do you want to go easy and try to see if we can get to Batchawana Bay?" I asked.

"I don't know," Buddy replied.

"Do you think we should call it a day and go back downhill to Montreal River Harbour?"

"I said I don't know!" Buddy said. He was frustrated. And disappointed.

The top of that climb would mark the end of our biking for that leg of our journey. We felt it best not to make his knee any worse. We weighed our options and decided to try to hitchhike a ride into Batchawana Bay, or better yet find someone headed as far east as Sault Ste Marie.

After an hour of unsuccessfully trying to get anyone to stop and another rainstorm threatening on the horizon, I phoned back to the Twilight Resort and Dan the owner kindly offered to come pick us and our bikes up with his truck. We retreated back to our lunch spot, and I set up our tent in a scenic spot beside the lake as the sun set. Buddy hobbled in and lay down to rest his knee.

I asked around to see if there was anybody driving east the next day. I found a friendly local, Tyara, who was headed to Sault Ste Marie and offered us a lift. We got a good sleep knowing we had a plan. The next morning I threw our bikes in the back of her truck, helped Buddy into the back seat and jumped in beside him. We ended up with a knowledgeable tour guide. Tyara was a descendant of settlers in the area dating back to the mid 1800s. Her parents and grandparents had lived on Roussian Island, off nearby Coppermine Point. She entertained us with third-generation stories of everything from shipwrecks to going to school on school boats.

Tyara dropped us off at the Howard Johnson Inn parking lot in Sault Ste Marie, where the Greyhound Bus would leave later that night. Buddy and I still had half a day until the bus was scheduled so I enquired about getting a room for a few hours. The request was met with suspicion from the hotel clerk, but I was able to get a place for the afternoon and early evening. We hung out there icing Buddy's knee. We had also been told the bus would only allow our bikes in their luggage holds if they were boxed, so I scrounged some big toilet paper boxes that I pieced together into sketchy looking homemade bike containers. My creations weren't pretty but after a king's ransom of duct tape that would have made Red Green blush, I felt like they would pass and hold for the bus ride.

With the aid of a wobbly-wheeled hotel luggage cart for a few back-and-forth trips, I ferried our bike boxes and then Buddy to the bus, and we boarded the Greyhound at midnight. We both slept pretty much the entire way of the ten-hour journey back to Thunder Bay, although it wasn't the most comfortable ride for Buddy with his sore knee.

Unbelievably, we found our original cardboard bike boxes still in their hiding spot at the Thunder Bay airport. They had remained there for an entire week.

"Should we be concerned about airport security?" Buddy said.

We ditched my Frankenstein boxes and transferred our bikes into the more secure and presentable boxes for the plane. I pampered Buddy in the airport by pushing him around in a wheelchair.

"Don't get too used to this," I said. "Shouldn't we be at a point with our trips where you are wheeling me around? By now I should be enjoying our yearly rides from a trailer that you tow around behind you."

Buddy just smiled and locked his hands together behind his head while he leaned back into the chair.

The guy's nametag who checked us in for our flight read: Paul Shaffer, which was weirdly suspicious considering David Letterman's Canadian sidekick was born in Thunder Bay. I asked him if he was spoofing, but he adamantly claimed it was completely coincidental. I remained suspicious.

Funny how I had started off the year wondering how I would hold up next to my fit son, then questioned myself with my wheel fiasco, and then ended the year distressing about Buddy instead. We flew home from Thunder Bay, got his knee checked out and luckily learned there was no lasting damage. It just needed time to rest and heal.

Seeing as to how a twenty-year-old knee can get sore, I made a note in my journal and a pact with myself to get at least a bit more biking in before we reconvened our journey again next year.

Year Ten Completed

Kms 3317 to 3931
Days 39 to 43

Thunder Bay to Sault Ste Marie (almost)

YEAR ELEVEN - Buddy 21 Years Old

TO THE NATION'S CAPITAL FOR ITS 150TH BIRTHDAY

First finishing our way to Sault Ste Marie. I shook my head while we were getting ready for this year's leg as I stared at my bike that was still in the box from last year's flight home from Thunder Bay. Had I not made a pact with myself? I had been physically active—I played hockey, went skiing a lot, hiked, and scrambled around at our cabin at the lake—but I just didn't seem to have or make time for biking. On the bright side, I laughed at the fact that I didn't have to repack my bike.

Buddy, on the other hand, had turned into an even more extreme biking maniac. He was lean and fit and his knee had quickly healed from last year. His injury seemed like a distant memory when I watched him do Parkour moves, briefly balancing on his hands before bounding off the edge of a wall and landing on his feet further below. He was living with a couple of his best friends in a small house in Edmonton that became board game central. He worked at a board game café and was as knowledgeable about games than anyone I knew. He had developed quite the knack for explaining games and simplifying them for people to enjoy.

Buddy had bought a fixed-gear bike off Craigslist that he stripped down to the basics to ride to the café and around town. He was in impressive bike shape and I again felt a bit scared for our upcoming journey. He had been crushing the hills last year, and if it wasn't for his knee failing him, I would have been chasing his pace the entire way. There was no doubt in my mind that he would be the lead for the coming year. I loved that I felt fulfilled by this development rather than sad in any way, but I was going to make sure that my wheels were on right so as not to give him any more of advantage than he already had over me.

As summer neared, so did our anticipation. It was Canada's 150th birthday, which gave us extra motivation to make it to Ottawa, the Nation's Capital. It would mean an ambitious ride. We would need to start out and finish our ride from Montreal River Harbour into Sault Ste Marie then continue with almost 1200 total kilometres of biking. It was our third year riding across Ontario and this year alone would represent a longer journey than the distance between Paris, France and Venice, Italy. Sound daunting? I thought it did.

Getting back to the hill where we turned back last year was not without complications. We found our best bet was to fly back into Thunder Bay and get back on the Greyhound. On the bus to Sault Ste Marie, our driver Tim was kind enough to pull out on to the shoulder and drop us at our exact spot. We got more than a few shocked faces peering out the bus windows while we unloaded our bike boxes in the middle of nowhere. I imagined a few people guessed that we had been kicked off, luggage and all.

We assembled our bikes on the side of the road and just like that, after a long flight to Thunder Bay and an even longer bus ride, we were on our way again. We set out towards Sault Ste Marie, a.k.a. "the Soo", and then proceeded to skirt around the city like we were Connor McDavid blowing by Soo Greyhound alumni Jake Muzzin. Didn't see us coming until we were gone. We rode past the Soo Finnish Nordic House and then out to Ojibway Park in Garden River. We tented there and woke up to a crimson hued sky on a squawking-bird-filled beach on St. Mary's River that connects Lake Superior to Lake Huron.

Close across the river was Sugar Island, Michigan. It was the nearest we had been to the U.S. during our entire trip since we rode along '0 Avenue' on the southern border of B.C. when Buddy was just eleven years old. I mentioned to Buddy that the St. Mary's River would be a far tougher ditch for someone to tunnel under. Thinking back to that first year of biking put a smile on my face again. I reminded Buddy how we had faced so many unknowns when we first started out.

"Remember your little BMX bike that you started out our journey on?" I giggled.

"I remember pushing it through the snow," Buddy said back.

We were moving farther and farther into Maple Leafs hockey country, but three of our stops showcased surprisingly different fans. Marco, the owner of Bucci's Place in Echo Bay, might have been the biggest Pittsburgh Steeler fan in Ontario with all his team's gear on display. Tonya at Cherry n' Top Bakery, wasn't a fan of raisins in cookies, but absolutely loved the Winnipeg Jets. And then there was the random guy sitting on a lawn chair outside of Bobber's restaurant in Bruce Mines, decked out head-to-toe in Vancouver Whitecaps gear and waving a Whitecaps flag. He tried to get us to kick his soccer ball around with him. I told Buddy not to be fooled, we might not see a Saskatchewan Roughriders level, but I was sure there would be plenty of Maple Leafs paraphernalia as we got closer to Toronto.

We had no shortage of things to gawk at biking around Lake Huron. It is the fifth largest freshwater lake in the world, with an incredible amount of nooks and crannies giving it the longest shoreline, 6150 kilometres, of any of the Great Lakes. That distance was astonishingly farther than the entirety of what we had biked across the country so far. Over 1000 shipwrecks have fallen victim to the lake, including the S.S. Manasoo, which after 90 years had been found just weeks before our trip. It had been located at a depth of 200 feet in Georgian Bay with an intact 1927 Chevy Coupe on board. Many felt the ship had been doomed as soon as they had changed the name from its original, S.S. Macassa, an act that mariners often thought could jinx a vessel with bad luck.

We didn't want to do any jinxing when it came to our weather. The area had been recently getting tons of rain, but we had full blue skies and calm winds. We heard plenty of warnings though on how easily storms over Huron turn vicious. In 1996, Hurricane Huron formed over the lake with satellites relaying images that resembled a tropical hurricane, complete with a thirty-kilometre-wide eye-of-the-hurricane. It brought back uneasy memories of the winds we biked through in Southern Alberta, so we consciously avoided talking about the weather altogether.

I made sure to point out the turn-off to Elliot Lake to Buddy.

"Your grandpa worked there when he was a young man," I said.

The 27-kilometre road north to Elliot Lake was paved now, but my dad remembered it as a rough gravel road back in his day. He had bought a sweet, 1957 gold and cream-coloured Bel Air that he babied and shuddered each time he drove it on that rocky road. It would have been nice for us to visit Elliot Lake, but it would have added a half day of biking and we already weren't sure if we were going to be able to complete our ambitious plan to get to Ottawa. In a salute, I tipped my bike helmet at the turn-off and left it for another time.

I felt my dad had indirectly been a part of the adventure Buddy and I were on because of how much his own adventurous spirit influenced me while I was growing up. He was equally comfortable in jeans with a chainsaw or in shorts with a book on a beach or in business attire doling out Canada pins on the many international trade missions he was involved in around the world. My siblings and I all shared a penchant for exploring, and I figured it was linked to our dad. I hoped I was passing on some of those same traits to Buddy. Cycles of life.

A bit further east, Buddy and I came upon an impressive art gallery in the log framed Serpent River Trading Post. It was one of the largest collections of First Nations art in all of Ontario. Alex, the Art Coordinator, was an endless source of interesting stories. He told us of an Ojibwe legend, *Mishebeshu*, a great lynx who lives in an underwater den near the mouth of the Serpent River, directly where it flows into Lake Huron.

When Alex found out that Buddy and I were father and son, he was delighted to tell us stories about his daughter. He shared pictures with us of his six-month old girl in a jumper and a jingle dress at the Genaabaajiing Pow-Wow. Cycles of life.

The Canadian Shield that we continued to ride through was mining country. The Sudbury area, which sits in a 1.85-billion-year-old meteorite impact crater, does an incredible $10 billion annually in mining. A staggering 1.7 billion tonnes of ore has been recovered around Sudbury over the years.

"1.7 billion!" I said to Buddy with my pinkie to the side of my mouth like *Austin Powers*. 40 billion pounds of nickel, 36 billion pounds of copper, 70 million ounces of platinum, palladium and gold, and 283 million ounces of silver. It is the richest mining district in all of North America. To make sure everyone knows this, Sudburians erected the world's largest roadside coin, a giant nine-metre 1951 nickel on the outskirts of town.

Buddy and I again got a kick over Canadians' odd obsession with having the world's largest roadside attraction of something or other. In B.C. we rode past the world's largest truck in Sparwood. That province also sports the world's largest hockey stick, cuckoo clock, fly fishing rod, cross-country skis, and totem pole. In Alberta we passed the world's largest putter by the world's largest bean guy, Pinto MacBean. That province boasts a long and eclectic list of the world's largest perogy, duck, spinning baseball bat, UFO landing spot, dragonfly, pysanka (Ukrainian egg), mushroom, badminton raquet, dinosaur, piggy bank, and beaver. And a special shout out to the world's largest kielbasa (sausage) in Mundare, Alberta, which sort of resembles something Clifford the Big Red Dog might have left behind. Saskatchewan has the world's largest bread and salt, bunnock (horse ankle), honey-bee, oil can, and a moose statue with enhanced antlers so it could outsize a controversial contender out of Norway. There was also a giant red paper clip with a great backstory involving a Montréal blogger who traded his way from a single paper clip all the way up to a house in Kipling, Saskatchewan. Manitoba lays claim to the world's largest pumpkin, fire hydrant, easel, curling rock, and mosquito (although it is beyond me why anyone would build a shrine for something whose talents seem to me to be buzzing-by-my-ear-when-I'm-trying-to-sleep-in-a-tent and generally just annoying us all for a couple months every summer). Winnipeg also has the world's largest vase of David Letterman fame. In Wawa, Ontario, we rode past the world's largest goose and then there was the nickel in Sudbury. We had a long way left to bike and wondered what else would be added to the list.

From Sudbury we branched south on Highway 69. Our route to Ottawa would be longer that way, but we had a chance to meet up with some of my cousins from the Barrie and Alliston areas. A group of them were travelling to meet us in Parry Sound.

On our way down the northeastern shores of Georgian Bay, our blue skies we had been enjoying ended abruptly. Rain pelted us so hard that it made my bike helmet sound like a steel drum.

"Can you hear anything?" I yelled as hard as I could at Buddy.

He couldn't hear me, so I took advantage and yelled, "I'm still faster than you!"

We slopped our way to the Moose Lake Trading Post and Lodge but arrived late and they had been closed for two hours by the time we got there. By chance, Rich Kaster, the owner, heard me tapping on the door. To be fair, my tapping might have been more like banging on the door with all my might. I think Rich took pity with how drenched we looked standing there in garbage bags, with head and arm holes poked in them, overtop of our rain gear. He set us up in a cabin overlooking the lake beside a long line of upside-down rowboats. When we got our wet clothes and shoes off, Buddy and I sat back to compare our pruned feet.

And then as fast as the rain came, it was gone again. The next morning we were back to bright blue skies for our remaining stretch into Parry Sound, where we were greeted by a large sign, "Home of 30,000 islands and Bobby Orr." Good chance Orr probably outscored the islands. Upon our arrival we discovered that we had inadvertently been travelling illegally for the last forty kilometres. The point where Highway 69 morphed into the 400 Expressway apparently prohibits bicycles.

Whoops! It was super nice new pavement with bigger shoulders of anywhere we had biked in Ontario, and we had ventured onto it very innocently.

We snapped a picture of our bikes in front of The Bobby Orr Hall of Fame to send to a cousin of mine who has had a hockey crush on the player since we were young. Then we joined my Ontario cousins at the local Boston Pizza. The first Boston Pizza opened in Edmonton in the mid-sixties by a Greek immigrant named Gus Agioritis. No one really knows why he named it that, but many think it was because Boston had a good team then and his neighbour was a Boston Bruins fan. Being in Boston Bruins' Bobby Orr's hometown and having Boston Pizza seemed fitting.

Because I lived on the other side of the country I rarely got a chance to see these cousins who had come to meet us, but was quickly reminded how much I valued our relationships. Seeing them on our bike trip brought back the importance of family front-and-centre. It meant a great deal to me to introduce them to Buddy. It was a proud moment for me from all angles. Cycles of life.

After a bushel of well wishes from our relatives for the rest of our journey, Buddy and I departed from Parry Sound and shamelessly ended up biking a short distance on the 400 again.

Whoops! It was super nice new pavement with bigger shoulders of anywhere we had biked in Ontario, and we had ventured onto it ~~very innocently~~.

My justification was that it was only for a short way and it had been difficult to find a biking alternative to get us to the road we wanted toward Algonquin Park. We pedalled fast and stopped looking over our shoulders when we got off the 400 at the turn-off to the Georgian Bay Travel Centre. From that point we would be able to head directly east. It would mean not biking through Toronto and area, but Buddy had been there previously on a family trip and we weren't all that keen biking in loads of traffic anyhow. Of the 2000+ kilometres that we would end up travelling across Ontario, it was the southern part we weren't biking that accounted for 94 per cent of the province's population. The roads we were travelling, the six per cent populated portion of the province, seemed more than busy enough for us on our bikes.

While we took a short break at the travel centre, I asked a guy getting off his Harley, who had come from that direction, how far we were from Toronto.

"It's 'bout a buck thirty-five," he gruffed.

"That must be miles, right?" I said.

"It ain't inches," he chuckled.

I then noticed he had Michigan plates. He seemed a nice enough guy so I didn't think I'd get punched in the nose and I made a slightly sarcastic, but light-hearted comment about Canada switching to metric in 1977.

He shot back right away.

"Easy there Huckleberry Hound. In '77 Keith Richards got himself 'rested in Canada fer heroin 'n cocaine. Last time I checked, Stones are still tourin', Keith's still playin' guitar, and we're still usin' miles."

I did not even know what to say to that. Huckleberry Hound? I guess I could have done worse, but my seven-year-old self would have preferred Speedy Gonzales.

I undoubtedly would have travelled a *buck thirty-five* and more in <u>miles</u> to see the Stones and April Wine at their famed, secret, live recording shows at the El Mocambo Tavern in T.O.

As Buddy and I got underway eastward, our reward was picturesque, curvy, rolling roads on secondary highways. After dealing with the Trans-Canada and the busy roadways we had been on all the way since Medicine Hat, it was a welcomed shift. Our biking pace remained similar, but everything else slowed down around us. Our route suddenly seemed peaceful, accentuating how much noise we had been dealing with. In the quiet of the early fall, it made for super riding. I was up to the pace challenge too. I was happy to be keeping up with my ultra fit companion, despite my lack of other biking through the year.

During our annual journeys we had plenty of side-of-the-road eating and baggie-filled snacks. However, we also had some memorable Canadian roadside dining experiences too. Our ride through the Muskoka region added two to that list. First at Katie's Cottage Law Canteen, a little gem of a homemade sandwich and soup place in Rosseau, where we filled up on delicious guacamole, grain, roast veggie wraps. The second was in Huntsville where Buddy and I enjoyed spiced lamb shanks and rice curry at 3 Guys and a Stove. When stops like those got thrown into the mix of ten or so hours on a bike, they had a way of standing out in a day.

The weather ping-ponged back and forth. We returned to dull skies and showers as we neared the western entrance to Algonquin Park. It was enough of a threat to be enticed by the Windrush B&B on a small, tree-lined, private lake. There had been so much rain in the past month that a beaver dam at the outflow of the lake had broken through due to high water levels.

Buddy and I had the entire lower floor to ourselves. We showered, put on our driest clothes, and sunk into their comfy couches to chill. Buddy in his toque and bare feet took full advantage and stretched fully out on his sofa. There was a flyer on the coffee table outlining the Algonquin Outfitter Muskoka River X, the world's longest single day canoe race out of Huntsville. It got us talking about races and events and such, and that prompted me to tell Buddy about a string of unusual sporting events I once attended back-to-back-to-back.

How Not to Get On the Racetrack at Indy

In a three-week period one May, when I was in my twenties, I ended up at three unforgettable events. Back-to-back-to-back spectacles. Each one with highly unexpected happenings.

The first was the Kentucky Derby, part of the Triple Crown and the pinnacle of horse racing. It looked impressive on TV. The build-up and hype, fancy hats, magnificent grounds, people dressed up to the nines and sipping mint juleps in the stately whitewashed grandstands of Churchill Downs. The event had a reputation of being a spectacle in sophistication.

Attending with general admission infield passes, however, was a different experience than any preconceived notions I had about the event.

The infield is a spectacle but had nothing to do with sophistication. After walking through the tunnels under the racetrack, my friend Jon and I came upon a well-manicured infield area, but there were no fancy hats, no one dressed to the nines, no whitewashed grandstands. Lots of mint juleps though, along with all other sorts of *potent potables*, as Sudbury's Alex Trebek would say. In simplest terms, it was a drunk fest.

The Cycle Of Life

I don't recall seeing that on the TV broadcasts.

I realized I was in for a unique experience as soon as we found our patch of grass that would serve as our home base for the day. The person next to us pulled off her shirt so she could peel off a flak jacket made of Kentucky-moonshine-filled zip-lock bags that was taped to her torso. There was no shortage of alcohol available for purchase, but it was impressive to see the ingenuity people undertook to bring their own booze. Kentucky has a rich history of bootlegging and it showed at the Derby. We even saw one guy digging to retrieve a bottle he had buried on an earlier visit to the site.

I definitely don't recall seeing that on the TV broadcasts.

As the day went on, surprises led to more surprises. With authorized and unauthorized alcohol flowing, so went public nudity. Perhaps it shouldn't be a surprise to find a correlation between alcohol consumption and public nudity, but at the Kentucky Derby? Turns out that Louisville sunshine + Kentucky moonshine + chants of drunken encouragement = an oddly impulsive willingness to flash.

I definitely and positively didn't see that on the TV broadcasts.

Through various races before the main event of the 113th running of the Kentucky Derby, "And they're off!" took on new meaning. As the infield turned wilder, I wondered if the people in the grandstands with the fancy hats knew what was going on down there.

Jon and I laughed about our eye-opening experience all the way back on our drive to Chicago.

A few short days later I was off to exceptional event number two at the Friendly Confines of Wrigley Field. I played hooky for an afternoon Cubs game, which turned out to be the unannounced return of the legendary Harry Caray to the broadcast booth after recovering from a stroke. It was on that Wrigley

Field visit that I heard my first live version of Harry's *Take Me Out To The Ballgame*. When Barry Larkin sent a fly ball out to Andre Dawson to end the top of the seventh inning, the crowed erupted in anticipation of Harry.

"Hare-eee! Hare-eee! Hare-eee!," chanted through the stands.

"Now, let me hear yah!" Caray sang back. The moment cemented the legend that Harry was. I can't see how anyone could have attended that game and see Harry in that moment in his famous spectacles, and not come away a Cubs fan for life. Take me out to the ballgame indeed!

Emotions peaked so high that no one wanted the party to end. In the bleachers, I was among a group of super fans, including Ronnie Woo-Woo who was a famous fan for his signature cheers. The talk was that Harry's return might even be enough to break the Billy Goat Curse that had plagued the Cubs since 1945. Unlike many other sport curse pretenders, this one had all the essential elements: a shunned goat being refused entry into a World Series game, a pissed off Greek dude whose ethnic heritage had centuries of experience in the curse world, and an actual incident when the curse was uttered, right on the front doorstep of Wrigley Field. Everyone floated out of the stadium on a glow of optimism and I was enthralled to have been a part of it.

I rode that high for five full days and directly into the debauchery of the third, and most surprising event of the three. My friend Tom invited me to the Indy 500, the largest attended single day sporting event in the world.

I am convinced that of the 400,000 or so folks that went to the Indy 500 each year in the 1980s, many returned home not knowing if there had been race cars there or not.

Dubbed the *spectacle of racing*, it was without a doubt the mother of all sport spectacles for a party.

The Cycle Of Life

We arrived the night before the event along with hundreds and hundreds of cars filled with people who had ascended upon the Indianapolis suburb of Speedway. All those with infield admission passes simply turned off their cars right in their lanes, lined up for miles away from the track gates, and joined the all-night party.

There was a wide array of characters on display, many who had long-standing annual traditions. My favourite was a crew dressed-up in black and white checkered overalls, like race-winning checkered flags, who pulled up in a station wagon painted in black and white checkers too, packed to the gills with beer—the car itself and the crew inside it.

The street party raged until nine o'clock in the morning when the Indy cannon fired to let everyone know that the gates were opening. Party-goers jammed back into their vehicles and joined the procession of cars and trucks heading into Speedway through a tunnel beneath the racetrack into the massive infield area.

The infield of the Kentucky Derby did nothing to prepare me for what I was about to see at Indy in the 1980s. A frat-like party the size of the population of Halifax, gone off the rails.

An hour into the race and eighteen hours into the party, we were back at our car to grab some beers and food when we saw puffs of black smoke drifting skyward. We ran to see what had happened, assuming there had been a crash on the track. There were emergency lights, but the closer we got we realized the smoke could not be coming from the track. The black and white checkered station wagon, the one from the night before, had been flipped upside down and lit on fire. Faint sounds of Kenny Loggin's *Footloose* was intermittingly spurting out of the radio in the burnt carnage. There was a row of guys roasting marshmallows on the smoldering mass that had been put out by the track safety crew. No one seemed remotely bothered that anything out of place had occurred. It was just part of the Indy craziness.

When we were able to fight our way to an infield fence, with cars flying by at over 250 kilometres per hour, it was tough to see much more than a blur. But I could feel the power of the cars in my chest. We managed to get a spot at Turn 3 for the final moments of Al Unser's come-from-behind win. And then a lady wearing nothing but cowboy boots and a cowboy hat, crawled out right on to the racetrack through a hole cut in the fence by fellow partyers. The race was over, but she waved her hat, stood tall, and welcomed the drivers past during the victory lap. I wonder how many views that would garner on social media these days. There were a lot of people at Indy who should be grateful there was no social media in the 1980s.

Three iconic venues—Churchill Downs, Wrigley Field, Indianapolis Speedway—hosted me for experiences that had to be in person to appreciate. I wouldn't have seen any of that on TV.

I think Buddy liked knowing that I would tell him some of the odder stories from my younger years without holding back. I knew he would rather be rock climbing, skateboarding, or hitting a gym than being a spectator at a sporting event, but what I was trying to get across was the embracing of a go-for-it attitude. None of those experiences would have happened if I didn't say yes to the opportunities. If nothing else, I was humouring myself again in my attempts to share underlying dad messages like that on our Cycle of Life. I liked to think it continued to turn into a nice ancillary aspect of our one-on-one adventure.

We slept soundly in the comfort of the B&B's soft beds, at least until the aroma of Lynn's homemade scones wafted down the stairs and got us up and moving. We were fascinated to see how

The Cycle Of Life

productive the beavers had been overnight, on their mission to fix their dam. Busy as beavers, in action.

We did some stretches and loaded our panniers on our bikes as soon as we could after breakfast. We were jazzed up for our ride through Algonquin Park, the loosely defined 'border' between Northern and Southern Ontario. Established in 1883, it's the oldest provincial park in all of Canada. It showcases some of the last refuges of original hemlock, yellow birch, and sugar maple forests in Ontario.

All our talk about beavers that morning made it hard to resist grabbing a couple Beaver Tails as we entered the western gate into the park. I don't mean the leathery, slapping variety, but rather the sugary fried doughnut version, drizzled with maple syrup. There was a roadside Beaver Tails stand in the parking lot right beside the Algonquin Bound Outfitters near the park gate. Jason, who did double duty between the Outfitters and Beaver Tails, told us that in the height of the summer that lineups of cars to get into the park could be hours long. There were so many people who asked to use the Outfitters' bathroom that they finally put up the Beaver Tails stand to take advantage of the crowds and convinced the park to supply a row of porta-potties along the highway.

Luckily for us we were there on a shoulder season. I had wanted to avoid *Blackfly Season*, ever since I read North Bay author, Giles Blunt describe it in his national bestseller of the same name. It sounded unbearable so September it was. It was late enough that we didn't have to concern ourselves with blackflies, and it came with the added bonus that we didn't have to deal with heavy vehicle traffic through the Park. It was, however, still early enough in the fall for the seasonal Beaver Tails stand to be open. Timing is everything sometimes. And that was emphasized for a far more enchanting reason when we started to see the bright reds, intense yellows, and vibrant oranges of autumn all around us.

There are no shortage of info signs in the park, highlighting facts about the history, area, flora and fauna. I read one about how there are over two thousand kilometres of canoe routes on Algonquin Park's lakes and waterways. I made note that it would be a fabulous spot to canoe sometime with Pam, who badly wanted us to get into canoeing. About halfway through the park, poetically, a lanky-framed moose clomped across the road in front of us. He wasn't startled at all by our presence and just slowly sauntered by, glancing over at us as if he was thinking, "What the hell are you guys doing here?"

Exiting the park to the east, Buddy and I took a short break at The Mad Musher for their coconut curry stir-fry, and surprisingly ran into Jason from Algonquin Bound Outfitters who had driven through the park on his way home from work. He was full of suggestions for camping.

"Every Canadian should camp on Crown land at some point," he said.

But later, when we couldn't find one of the better places he had suggested, and it started to get dark, we defaulted to the Riverland Campground in Madawaska.

The following early morning on our way to Barry's Bay, on a gentle downhill section of Highway 60, Buddy and I spotted something looking out of place on the highway ahead. When we got close, we were taken off guard to find a massive turtle in the centre of the road. Buddy jumped off his bike to check on it.

It was a giant Snapping Turtle. A wild looking prehistoric reptile, complete with a huge shell, over a foot and a half long, and a spiky tail. These crazy looking creatures can live over a hundred years and hold their breath for over ten minutes while swimming underwater. The longer the spiky tail, the faster they can swim and an indicator of how aggressive they can be.

This guy sitting on the road had a very long tail.

"He's alive!" Buddy exclaimed.

"He's going to get smuckered by a truck," I said. "See if you can get him moving."

The Cycle Of Life

"I don't think that is going to happen anytime soon," said Buddy.

"Well, pick him up and take him to the side of the road so he's safe."

"I don't know. He's really big." Buddy got out his phone to take a picture.

"Aw come on. Help the poor guy out," I said.

Buddy crouched down over the turtle. "I don't think so. Not sure I even want to touch that thing, he's pretty scary."

I jumped off my bike. "Oh man, ya big chicken, just pick him up and move him," I said.

I bent down to move the turtle myself. "Holy $@#&%, I'm not sure I want to touch him either."

"Who is the big chicken now?" Buddy said.

The turtle was huge. He had a big head, a long neck, and I could not believe how long his spiky tail was. I could not blame Buddy for not wanting to touch him. The turtle looked…well…mean.

I had to do something. The turtle was going to get creamed by the next vehicle and I also had my pride on the line by goading Buddy moments earlier. I pulled my bike gloves over my fingers and reached down to grab the sides of his shell. He was heavier than I expected, I guessed over 15 kilograms (over 30 pounds). I had him only inches off the ground when all four of his legs violently shot straight out, with paws as big as my hands and with freakishly long claws, fully extended. He lunged his neck around to snap at me with his ominous beak-like jaw. I jerked backwards unevenly and the turtle flipped out of my hands and onto his back. His shell now against the road, body exposed, claws thrashing furiously and beak snapping. If I thought he looked mean before when he was perfectly still, on his back he was straight up vicious.

"So, what are you going to do now, Mr. Pet Detective?" Buddy laughed.

Knowing the turtle was vastly more aware of my intentions to grab him, I was skeptical to reach for him again. Luckily, still no vehicles had gone by. I grabbed a thick branch from the ditch and used it to slowly push and shell slide the turtle to the shoulder of the road. I hoped the sliding wasn't damaging his shell, but that thing seemed rock hard, and I didn't know what else to do. The turtle was not happy, but he was otherwise helpless. When I got him off the pavement, I worked the branch under his shell to flip him back upright, but the end of the branch broke off from the sheer weight of the turtle. I wedged it further underneath and succeeded on my second attempt. The turtle flipped back right side up and resumed his "I'm-not-moving" position, except for his slow-moving head, swaying back and forth, following my every move. He still looked mean. I do not think the turtle and I bonded over the rescue, but at least he was safely off the road.

My bike gloves completely reeked from just touching the turtle. It was a putrid smell like rotten spinach. I took them off and hung them on the frame of my bike. I washed and rubbed my hands in the grass and grabbed a second pair of bike gloves I had packed. As we pedalled away, a truck roared over the hill and whooshed by us down the road. That would have been a mess.

When we popped in for an ice cream and Cottage Cronuts at the Cottage Cup in Golden Lake, the owner Amanda, who was pregnant and expecting soon, told us that there were a lot of turtles on that stretch of road. From our description of its size, another patron guessed our turtle friend had to be over 100 years old. I hoped I was that feisty if I ever got to be that age.

The Eganville Granary was also over 100 years old. It was a huge barnlike building that had been converted into a German cuisine inspired restaurant. We stopped there for rouladen and schnitzel. Buddy also had apple strudel, which he thought was quite good, but didn't think it was going to win pie of the year. With a thousand kilometres on our tires since our starting point that year, he'd had plenty of pie stops. He listed off his podium selections of the year:

1. Sharon's peach pie & cream at Lake Lauzon.
2. The Cookhouse at Batchawana Bay for their homemade strawberry apple pie.
3. Noel's Place Chummy's Grill, on the east side of Sault Ste Marie. Our first blueberry pie since the first-year journey.

I threw in an honourable mention to the McKerrow Trading Post for their fudge. It wasn't pie, but it had been delicious and gave me a much needed boost on our day into Sudbury. I was somehow keeping up with Buddy in terms of biking, but I could not keep up to him on the pie front. He was so lean and trim it was hard to imagine all that pie in him.

We crashed that night on the doorstep of Noah's Ark.

"Who knew all these years that Noah's Ark was in Cobden, Ontario?" I said.

The Logos Land RV Park, originally built as a Christian campground, has an ark replica, complete with elephants, zebras, giraffes, and more at its entrance off the highway. In addition to being an RV Park, it's also a summer destination for family campers looking for a waterslide. For us it was a timely tenting spot, and our early stop gave us a chance to get caught up with our journals with one day left until we got to Ottawa.

At dusk we saw a shooting star. I mentioned to Buddy that maybe Marc Garneau might not have been the first Canadian in space. My convoluted reasoning was that Dan Aykroyd was from Ottawa. There were rumours that Aykroyd saved Carrie Fisher from choking during the filming of *The Blues Brothers* and that they became engaged to be married—which meant that there likely had to be Canadian fingerprints all over Princess Leia—and that meant we almost had a Canadian married to Princess Leia—and Princess Leia's father as a young Darth Vader was Canadian

Hayden Christensen—and all that happened a long time ago in a galaxy far, far away ...

"Go to sleep," Buddy interrupted.

Turns out Logos Land was not the only quirky theme spot of the area. Just down the road was Storyland. The 175-acre park had closed down over a decade earlier, but people who grew up in and around Ottawa got a nostalgic look in their eye when Storyland was mentioned. In its heyday it boasted mechanical, Disney-esque rides involving the likes of Snow White, Humpty Dumpty, Cinderella, Rapunzel, Hansel and Gretel, and Alice in Wonderland. But the place was completely dismantled when the book closed on them for good in 2011.

We rode our entire last day along the Ottawa River. As we biked through Braeside, we could hear a dude practicing his bagpipes for blocks and blocks. For a couple of guys passing by on bicycles it was a cool change of pace, but for how far away we could hear him, Buddy and I speculated that his neighbours might have a different opinion.

Mid-afternoon we made our way into the heart of the Nation's Capital and Parliament Hill. High above the Peace Tower, the Canadian flag was shining in the sun.

The happenchance that this leg of our Cycle of Life took us to the Nation's Capital on Canada's 150th birthday was cool. We put on our red and white biking shirts for our arrival. I put my arm around Buddy's shoulder and gave him a big hug in front of the Parliament Buildings.

We spent a whole day riding around the Capital doing Canadian tourist things. Ottawa is tremendous for cycling, especially along the Rideau Canal where, even though it was summer, I could not stop myself from picturing that quintessential Ottawa winter activity of skating the Canal. Buddy and I visited the National Gallery of Canada, obsessed over gelato at the insanely popular Stella Luna Gelato Café, and played Galaxy Trucker at the Loft Board Game Lounge with a Down To Earth Craft Beer from Ottawa's—appropriately named for us—Bicycle Craft Brewery. A long-haired guy selling 'signs' in Confederation Park got me humming Ottawa's Five Man Electrical Band tunes in my head. And then, courtesy of MP Mike Lake, we also got in on a tour of the neo-Gothic Parliament buildings to top off our visit to the Capital.

Ottawa was a strategic point for us on our cross-country journey, sitting on the Ontario and Québec border. It was one of the reasons why Queen Victoria selected it as the Capital all those years ago. At that time, it was just a small logging town. An American newspaper even quipped that it would be safe from attack because Americans would get lost in the woods trying to find it.

In the evening, we met up with the perpetually smiling Canadian author Margaret Webb. She had ventured up from Kingston with her partner Nancy to join us for a year-ending celebratory dinner in the ByWard Market district. Margaret is a wonderful author, screenwriter, and fitness inspiration, but most importantly to me, she is my cousin. I was thrilled that Buddy had the chance to meet them both. It had been a long time since Margaret and I had seen each other so it was especially nice to have an evening to get caught up on biking, the recent flood waters in the area, fitness, food, and of course family. For this reunion to happen during our bike trip made it all the more special.

After dinner we all strolled to the Parliament grounds to take in a light and sound show illuminated on the walls of the impressive Centre Block building and the Peace Tower. The birthday year presentation, *Northern Lights*, had been created specially to commemorate Canada's 150 years of history. The people who put it together did an amazing job. It was cool, but we did think it a bit campy in perhaps a good Canadian way. Buddy and I chuckled that it was a very fitting 'Oh' Canada thing to cap our journey to the Nation's Capital. Our trek to date now totalled 5000 kilometres of *Canadiana* biking across five provinces. A celebration indeed.

Year Eleven Completed

Kms 3931 to 5123
Days 44 to 50

Montreal River Harbour
(outside Sault Ste Marie)
to Ottawa, Ontario

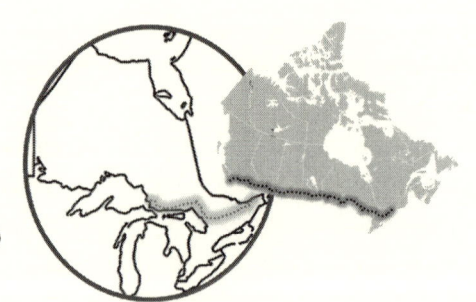

YEAR TWELVE -
Buddy 22 Years Old

THE POUTINE RIDE

East Out of the Nation's Capital. We were about to venture farther east than Buddy had ever been in Canada. He had now been to Ottawa twice; last year's biking and once as a five-year old when we did a family cross country train trip. On that occasion we joked that Buddy walked all the way to Ottawa, after racing up and down the train cars non-stop on the three-day journey.

As a parent, I'm not sure any of us can pinpoint exactly when it happens, but at some moment it becomes unavoidably evident that your kid isn't a kid anymore. Buddy was long past a boy running up and down train cars. He was a sharp, good-looking, well-rounded young man with a bright future. I was lucky to have the friendship he and I had developed. I thoroughly enjoyed every time I went over to his place and saw the latest pursuits of him and his roommates. Exploratory cuisine, mead brewing, new homemade furniture, creative cocktail nights, marathon board game sessions, and even a snow-packed toboggan course down the steps out their front door. When Buddy visited us, his free-wheeling nature even had our family dog convinced that he was simply just another puppy to play with.

Prior to us recommencing our journey, Buddy had taken a trip to visit a friend in Copenhagen. It marked his first time to Europe. He also arranged a layover in Iceland to explore Reykjavik. I was glad he was getting a chance to do things like that and see other parts of the world. He enjoyed his trip, although it contributed to his increasing questions regarding how appropriate leisure travel is overall. Some of the more opulent aspects involved with far-reaching travel and interruptions to his daily life were tough hurdles for him to put to the side. Our talks about his feelings towards it had me wondering where our biking into eastern Canada would fit. He never questioned the biking aspect of our journey as it was pretty grounded, but every once and a while Buddy did raise concerns on our travel to and from the eastern provinces and also how our trips put a hitch in his daily routines of home. In general though, at least for the time being, Buddy remained keen on our journey. We chatted about things we were both looking forward to doing in Québec, poutine stops being one of them.

The exact origin of poutine in Québec remains a bit hazy. One of the more popular theories tells of a restauranteur, Fernand Lachance and his customer Eddy Lanaisse. One day in 1957 Lanaisse asked Lachance to throw some cheese curds on top of his French fries. The story goes that Lachance said, "*Ça va faire une maudite poutine*," roughly meaning "that's going to make a damn mess." A restaurant in Drummondville, Québec, Le Roy Jucep, might have issue with the Lachance tale as they claim Jean-Paul Roy as "*l'inventeur de la poutine*" in 1964.

Regardless, Buddy and I looked forward to a few tasty stops on our travels through Québec. You can get poutine everywhere across Canada nowadays, but it seemed like something we should partake in while we rode through la belle province. Who could possibly know poutine better than Québecers?

The dish even played a role diplomatically for Canada. Rick Mercer, in his *Talking to Americans* segment on This Hour Has

22 Minutes, got then President George W. Bush excited to think that Prime Minister Jean Poutine supported him.

Leading up to our trip, I was lured into checking out what connoisseurs heralded as the three key components of poutine. First, the french fry itself, which should be not too thick or too thin, crispy on the outside, soft on the inside. Second, cheese curds should be so fresh that they have a rubbery or springy texture. The older the curds, the less elasticity they have from the protein fibres, and the less they squeak. Fresh curds should produce a squeaking sound with every bite. Third, the gravy must be just the right consistency, not too watery but thin enough to find its way through and around all the fries. The gravy should be brown, rich, and flavourful. We decided to utilize that criteria and to critique as many places as we could while in Québec.

Buddy reminded me that it was 'poo-tin', not 'poo-teen', if I wanted to sound Québec*ois* and not like I was from west of the 100th meridian. And certainly not *'poutain'*, like maybe an American might say. That kind of mispronunciation lends itself to good fodder at *casse-croûte* snack bars, raising eyebrows at the random swearing or quest for a prostitute.

I found an alarming stat that Joey Chestnut holds the world record for eating eleven-and-a-half kilograms of poutine in ten minutes. Squeaky cheese or not, that is a gross amount of poutine. Chestnut was also the guy who won all the Nathan's Hot Dog Eating Contests on Coney Island.

"How exactly is that guy still alive?" I said to Buddy.

"My metabolism is good, but his must be other worldly," Buddy said.

Our Ottawa flight arrived early in the evening and we immediately jumped on our bikes for a thirty kilometre ride to the Poplar Grove campground. It was not our most direct path, but we wanted to be out of the city and in our tent for our first night. It also positioned us for a stellar route of biking the next day on the Prescott-Russel trail, an abandoned tree-lined railway that took us past Vanleek Hill.

When we finished off our last section of Ontario and crossed into Québec, we enthusiastically made a toast with our water bottles yet again.

"Province number six!" Buddy exclaimed.

"*Salut!*" I shouted back.

Just outside Rigaud, we camped at a high-end RV resort. Their primary clientele was big RVs, but the camp operators were friendly and willing to accommodate our tent. We were however, taken aback when they charged us the same rate for our little tent as a big RV. They tucked us in the back of the property in an add-on area down a steep gravel road and on the shores of *Rivière Raquette*. We were the only ones down in the small remote area that had a plastic porta potty for services. We had no vehicle. We had a tiny two-person tent. But we still paid full pop. Pricey bike camping, but we were content to have a place to camp and the location was ideal – leaving us only a short ride to Montréal the following day.

Our secluded spot by the river was not secluded in terms of mosquitoes. We looked like we were in a cartoon setting up our tent, jumping around like idiots, constantly moving and throwing our arms all about. The mosquitoes were so thick that they would get in our mouths if we started to talk. We couldn't relax until we were hunkered down inside our tent, where we could still see throngs of the little nuisances buzzing all over the outside, trying their damnedest to get at us. But by then we were snug as bugs and out of their reach.

We didn't waste time the next morning. Mostly to avoid getting swarmed again, but we also wanted to get into Montréal early enough to have the majority of our day to poke around the city.

We crossed to the east side of the Ottawa River over the Galipeault Bridge, onto the island of Montréal. As we next rode along Lakeshore Drive, through Beaconsfield, we figured it had to be one of the more pleasant routes into the heart of the city. We saw more bikers on that stretch than we had anywhere else on our entire journey across Canada so far. Casual cruisers, road bikers clad in race jerseys, and determined commuters. Everybody was out taking advantage of the bright, warm day with the sun glistening off the St. Lawrence.

Making it to the St. Lawrence marked another Canadian milestone for us. The waterway plays an incredibly important role for our country. The St. Lawrence Seaway stretches an impressive six hundred kilometres from Montréal, all the way to mid-Lake Erie. The whole of the Great Lakes – St. Lawrence Seaway is a whopping 3700 kilometres. There are fifteen locks, thirteen Canadian and two American, that enable vessels to gain 170 metres (570 feet) above sea level. It can amazingly accommodate ships that are 225 metres (740 feet) long and boat beams that measure almost 24 metres (78 feet).

Directly across the St. Lawrence from us was the Onake Paddling Club, where the great Canadian kayaker Alwyn Morris got his start. Morris, considered one of the most influential Indigenous athletes of all time, gave rise to all Canadians with his gold medal and eagle feather salute atop the podium at the Los Angeles Olympics in 1984.

Edging around numerous construction zones, Buddy and I biked in snail-like fashion into downtown Montréal and found Hôtel Le Dauphin, our accommodation and base for the rest of the afternoon and evening. We checked in early and took our bikes up to our room before heading out to explore the city. Québec has the most estimated cyclists per capita of all the provinces, but unfortunately that means they also have the biggest market for stolen bikes. Vélo Québec estimated that upwards of 25,000 bikes are stolen every year in Montréal alone, and we didn't want to add two more to that total.

Out on the town, we first strolled past McGill University, where Canadian law professor, John Humphrey, came from to create the first draft of the world changing Universal Declaration of Human Rights for the United Nations. Eleanor Roosevelt famously referred to it as the "Magna Carta for all mankind". One more contribution to the world that Canadians can be proud of.

While we worked our way over to Old Montréal, I said to Buddy, "Trivial Pursuit question for you - What is the seventh highest selling board game of all time?"

"I'm guessing from the way you're asking that it is Trivial Pursuit," he said.

That had not really worked the way I hoped. I didn't even bother with my follow up trivia question, "In which Canadian city was Captain Kirk born?"

Trivial Pursuit was the early 1980s brainchild of a couple of Montréal friends. Their original version went on to sell over 20 million copies and garnered nearly $800 million in sales in 1984 alone. It outsold Monopoly in the '80s. Not bad for a trivial little friends' get together over a few beers.

Buddy wasn't short on energy, and he bobbed along on our walk through the historic cobblestone streets of Old Montréal, one of the oldest urban areas in North America. It felt great to be off our bikes for the afternoon.

When Mark Twain visited Montréal in 1881, he referred to it as the city of a hundred steeples and is credited with the quote: "This is the first time I am in a city where it is impossible to throw a brick without breaking a church window."

Two of the city's most remarkable steeples flank the entrance to the Notre-Dame Basilica, the first Gothic Revival style church in Canada. Built in the 1820s, it is admired worldwide. Even the church's famous pipe organ joined Canada fourteen years before Alberta and Saskatchewan did. Buddy and I took in an imaginative laser light show, AURA, on the Basilique's stunning ceiling and 35 metre (115 feet) high domes. I whistled Montréal's

Leonard Cohen's *"Hallelujah"* as we walked out of the building and down its front steps.

We had a late afternoon meal at Jardin Nelson, in their charming brick-walled courtyard shadowed under giant oversized upside-down rain-catching umbrellas. Years earlier I had been taken there by my friend and colleague Daniel Lavallée, the Executive Director at Ski Québec Alpin. On that occasion we had been served water in a unique bottle that I thought Pam might like as a gift from Old Montréal. After lengthy negotiations, I ended up talking the manager into reluctantly selling me the bottle for twenty-five dollars but wasn't sure how I was going to get it home. It was 2001 and two weeks after the terrorist attacks in the United States on 9/11 and security was on high alert. My route had me changing planes in Chicago too. Airport security ended up snapping the tiny file off my nail clippers, but somehow let me take the glass bottle on board. Unfortunately, any pride I had in my valiant efforts and unique gift faded soon after I got home. A week later, I was greeted in Ikea by a whole wall of the exact same bottles on sale for $4.99 each.

On my visit to Jardin Nelson with Buddy, I didn't haggle over any water bottles. The courtyard with live jazz was special all on its own. We were soothed by a tribute to Montréal's Oscar Peterson, the *Maharaja of the Keyboard* as he was referred to by Duke Ellington.

Later that evening, Buddy and I determined that no trip to Montréal would be complete without a visit to one of the city's delis for Canada's most famous sandwich, Montréal smoked meat—*viande fumée*—a masterful combination of cured corned beef and pastrami on rye bread, smothered in zesty mustard. Since the 1900s, Jewish delis in Montréal have been serving up this succulent sandwich to adoring patrons. Debate remains whether the first was at Schwartz's Hebrew Deli or at Ben's De Luxe Delicatessen, but Marie at Hôtel Le Dauphin *insisted* that Rueben's Deli was the place for us to go for authenticity. If you are ever looking for an argument in Montréal, wear a Maple Leafs jersey or suggest aloud which deli has the best smoked meat. Marie's co-worker piped up, adamant that we should visit Wilensky's for the Wilensky Special that Anthony Bourdain so ostensibly loved. We quietly backed away from the two, who had by then entered their own debate. The shorter walk down Saint Catherine Street to Marie's suggestion won out for our twilight snack. It was so delicious that we stocked up for our next day's lunch by taking two more of their storied smoked meat sandwiches, complete with sides of fried pickles to go.

Perhaps overstuffed, but fully satisfied by our tour of Montréal, we returned to Le Dauphin to crash. When I went to the elevator, I saw Buddy sprinting for the stairs. I had to run down the hallway just to make our spur of the moment race close. Being a kid moment like that was always fun. It set me up to tell Buddy about a special race I once participated in – with maybe a bit of a message on the benefits of staying young at heart.

How to Beat a World Cup Ski Racer

In 1988, in Leukerbad, Switzerland, Felix Belczyk edged out hometown favourite Pirmin Zurbriggen by 49 one hundredths of a second, in front of a sea of snare drumming, cow-bell clanging, red parka-wearing Swiss fans, to become the first ever Canadian to win a World Cup Super Giant Slalom – Super-G. He joined the likes of Ken Read, Steve Podborski, Dave Irwin, Todd Brooker, and Rob Boyd as Canadian Men World Cup Winners. On that day, Felix stood at the top of the podium, as the best skier in the world. All of us Canadians stood a bit taller out in the world, thanks to Felix.

His historic win also made it all the more gratifying for me when I took down Felix in our own head-to-head race a decade later. It was even in a Super G.

Well, sort of a Super G. And sort of a race. And he might still claim he beat me. But why let details get in the way of the gloriousness of my victory.

Through 15 years in the ski industry, I amassed a long list of untradeable moments on the slopes with some of the best people I know—but one particular occasion with Felix, when we were in our thirties, stands out as one of my favourites.

It was at an infamous ski race that I helped organize called the Tequila Cup at Mt. Washington on Vancouver Island. The race involved a double knock-out, double pro-bump, dual-slalom sprint format that Felix won. No surprise there. But even Felix knew where the priorities of the day lay. The event was known for the race but, well, known a whole lot more for the Jose Cuervo Tequila sponsored après-ski party.

By the time midnight rolled around, and B.C.'s 54-40's *'I Go Blind'* appropriately blared a warning of things to come, many at the party had gone through all four stages of tequila.

1. I am really happy.
2. I am really good-looking.
3. I am bullet proof.
4. I am invisible.

Sometimes Jose Cuervo himself comes to life and makes an appearance.

We all still seemed visible, but likely teetering on bullet proof when I leaned over to Felix and proposed a grand idea. Perhaps again putting into question the advice that "Nothin' good ever happens after midnight." Twenty minutes after midnight and a radio call to the night snow grooming team; I had arranged for Felix, me, and our friend Andy to get a lift up the mountain on the back of a snowcat, with each of us clutching a GT Racer—a kid's snow slider that you sit on like a tricycle and steer as you scream down a hill—or at least you think you can steer when an imaginable Jose Cuervo rides shotgun and squeals with delight as he peers over your shoulder. We were on our way to the peak for what we were contemplating to be the ultimate Tequila Cup race.

With the full moon glinting off our shot glasses for one last toast to Jose, we shot off down the slopes on our sleds. Laid out ahead of us was our own private Super G track of fresh groomed corduroy, covering the entire vertical of the mountain. Felix and I soon lost Andy to shrieks behind us on the second pitch, but that was quickly drowned out by Jose Cuervo's boisterous encouragements and mischievous laughter taunting us to go faster.

It was epic. I was locked in an intense back and forth, head-to-head, neck and neck, nose-to-nose, battle with a national ski racing hero. Felix and I exchanged leads multiple times down the hill, both of us giggling like little kids, neither of us pulling ahead too far or losing the other in our sights. On the last stretch to the finish line, I swear I heard Jose doing Speedy Gonzales shouts of *Andale* and *Arriba*. It was the boost I needed and pushed me from bullet proof to invisible for the briefest of moments while I shot by Felix to take the lead. The race was so close that to this day, you might get differing opinions from Felix and me on who in fact won our infamous duel—but in my books—Felix had his world-beating Super G win at Leukerbad, Switzerland to cherish and I had my Super G win at Mt. Washington on Vancouver Island. I like to think that raises into question who the ultimate champion was. (*wink wink*)

However, when the next morning arrived far too early, it was Jose who harshly reminded both Felix and me that Jose was the only winner, in his fiesta to siesta way of doing things.

We did find Andy by the way, but never ended up finding the GT Racer he had been on. It had been hurled off into the dark unknown when Andy crashed, never to be seen again. I always figured Jose claimed it and still uses it on occasion to invisibly swoop in the moonlight past unsuspecting late night mountain revellers, laughing away as only Jose Cuervo can.

Buddy had met Felix a number of times over the years, so he could readily imagine how much fun he would be on the mountain and wasn't too shocked by our antics. "Stay young at heart," I said to Buddy and thought was worthwhile to remind myself, too.

On our next morning in Montréal, Buddy and I packed our smoked meat sandwiches in our panniers, checked out of our hotel, jumped on our bikes, and headed out of downtown.

"I love the vibrancy of Montréal," Buddy commented.

"I think it is Canada's most cosmopolitan city," I agreed.

I was glad that Montréalers *were* finally able to get out of the financial hangover of the $1.6 billion debt that handicapped the city for decades after hosting the 1976 Olympics. A tad more than the $125 million budget to which then Mayor Jean Drapeau famously boasted, "The Olympics can no more have a deficit than a man can have a baby." The city's debt pregnancy, which lasted for a thirty-year term, suggested otherwise.

Buddy and I were disappointed to leave Montréal without getting to visit Gibeau Orange Julep, the world's largest orange. It seemed odd to us that claim belonged to a city in Canada. The orange is so big that when it lights up at night, commercial pilots say they can use it as a landing marker.

With a few last looks back on Montréal from atop the Jacques Cartier bridge, we crossed over the St. Lawrence. Parc Jean-Drapeau was on the island in the river beneath us, home to Circuit Gilles Villeneuve, Montréal's famous Formula One Race Track named after the world popular Canadian race car driver who sadly died in a crash at the Belgian Grand Prix in 1982. 13 years after that sad day, race fans went bonkers at Circuit Gilles Villeneuve when Jean Alesi won in the same #27 red Ferrari that had been driven by the Canadian icon. Fun fact: Alesi ran out of gas on his victory lap and had to hitch a ride on the back of second place finisher Michael Schumacher's car to get to the winner's circle.

Once over the bridge, Buddy and I were on the southside of the St. Lawrence Seaway for the first time on our journey. Through all of Ontario and our first part of Québec, we had been on the north side of the Great Lakes and the Seaway. The decision to bike the southside of the river turned out to be *magnifique*, with a charming blend of bike paths, less travelled roads, historic old churches, green pastures, red-barned farmyards, delectable poutine stops, and treasured little towns. The biking was flat and fast, all while bordering the grandeur of the St. Lawrence.

We didn't wait long to tuck into our high-stacked Montréal smoked meat lunches at a picnic table in a treed park alongside the river in Contrecœur. The sandwiches and side pickles were nearly as scrumptious the second day as the night before. Beside the park was a small boutique that featured delicately hand-painted pysanky eggs, by the Québécois artist, Flora Marie-Lily White. The designs

The Cycle Of Life

were incredibly intricate. Flora was my mom's name, who I enjoyed many childhood Easters with painting Ukrainian pysanky. I took it as a sign of her being part of our Cycle of Life journey. I would have bought one of the eggs but was certain it would not survive my pannier. I got lucky all those years ago with the glass bottle, but a fragile eggshell on my bike sounded far too precarious.

It rained off and on for most of the afternoon and there did not seem to be many camping options on our route on Highway 132. We eventually found an out-of-the-way spot, Le Camping du Port St-François, on the outskirts of Nicolet, but a good portion of the campground was flooded. We found a higher spot to pitch our tent near a homemade outdoor gym set-up which doubled as a handy drying rack for all our stuff—clothes, camping gear, sleeping bags, ponchos, shoes. We spread it around on every single work-out station. When we left in the morning, we couldn't find a campground operator so we put money in a makeshift, taped-up paper envelope and slipped it under the office door.

We were biking in maple country. Streaks of red and yellow maple trees covered the hills on both sides of the river. And locally tapped maple syrup covered our massive breakfast at Restaurant Rôtisserie Guay, located in the shadow of the bridge to Trois-Rivières, the only bridge across the St. Lawrence between Montréal and Québec City.

Québec maple syrup producers account for over 70 per cent of global maple syrup production, harvesting over 12 million gallons yearly—enough to fill the gas tank of every vehicle in Trois-Rivières ten times over. It was in Trois-Rivières that three men were found guilty of the theft of an estimated $18.7 million worth of maple syrup, said to be the largest theft investigated by the Sûreté du Québec, the provincial police service. "Stealing from thieves is not stealing," the accused said, defending it as an act of rebellion against the federation who controlled and monopolized the maple syrup markets. A total of 9571 barrels of maple syrup were drained and filled back up with stream water. It sounded like a Québécois case worthy of Chief Inspector Armand Gamache, of stellar Canadian author Louise Penny fame.

We continued along the southside of the Seaway on Boulevard Bécancour and rue Marie-Victorin. Buddy and I didn't stop for any breaks until midday, when we spotted what would turn out to be our favourite poutine stand of the trip - the little red and white food trailer La Roulotte à patates de Gentilly. With an amazing 70-year history, we figured if anyone was going to serve up poutine as it was meant to be, it was going to be them. Perfect fries, rich brown gravy, and super squeaky curds. *Très bonne poutine avec frites maison!* Rough translation: Yum!

Later that day, we nailed our second fantastic camping spot in a row directly on the banks of the St. Lawrence, at Parc de l'Île in the charming little town of Leclercville. The combination of it being September, few campers, mid-week, and a bit chilly, played out well for us. We were the only ones in the entire campground. Buddy and I worked together and pitched our lone tent at the end of a sandy peninsula where the Chêne River flows into the St. Lawrence. The shining silver steeple of the town's church loomed on the hill above us. We also had a short walk to Le Sainte-Emmélie resto-pub from where we could see our tent from the terrasse. We feasted on scallops prepared with maple syrup (of course) and recommended by the owner, Caroline. The seafood was accompanied with *La Saison du Tracteur*, an opalescent Belgian Saison style beer brewed by *Le Trou Du Diable* in Shawinigan. A decade earlier on our journey, Buddy and I were sharing juice boxes, now we were sharing local beers. Buddy capped his meal by scoring his selection for the best pie of our travels through Québec, a chocolate pie served with a raspberry sorbet and white chocolate liqueur. I had to steal a bite; dad tax. *C'etait merveilleux!*

The next day we made it all the way to Québec City, crossing back over the St. Lawrence via le Pont de Québec on its 100th anniversary year. The structure remains the longest cantilever bridge in the world. In 1919 when the riveted steel truss bridge was completed—the same year baseball great Jackie Robinson and Prime Minister Pierre Trudeau were born—it was the longest bridge of any kind in the world. But it was not without tragedy. During construction, portions of the bridge collapsed, twice, and 89 individuals lost their lives, 33 of them being Mohawk ironworkers from nearby Kahnawake.

Arriving in the Québec capital, we had completed another 516 kilometres, bringing our Cycle of Life journey total over 5600 kilometres. Each year now, Buddy set new marks to the farthest east he had been in Canada, which maybe excited me more than him. I found it admirable he didn't need those kinds of badges of accomplishments for gratification. *Ca c'est de la classe.*

The last time I had been in Québec City was for a NorAm ski event at Le Massif de Charlevoix on the banks of the St. Lawrence.

"Not only do you still have an old grey long sleeve t-shirt from that event, but you wore it yesterday," Buddy said, shaking his head.

What could I say? I liked that shirt and it was great for biking.

Buddy laughed, "It was the same shirt you were wearing on the illustration I drew of you for your birthday present seven years ago."

To avoid more abuse, I didn't say how old the shirt actually was. Because it was much more than seven years.

The timing of our return flight home gave us two nights and a full day to explore Québec City. I woke up the first morning, jumped in the shower, and was more than a little shocked to find a tick burrowing half-way into my armpit. I most likely had picked up the little bugger during our biking or camping the previous days, and it had latched onto me while I slept. Québec's tick population and Lyme disease had been reported to be on the rise in recent years. Fortunately, the tick popped out easily enough and that was that. We wheeled over to Sport Olympe bike shop to score some bike boxes for our packing, took them back to our motel, and then headed into the heart of the city.

The September blaze of red and orange on the maple trees presented our most camera worthy city since our start in Victoria.

I chased Buddy up the hills to *Cap-Diamant* lookout, at the city's quarried sandstone La Citadelle de Québec, for a 360-degree panoramic view. Known as the Gibraltar of the Americas, the fortification is the oldest military installation in the country. With its strategic location high on the banks overlooking the mighty St. Lawrence, it could easily be seen how it played a key role in the defence of the area in the early history of Québec and Canada.

From that high point to the city, I followed Buddy down a path to visit the historic, fortress-like Château Frontenac. It has famously become the world's most photographed hotel with its stone and brick towers and turrets, steeply pitched roofs, and ornate gables.

We took our time meandering around the tightly quartered streets within the stone walls of the historic Lower Town, *Basse-Ville*. Buddy got a laugh when I almost took a tumble, not paying attention to the cobble-stone road while I was absent-mindedly looking up at a row of whitewashed, stone walled buildings.

A juggler performing on one of the street-corners near *Maison Jacquet*, the oldest residence in the city that was built in 1675 and is now home to the restaurant *Aux Anciens Canadiens*, got me thinking about Guy Laliberté busking on those same streets while he and Gilles Ste-Croix formed their initial ideas for Cirque du Soleil. Humble beginnings to the present day mind-blowing, imaginative shows that have astonished over ninety million people worldwide. The first time I saw Cirque du Soleil, I was so mesmerized by what I had witnessed that I returned the next night with a then eight-year-old Buddy. We sat in awe of the physical feats and the beauty of how it was all choreographed into a wondrous storyline to showcase those incredulous talents.

Our dad and son day in Québec City also involved a cuisine challenge. Over the years, Buddy had turned into quite the foodie. He had an appreciation for good food and how it was prepared. When choosing where we would eat that day, we recognized how the two of us employed two generationally different methods of finding and selecting restaurants.

"I like to ask around, talk to a few people, hear what they have to say," I said to Buddy. "If I am on vacation, I like to see what catches my fancy while walking around, sometimes checking menus posted outside the establishment. I often go on my gut instinct of the vibe I get off a place."

Buddy, on the other hand, said, "I go straight to evaluating places online. I read the reviews. I look at images of the food presentations. I look over online menus. I see what some of the more discerning voices say about a place. Then I go directly to the place I've chosen."

My way was more time consuming, but I liked to think the process itself was half the fun. It often led to something quirky and getting to know the community a bit better. It gave me the feeling that I was more involved in the selection process as opposed to relying on what others thought. It felt less contrived and more adventurous.

Buddy's way was immensely more efficient and he felt it led him to the best restaurants and left less to chance. He spent about ten minutes searching and still felt he was equally as involved in the selection process. He preferred to spend less time looking around at places and more time knowing precisely where he wanted to go. He felt it was less willy nilly.

But it was my willy nilly way that led us to *Maison Livernois Distillerie* in the middle of the afternoon while we strolled through Old Québec. I was enticed by the building, then the atmosphere, then the chat with the hostess. The place was eye-catching with stone walls, thick wood tables, and an elegant long back-lit bar. There was an easygoing feeling to the place and Emily, our server, was upbeat. Buddy and I indulged in maple-rosemary duck wings and *Québécois* triple-style golden ale, La Fin du Monde. It was an extremely cool space and we both enjoyed the food.

Buddy's more robotic way, I contended, led us to *Le Clocher Penché Bistrot* on rue Saint-Joseph later that evening. A highly rated, staff-owned and operated restaurant that Buddy had found online. It was a quaint little corner bistro with white linen tables, an open concept window to the kitchen, and a cozy bar with fun portraits of their staff high on the wall behind. Every one of their specials written on the blackboard sounded delicious. It was obvious they were well-connected to their agri-food suppliers. It was a brilliantly crafted meal with exquisite carpaccio de veau and saumon fumé maison, prepared and served by Julien and Matthieu. They take their cocktail craft seriously as well and I tested their outstanding Old Fashioned while Buddy had a White Negroni, with Suze liqueur, because he could only get it with Campari back home. It was definitely an extremely memorable meal.

Buddy and I whole heartedly agreed we had each found fantastic places. I admitted I would remember the food from *Le Clocher Penché Bistrot* for a long time. We were glad to have gone to both restaurants back-to-back and how they ended up nicely complementing each other.

When we started our journey a dozen years ago, we would have defaulted to my approach as I was the adult leading us around. It was nice to share that now, and it opened my eyes to new places through Buddy's process that I would have likely missed altogether. Cycle of Life. His adventurous approach to dining thrilled me.

When leaving Buddy's restaurant of choice, we spotted The MacFly Bar Arcade, a brightly coloured, music-filled, nostalgic joint filled with retro arcade machines from the 1980s and a wide array of vintage pinball machines. We chanced inside and grabbed a couple beers in the fun find. Québec's Arcade Fire cranked out *Afterlife* while we played a few games of *Donkey Kong Jr*.

We wrapped up our evening back at our motel before our flight home the next day.

Buddy said, "I think Québec City is one of my favourite spots on our journey ... so far."

"Thanks for making it a special spot for me too, Buddy," I said back.

It was another night on our trips when I fell asleep smiling. Our enjoyable restaurant experiment had me thinking about the whole idea behind our Cycle of Life journey. Buddy had gone from a little boy to a young man. We had come a long way. He influenced my decisions now as much as I did his. I was already looking forward to seeing which restaurants Buddy would choose on our future legs.

Year Twelve Completed

Kms 5123 to 5642
Days 51 to 55

Ottawa to Québec City

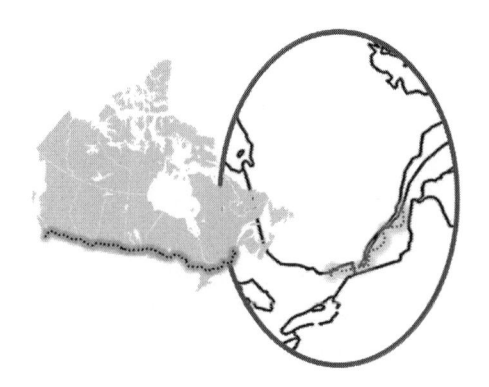

YEAR THIRTEEN - Buddy 24 Years Old

THE LOST YEAR

#CovidSucks!

YEAR FOURTEEN - Buddy 25 Years Old

LOUP-GAROU AND INTO THE MARITIMES. 'MAGINE!

Getting underway again from Québec City. We had made it through bizarro time - learning about 3-ply masks, self-isolation, PPE, N95, quarantine, hepa filters, vaccination efficacy, transmission, flattening the curve, and social distancing. We developed a new vocabulary. Suddenly we were living in a different world.

During the first wave and first shutdowns in Canada, Buddy and I initially contemplated still making our trek. Everything was completely shut down and we knew we could isolate ourselves on our bikes and in our tent. We got as far as planning to drive our van to Québec, a bike route to Moncton, and reserving a one-way car rental to get back from Moncton to Québec City where we would jump in our van again and make our long return drive home. It sounded safe to us and others, and perhaps a productive use of time while the world went on pause. And then New Brunswick pulled the bikes out from underneath us and announced the closing of their border with Québec. And then Québec followed suit and closed their border with Ontario.

And suddenly, like for so many people, the entire year slipped by.

But the Cycle of Life had to keep on, right? Even a pandemic can't hold back everything forever, right? Right?

As all the shutdowns moved into their second year *(*spits on ground*)*, Buddy and I were wondering if we would be forced to delay another year. While we waited for restrictions to lift, I was also nervous about my left knee as I had torn a ligament while skiing near the end of winter. I had some angst over how far I could bike. It healed well, but I figured the more time it had to mend the better.

A potentially bigger stumbling block was Buddy's growing uneasiness towards leisure travel in general. If anything, through the COVID-19 challenges, Buddy's desire for routines had intensified and he was placing greater emphasis on building a life that didn't need far-reaching excursions to garner happiness and satisfaction. My approach to free time had been quite different when I was his age, but I could see how interrupting routine by travelling could be counterproductive to how he wanted to live life. It renewed some nervous questions for me regarding where he stood on our Cycle of Life.

Initially, I thought our trip might be at odds with one of the underpinnings that I had based our whole journey on: my desire for Buddy to foster an appreciation for adventure. However, I came around to asking myself if I had developed some tunnel vision on that matter. I considered that maybe a different approach might not necessarily be a lesser one, as I clearly learned from our restaurant choosing methods in Québec City. Once again, I was seeing my son's views act as a catalyst for me to broaden my own thoughts. And in this case, bringing me around to where I started to realize and appreciate more the strong spirit of adventure that Buddy had developed in his own way. It had just manifested for him in a different fashion than me. My little epiphany reframed my thinking. Instead of being in a place where I was questioning one of the key aspects of our trips, it made me even more proud about what we were accomplishing with our Cycle of Life. I said all those years ago that 'it was about the journey, not just the destination'. This had become an opportunity to espouse a fuller version of that notion. Our annual forays were presenting me with a platform to understand my son better and create a stronger bond between us. How adventurous was that? What more could I ask for? Wasn't that one of the most important parts of what our journey had always been meant to be about anyhow? I was inspired to be realizing that our Cycle of Life had come to a point where I may be learning as much from Buddy as he was from me.

Even though the travel distance to our starting points had increased, and conflicted with some of Buddy's viewpoints, I was nevertheless relieved to learn that within those sentiments he still possessed a desire to complete our journey. I also saw that he recognized how important the trips had become for me, and I think that made it easier for him to look past some of his potential travel objections. I appreciated that. It exemplified how he had come to understand me better from our journey too.

Above all else, it was most gratifying to realize that we both loved spending time with each other. For me, it was the most special part of what we had built together through the years. It was evident to me that we both had an appreciation of what we were accomplishing together. We were anticipating the completion of our cross-Canada adventure, each in our own way. And, it even had us noodling already what we may do together in future years.

As summer took hold, opportunities for us to bike in a pandemic were opening up—at least a crack.

In mid-September, Buddy and I decided to go for it. We packed up our bikes, our gear, our masks, a knee-brace compression sleeve for me just in case, hand sanitizer, and our vaccine passports. We made our arrangements to get back to Québec City. A few months prior to the first lockdown, Buddy had moved to Calgary, and then decided to go back to Victoria while everything came to a standstill. It meant we were on different flights to start our yearly outing. On one hand it seemed odd to not be travelling together, but I could certainly appreciate the symbolic nature of my son growing up and living in a different city emerging as our circumstances along our Cycle of Life.

I took both our bikes on my flight and arrived at the Jean Lesage International Airport in Québec City about three hours before Buddy. My plan was to casually unbox our bikes and put them together so that we would be ready to roll when Buddy arrived. But the airline had a different idea. Buddy's bike box showed up with a big flap of cardboard torn away on one side. Luckily, most of his bike was in good shape. Unluckily, the stem on his handlebars was not. It was a Sunday afternoon. I soon realized that it was going to be hard to locate a place that would have the part we needed.

I found a Mountain Equipment Co-op (MEC) store that was open on Sundays and had a well-respected bike department and repair shop. I crossed my fingers and loaded our bikes into the back of a taxi van for the 15-minute lift to the store. I asked my driver his name. "Gilles," he said abruptly and indicated he did not speak English. He was standoffish until I complimented him on his baseball cap. Our icebreaker was the Expos. I reminiscently rattled off the names of Cromartie, Dawson, Gullickson, Reardon, Rogers, Lee, Carter, Wallach, Oliver, Alou, Walker, Grissom, Guerrero—even Pete Rose –and we were like best friends after that. "Oui, Oui, Oui!" Then silence again, but best friends.

Unfortunately, MEC didn't have the handlebar stem I needed for Buddy's Trek bicycle. The part was not common. Leo in their repair shop went well out of his way to explore alternatives, but it looked like we would have to wait until after the weekend for specialized bike stores to open. It was still a couple hours before Buddy arrived, but I thought it would be best to stay where I was and wait for him to cab over to me so he could help me with the bikes. I browsed around the store, picked up some fuel for our backpacking stove, and phoned around for accommodation options. Then, just prior to the store closing, Leo found me and was thrilled to say he had scrounged a replacement stem off another bike in their back storeroom. With the staff about to lock up, he was sorry he wouldn't be able to help me swap everything out, but at least he had found the right part.

I went to work in the parking lot and was halfway through getting Buddy's bike in order when he rolled up in a taxi. After big hugs, we finished the repair together. What I thought was going to be an easy-paced few hours setting up for Buddy's arrival and getting us off to a smooth start, turned into a scramble.

It was a relief when we finally got to pedalling. However, with the time it had taken to complete all the repairs, dusk had started to set in. We obviously were not going to get as far as we originally planned, but we thought we should try to at least get ourselves across the St. Lawrence to Lévis. We hopped on a bike trail that took us alongside the St. Charles River and wound its way around Old Québec City. It led us directly to the ferry terminal for the one-kilometre crossing of the St. Lawrence.

Once we were onboard and went up to the upper deck, another passenger had an iPhone playing a moving piano piece that I was told was Jean-Michel Blais, a Québécois pianist and composer. I thought it was the perfect soundtrack for the moment. Buddy and I standing by the railing and looking back at Québec City above the river, with all its lights glimmering off the water.

It was quite dark when Buddy and I deboarded and got going on the bike paths on the south side of the river. The Lévis Motel however, was far from dark. It was lit up in pink neon for us, like a Vegas beacon.

Being a Sunday evening, our food options were slim by the time we arrived. We didn't have any luck with delivery services either. I dug into my pannier and pulled out our stove and a dehydrated pack of backcountry stew, spaceman food as Buddy called it. I boiled it up outside our motel room door. We had to laugh at our unexpected start to the year—damaged parts, biking in the dark, and back-up dining. Our tiny room made us giggle too. With our bikes inside, we had to perform acrobatic moves to get to and from our bathroom. But we went to bed thankful that we would be riding the next morning and not delayed another day dealing with repairs.

We slept in quite late. We eventually headed east on Highway 132 and made our way along the southern shores of the grand St. Lawrence, passing through little villages and towns, each with their own silver-spired church standing high like sentinels above the other buildings.

We stopped when we came to our first possibility for food, Casse-Croute Le Phare, a small roadside food stand with green picnic tables off to one side. We feasted on a breakfast for champions to kickstart our first morning, pizza *la gourmande* and poutine *viande fumee*.

The stand's owner, Corrine, somehow talked Buddy into a coconut tarte to cap off his meal.

"I like food," Buddy said.

"It must take you 27 bike trips to get your groceries home," I said, always in amazement at how much Buddy could pack away.

Mid-twenties, fit, and a world class, elite digestive system.

When we got back on the road, Buddy and I noted again the large number of houses that had above ground backyard pools. We had first seen it biking from Montréal to Québec City. It turns out that Québec has more backyard pools per capita than anywhere in North America. Even more than California. A Globe & Mail report estimated there was a pool for every 26 Québecers, compared to a pool for every 31 Californians.

Our route took us through the artsy village of Saint-Jean-Port-Joli. For over a century, in large part due to the intricate work of the Bourgault brothers, the little town had built a reputation for being home to wood carvers. Almost every yard we passed had a sculpture of some sort.

As we made it farther east, the St. Lawrence continued to widen. Our bikes looked smaller and smaller against the backdrop. It was over twenty kilometres across to the northern side when we camped at Rivière-Ouelle. The long views made for an idyllic tenting spot, complemented with a helpful camp shelter that we had all to ourselves, patio furniture and outdoor sink included. It was chilly out, but we padded on an extra layer of clothing to lounge around while we sparked up our stove again for some hot tea and boiled Pad Thai spacefood.

I woke the next morning, quietly crawled out of our tent, and went for a walk by myself down the shoreline. My hamstrings were tight, so I moved in goofy long strides to stretch them out. It was early enough to watch the sun rise with red glows stretching across the St. Lawrence and lighting up the green filled hills on the far side of the river. I found a drift log to sit on, above a marsh area alongside the river's edge. It was filled with birds. I know there are special places around the world, but when it comes to sunrises and sunsets, I can't imagine there is a country that has the diversity and beauty that Canada has to offer.

After Buddy emerged from the tent and we got rolling, we passed a number of eel weirs. The entire region has a long and rich history of eel fishing, in nets set with long sticks along the St. Lawrence that take advantage of big tide swings and the eels' fascinating migratory pattern. Like salmon, eels live in both saltwater and freshwater, but in a completely opposite life cycle. Eels are catadromous, meaning they are born in saltwater, migrate to freshwater to grow, then return to their saltwater origins to spawn and die.

There are plenty of east coast seafarer stories about giant eel monsters attacking vessels, but Buddy and I had become far more aware of a different monster that had history around this part of the province. Articles published in *La Gazette de Québec*, dating back to the 1760s, warned of loup-garou, a werewolf, who roamed the land around Kamarouska. As we biked from Rivière-Ouelle to Kamarouska, the inselbergs—isolated hills—that jutted up on an otherwise flat river valley made it look like just the kind of place where werewolves would like to hangout. One of the more famous inselbergs is Devil's Tower featured in *Close Encounters of the Third Kind*. The unique land formations along the St. Lawrence are not nearly as dramatic as that one, but the two big outcroppings coming into Kamarouska made it easy to imagine torch bearing, pitchforked villagers desperately attempting to dart through the farm fields between the two prominent hills.

"It could be right out of a Dungeons and Dragons," Buddy remarked.

We stumbled upon a great breakfast spot in the village of Kamarouska, the Café Du Clocher. The restaurant, with its red roof, treed courtyard, red picket fence, red framed doors and windows, embodied the quaintness of the entire village.

"Just the kind of quaint place one might find in a werewolf story," I said to Buddy.

We were greeted at the café by Phillippe, and after producing our vaccine passports and ID, we were led to a patio table with a view across the St. Lawrence.

I pointed out to Buddy that Phillippe—looking debonair in a dinner jacket, a silk cravat, pocket square, and a suede leather vest—looked like he could have stepped right out of Taika Waititi's vampire satire film, *What We Do In The Shadows*.

"If someone was a werewolf in Kamouraska, that stylish outfit would be exactly what they would wear," I told Buddy.

"Knowing that we were vaccinated could be useful info too," Buddy chimed in.

I asked Phillippe if he had heard of loup-garou legends in Kamouraska, but he said he had not.

"That's exactly what someone would say if they didn't want anyone to know about werewolves in Kamouraska," I exclaimed to Buddy.

On his next visit to our table, Phillippe continued the conversation. "I haven't heard those tales about Kamouraska, but I do love loup-garou. Very sexy."

Buddy and I looked at each other wide-eyed. We were thinking the same thing. That is exactly what someone would say if they *were* a werewolf in Kamouraska.

Phillippe was awesome and our breakfast was delicious. We had bagel et anguille fumée, smoked eel, of course. Phillippe suggested that a good route for us to bike out of town would be on Mississippi Street. He said it was really nice for biking. But we remained on the main roads, just in case those directions were what loup-garou from Kamouraska would say to a couple of unsuspecting visitors inquiring about werewolves we missed the turnoff.

Not loup-garou, but we rode alongside a moose sauntering in a field beside the highway as we made our way out of Kamouraska. We were guessing that it wasn't a zombie-moose like in Ontario though. Maybe not Bullwinkle-friendly, but Québec highway signs confirmed that we were back to happier moose again. I suggested that maybe the moose are angry in Ontario because the Leafs haven't won a Stanley Cup in so long.

We biked past *Le Perchoir du Cirque* near Pointe-Séche, a grouping of oddly shaped glass and wood cabins perched on the sides of the cliffs that rose up behind Kamouraska. We were told that from the beds in those cabins, people could see full moons through sky lights. With loup-garou fresh on our minds, it seemed coincidental and a little suspicious.

About 30 kilometres further, we said farewell to the St. Lawrence at Rivière-du-Loup and branched southeast toward Petit Témis Linear Interprovincial Park. It marked the beginning of our last stretch in Québec. Built on the abandoned Témiscouata

Railway, which first operated in 1885, the Petit Témis now offers a bike friendly, 134 kilometre-long, finely graveled, rock dust path all the way from Rivière-du-Loup to Edmundston, New Brunswick. The trail is dotted with various break spots and camping areas that are spaced out about every 20 kilometres or so. The steepest grade is 4 per cent so it is super accessible for everyone, and on a weekday in September it was brilliantly unpopulated.

The only other people we came across that afternoon were a couple who were on a weeklong bike excursion. We met them at the Station Saint-Modeste, a cute little building which had been converted into a trailside snack shop. It had closed for the season, but it had a water station and picnic tables. We chatted with the two for awhile before they headed out on the trail ahead of us. We hung back and took advantage of the tables for our backpack-stove dinner.

We caught up to the couple about an hour later and saw they had set up their tent in a nice, dedicated camping area, Camping de la Rivière des Roches. There were four other tenting spots, but Buddy and I decided to push on to the next site 20 kilometres further. It was getting late, but we thought being one of only two groups on the entire trail, we could afford to spread out more than a few feet.

But wouldn't you know it, a short distance later it started to rain. And then as it got darker, we somehow got branched off of the Petit Témis route and ended up on a side road that detoured us for about four kilometres. By the time we backtracked and found the right path, we had to finish off our last riding in full darkness. Again. Distance has a way of feeling farther in the dark and the rain, but we eventually found our destination, Camping du Ruisseau Beaulieu. There were three wood planked platforms for tents in an otherwise rocky area beside a creek. Since our small backpacking tent was more suited to be set up on ground, we pitched it right on the side of the trail. The ground was soaked, but flat enough.

The Cycle Of Life

The rain stopped during the night. We woke to heavy grey overcast skies and big sloppy puddles all around our tent.

We packed up our gear and trekked out along the old rail line into *Saint-Louis-du-Ha! Ha!*, the only town in the world to boast not one but two exclamation points in its name. Like many who visit *Saint-Louis-du-Ha! Ha!*, we took a few pictures in front of their sign, and then stocked up on a few grocery items at Épicerie Chez Nancy.

We wound south on the rail trail along the west side of the 45-kilometre-long Lac Témiscouata, with deep blue waters surrounded by deeper green treed hills. We were met with a tranquility that made it hard to fathom the need for the outposts that were built in the area during a border conflict between the British North American colony and the United States in the 1830s. Had what they called the Aroostook War gone a different way, the whole region we were biking through would have become part of Maine. Locals referred to it as the Pork and Beans War after the favourite food of the lumberjacks who were fighting over who had the right to harvest valuable timber. The incident was eventually resolved with the Webster-Ashburton Treaty and resulted in the border lines that are still in effect today. The almost 13,000 square kilometres northern portion of the disputed lands that were awarded to what would eventually become Canada, provided a key connection between Lower Canada and the Maritime Colonies. It also fortuitously gave Buddy and me some fantastic biking terrain along Lac Témiscouata.

Our last stop in the province of Québec was for pumpkin soup at Amarante épicerie ecologique in Témiscouata-sur-le-Lac. After which I chilled while Buddy did handstands and bounced over things in the parkgrounds by the lakeshore. We then got back on our bikes to continue along the water's edge, riding over old rail trestles that brought back good memories of the rail lines we biked through British Columbia.

Late that afternoon, our trail crossed under a timber framed archway that marked the border between Québec and New Brunswick. Buddy and I had officially made it to our seventh province. We did a little jig and took a moment to pee while straddling the border. We both had to go and didn't want to show favour to one province over the other. We weren't sure if peeing on or not peeing on would show preference anyhow.

We loved our biking through Québec, but we were thrilled we had reached the Maritimes. It seemed like such a far-off place when we were first setting out from the west coast.

Along with Ontario, Québec and Nova Scotia, New Brunswick was one of Canada's first four original provinces. It was the birthplace province of the only British prime minister to be born outside of the United Kingdom, Andrew Bonar Law. And more impressively, it had the most breweries per capita of all the provinces.

We remained on the Petit Témis trail for 15 more kilometres, until we were adjacent to the base of the Mont Farlagne ski area on the hills near Edmundston. At 352 metres above sea level at the peak, it was the second highest ski area in New Brunswick. The business had recently been purchased, and saved, by local investors for $900,000, making the whole thing less expensive than splitting a condo in Whistler.

Edmundston is situated alongside the Saint John River which separated that part of New Brunswick from Maine. After the Aroostook War, an American industrialist who had built sawmills on the Edmundston side declared the area an independent state named the Republic of Madawaska. It was never legally recognized, but to this day the mayor of Edmundston also holds the title of President of the Republic of Madawaska. Buddy and I rode past a house with the Republic's Eagle Flag still flying high.

We had pushed hard the previous days and I sensed we needed a break, especially after our wet, trail side camping spot the night before. We got a room at the Days Inn on the eastern outskirts of Edmundston and ordered in a feast of bar-b-qued ribs.

While we waited for the delivery, I delved into a story with Buddy about a creative way that once got me and a friend into the Super Bowl. It had some elements of anything is possible perseverance messaging that I thought might be fun to relay.

How to Get on the Field at the Super Bowl

My long-time friend Tor and I were diehard Chicago Bear fans and caught up in the granddaddy of all football rivalries: Chicago Bears versus Green Bay Packers. One fun-filled Monday Night Football evening, we started joking around about finding something ugly in Green Bay Packer history for every single day of the year. It led to a big research project that culminated in quite a unique sports calendar, depicting a full 365 days of Green Bay Packer blunders, losses, fumbles, firings, questionable decisions, bad trades, weird things, and just plain ugly days that befell the Packers over the last century. We knew it struck a chord when the powers-that-be of the Chicago Sun-Times, the largest circulated newspaper in the world in the nineties, offered full-page colour ads to sponsor the calendar. And then unbelievably the Chicago Bears asked us for copies for Coach Wannstedt to put in the players' locker room leading up to their game against the Packers that year. We figured not bad for a couple guys who looked up a bunch of goofy football lore.

When the Packers, sadly for us, made it to Super Bowl XXXII in San Diego, I wanted to see what the response to our calendar would be at the holy grail of football games.

I was a director of marketing at a ski resort at the time and had a long list of contacts with some of the same companies in the beer, banks, soda, and car worlds that dominate Super Bowl sponsorships. I thought for sure one of those connections would be able to come through with tickets. When Tor ended up not being able to go on a trip at that time, my friend Kevin who was a ski shop retail manager jumped at the chance and came on board with his own list of contacts. Super Bowl tickets are hard to land at the best of times, but Green Bay fans were losing their minds over this one. We hadn't secured tickets yet, but Kevin and I figured we would go anyway and see what luck we might have on the ground in San Diego.

On game day, we got to Qualcomm Stadium early. We parked our rental car smack dab in the middle of the lot, our trunk full of Green Bay spoof calendars. Still with no tickets, our rough plan had become to sell enough at $10-a-calendar to help us with our way into the game.

Unfortunately, Packer fans had descended on California in droves and were driving scalper prices sky high. Tickets were well over $1000, USD, for average seats. Those prices would be considered a steal today, but back then it was record setting insanity. We were going to have to sell a whack of calendars.

We decided to give it a shot, heading out with 50 calendars each to start. I sold my entire batch in less than half an hour. Football fans appreciated the amount of research put in. People snapped them up for Super Bowl souvenirs and for presents for friends at home.

Kevin had a different experience. Within five minutes, he had been confronted by security and had his calendars confiscated. He was done, but happy regardless just to be part of the Super Bowl tailgate parties that had started to shape up.

I decided to keep going until someone told me to stop. Each time I returned to the car to load up

The Cycle Of Life

with more calendars, Kevin had loaded up on more bar-b-ques and beer.

By noon, I was sitting on $2000 (USD!) in calendar sales and thinking that game tickets might actually be possible. However, the amount of beer being consumed by fans was rapidly removing constraints on their wallets. It helped with my sales, but to my dismay, nosebleed seats in the absolute worst spot in the stadium were now going for over $2000! USD! For single seats! In the nineties!

While I mulled over the developments, I made my way over to the limousine section. One of the head honchos for Coca-Cola in Southern California loved my story about selling calendars to get into the Super Bowl. As a program seller strolled by, he dropped an attention-grabbing nugget of information. He told me that the official game program sellers were from different San Diego sport groups, raising funds for their programs, and got to go into the stadium for free.

Lightbulb! My entrepreneurial wheels kicked into overdrive. I zoomed to catch up to the program seller, a college fastball student named Beth. She was clad in an oversized, white Super Bowl shirt (with Super Bowl XXXII displayed down the full-length green sleeves), a blue San Diego Super Bowl XXXII apron (with a front pocket for holding cash), and a big "Official Super Bowl Program $5" button (which added an official air to her get-up). My lightbulb turned chandelier when Beth said that she and her other program-selling best friend were not football fans and not planning to watch the game. I offered $100 to each of them for their uniforms. They were thrilled with the transaction. I was more thrilled.

Kevin was glowing. A little bit from my idea, but mostly from a full day of tailgating by then. He and I headed towards the stadium gates, decked out in

Super Bowl program selling shirts, program aprons, and big ol' "Official Programs $5" buttons.

Kevin said, "I don't think this is going to work, but these are pretty cool Super Bowl souvenirs."

We waltzed directly in while Jewel was belting out the National Anthem. No one said boo to us. 1998 security. Try doing anything like that today. Back then, I even carried a backpack in. Kevin lifted me off the ground with a hug, he was pumped up.

We found an empty wheelchair zone at the top of one of the seat sections and parked ourselves at the railing. Just prior to the end of the first quarter, the game was tied 7-7, I ran out to a bank of payphones. Cell phones weren't a common thing in those days.

"We're at the Super Bowl!!!" I called everyone I knew until I ran out of change.

Everything had been going so smoothly. When I got back to Kev, he was in the same spot, but four other guys had moved in behind him with their backs against the concourse wall. One of the guys said to Kevin, "Hey, fella, I said you can't stand there."

Kevin was a gentle giant kind of guy without a bad intention in his whole being. Quite innocently, I thought, he did a *Baloo the Bear* and wiggled back and forth between two of the guys.

"Well how about if I stand here with you guys?" he said, in an overtly friendly tone.

Kevin's day abruptly turned upside down. They were undercover police whose nerves were either frayed from endlessly dealing with drunk football fans or they were not fans of *The Jungle Book*. Either way, they had Kevin spun around with his face against the wall and handcuffs going on behind his back. I looked on, bewildered, it happened so quickly.

"Your pal here is being arrested for disorderly conduct and I can tell ya' he won't be watching any more of the game today," said one of the officers.

I was bluntly told that Kev would be taken to the downtown jail from where I could 'collect my friend' when the game was over. I pleaded and protested to no avail. They hauled Kevin away. Shell-shocked, I retreated back to the railing.

A quick recap of our situation: I was well over $3,000 in calendar sales by then, we had amazingly found our way into the Super Bowl, Kev was now in a downtown jail, and there was absolutely nothing I could do about it until after the game. Me sitting in a jail lobby certainly wouldn't help Kevin in any way. I figured I might as well keep watching the game.

At half-time in the concourse, with the Temptations crooning away on the field, who did I bump into? The Coca-Cola exec from the limo.

It took a moment for him to register.

"You got in!" he stuttered in disbelief.

I told him the abridged version of our story.

"We have your calendars in our suite! Man, you need to watch the second half with us!"

So...as Kev served time in a downtown cell, I hung out in one of the premiere suites at Super Bowl XXXII being treated with pseudo-celebrity status. To cap things off, the Denver Broncos scored a winning touchdown off a botched time management call by then Packers' coach Mike Holmgren, an event destined to be part of any future editions of our calendar.

When the game ended, Kevin was obviously on my mind, but sheepishly it didn't stop me from accepting my Coca-Cola hosts' offer to join them, with on-field passes, for the post-game celebrations. Somehow a guy who wore a program sellers' shirt to sneak into the Super Bowl, ended up being a football toss away from Tyrell Davis when they presented him with the MVP trophy.

I got a picture of myself with John Elway. Kevin got a mug shot.

I scored a lanyard with a Super Bowl On-Field Pass. Kevin had his shoelaces and belt taken away.

My newfound Coca-Cola friends invited me to head out on the town with them. Kevin was continually asked if he had any cigarettes to bum.

Kevin eventually got released at 3:00 a.m. along with his other cell mates, out the back entry of the jail. He looked disheveled, with a 'prisoner number' marked in felt pen on the back of his left hand, his shoelaces and belt draped loosely in his right hand, and his laceless running shoes flopping on his feet like snowshoes. To this day, he still cherishes his Super Bowl story. Each of us love our sweet-souvenir Official Program Seller Super Bowl shirts and now BBQ aprons. The calendar sales covered both of our entire trips including airfare and accommodations. The experience…priceless.

Kevin says the whole thing was awesome.

I tend to say it was more awesome.

Buddy got a few more details out of me while we made quick work of the ribs when the delivery arrived. Our calendar project was never a massive financial win. I don't think we made anything after we added up all our production costs, but not everything is about money. It led to a few one-of-a-kind experiences. The Super Bowl only being the cap on it all. I felt fortunate that we rolled with a fun idea and it uncovered a series of untradeable tidbits of life. I figured that was a worthy notion to share with my son through one of my stories.

We had a sleepy start the next morning as we biked out of Edmundston. There were some odd New Brunswick road signs that has us baffled. One had a depiction of some sort of swirl and no words. We could not figure out what it meant. We laughed that we couldn't find someone who knew what the numerous signs were for. It took us nearly half-way across the province before we eventually found out that the signs indicated fiddlehead foraging spots. Turns out that New Brunswickers are so enamoured with fiddleheads that they host an annual Fiddlehead Festival, dub one of their towns the Fiddlehead Capital of the World, lay claim to the world's largest fiddlehead at 24 feet tall, and display swirly highway signs to let you know when you're in a good picking spot. New Brunswickers pay a lot of attention to their fiddleheads, apparently more than their road signs.

The front wheel on Buddy's bike developed some play. We couldn't determine if it was a bearing problem, a frame issue, or something that had gone off-kilter from riding the road touring bikes on all the trails around Lac Témiscouata. When we made it to a little bike shop situated in the Grand Falls Home Hardware, the repair guy Eric did his best to help us figure it out. We almost bought a new wheel for the bike, but hesitated when we decided it likely wasn't a bearing issue after all and considered that the bike wheels at the shop would be a downgrade on the wheel that was already on his bike. We ended up adding washers on one side of the bike fork and realigning the wheel as best we could to eliminate almost all the wobble. It did the trick.

South of Grand Falls we chose the less used River Road along the west side of the Saint John River, and we hardly saw another vehicle. We biked around all kinds of roadkill though, the most we had seen on our journey—small rodents, rabbit, porcupine, racoon, cat, coyote, duck, and even a fish somehow.

We tried to stick to paved roads and avoid trails in case they were affecting Buddy's wheel. However, when we came to the Aroostook River near the spot where it joins into the Saint John River, we made the call to bike one short section of an abandoned rail trail to take advantage of a scenic shortcut across a long-curved trestle bridge. By doing so we were able to connect to secondary Highway 130 and continue our route south along the west side of the Saint John River.

We were surprised when it was Buddy's knee that needed attention, not mine. We were not sure if it was from the way his bike was set up with the new handlebar stem, the play in the wheel that had earlier developed, or the strain of a few long days of biking, but one of Buddy's knees was starting to feel sore. This time felt different to him compared to the time he had problems along Lake Superior. He wasn't overly worried, but the fact that I had brought a knee brace with me was a nice coincidence. It was a bit big on him, but he positioned it over top of his sweatpants and it seemed to help.

With bikes and knees breaking down through the day, we were glad to coast into the River Country Campground and finish our first full day of biking in New Brunswick. We arrived at dusk and were greeted by a sign on the door of their welcome building with instructions to ring the bell if nobody was present. We rang a few times, but no one came. We strolled into the campground and immediately found out why, there was no one around at all. All the picnic tables were propped up, garbage cans removed, and bathrooms locked, except one porta potty that we were happy had been left open. Other than not posting a 'closed-for-the-season' sign, they had done a bang-up job of shutting down and it wasn't going to matter how many times we rang the bell.

The good news was we had the pick of the place for our tent, so we chose the softest ground we could find in the whole campground. With no picnic tables around, we sat on the playground equipment, broke out our stove again, and dined on Spicy Chicken Curry. The geese overhead were honking so loud that we had to shout to hear each other.

Buddy still wore my brace the next day, but his knee seemed okay as we worked our way into McCain Foods country. We biked past the Potato World themed park. Then crossed back over to the east side of the Saint John River and into the town of Florenceville-Bristol, the French Fry Capital of the World and official home to McCain headquarters, the largest French Fries producer in the world.

McCain reportedly produces over one million pounds of potato products per hour. Per hour! They do business in over 160 countries around the globe, all from the little company that started out in the town of Florenceville-Bristol, with a population of about 1600. In town, we were unsuccessful finding a better fitting knee brace for Buddy, but we did get ourselves deliciously prepared local potatoes at On the Boardwalk Café, owned by none other than Allison and Clare McCain. Allison was the son of Andrew, one of the four original McCain brothers, and now the chairman of the whole McCain operation. Buddy and I figured that made him the world's Potato King. And that meant we were feasting on some of the King's potatoes.

We found a drugstore about 20 kilometres further south in Hartland, where Lana was super helpful finding the right knee brace for Buddy. My compression sleeve had worked in a pinch, but Buddy said the new one supported his knee far better. Most people remember Hartland for its famous bridge. We would mostly remember it for finding a knee brace. The bridge is super cool though with its sign that states, "You are now entering the longest covered bridge in the world. 1282 feet."

Hartlanders happily tell three legends about the bridge. First, Sal the flying salmon who once jumped over the bridge. Alden Nowlan, the famous New Brunswicker poet, while he was a reporter for the Hartland Observer, even wrote about Sal's feat. Some say Sal was spooked by the shadow of the covered bridge. Some say he was just showing off.

Second, horses in Hartland were trained so well they would stop half-way across the river to provide a kissing moment on romantic carriage rides on the bridge.

And third, if you made a wish on one side of the bridge and held your breath until you got to the other side, your wish would come true. Thanks to some pretty smart horses, with kisses on the wish list, I supposed some only had to hold their breath to the halfway point for their wish to come true.

"Want to try holding your breath across the bridge on our bikes?" I teased Buddy.

He reminded me how he used to hold his breath past graveyards when he was younger. "Oh, I know," I said. "You got your sister so worked up about it that I thought she was going to pass out once."

After Hartland, the temperature started to soar. The sun directly in our faces made it feel even warmer. We got some reprieve at The Strawberry Hill roadside farm, not from their strawberries, but from devouring half of a fresh picked watermelon each—a perfect treat for a couple of sweat-soaked bikers.

At Woodstock we crossed over the Saint John once more. The river bends toward the east there and so did we, following its southern shoreline to the Woolastook Park campground. Their full-time RV area was operating and full, but like our previous night, the rest of their facilities and camp sites had closed for the season. I imagine a lot of campgrounds had a tough go over the past two summers with all the restrictions due to COVID-19. We got the green light to stay overnight and had the area to ourselves, except for the geese who left plenty of *proof* all over the place that they had taken full advantage of COVID and the park being closed. We managed to find a clean patch and a brilliant spot for our tent that overlooked the river.

Buddy warmed my heart that evening when he asked what we should do together after our coast-to-coast bike journey was over. He had been thinking of a ideas. I smiled so much my cheeks hurt. He suggested that maybe we could do micro-brewery tours together. Cheers to that I thought! It sounded good to my legs too. I imagined his wish would be for it to be more local for him in nature, but I didn't ask. I was just thrilled about the prospect of us continuing with more adventures together.

Buddy and I were down to our last drops of water in the morning, so we wheeled into the Upper Kingsclear Fire Hall to see if we could get replenished. The crew was in early for a training session and they jumped at the chance to help us out. They told us their water tasted awful, so they fantastically loaded us up with ice cold bottled water from their fridge.

When we made it to the outskirts of Fredericton, Buddy and I took a good long break at Porter's Diner for their Truckers' Breakfast Special. All the walls and booths were packed with pictures of Paul Porter racing in his '55 Bel-Air and other car photos that people had donated over the years. The place was packed with customers too. They even had added a bakery stand inside their front doors to help get them through the pandemic. It was encouraging to see how resilient some places had been during tough times.

Unfortunately, Buddy's knee had grown sorer. We considered the possibility of flying out of Fredericton, but he felt the brace was helping and he wanted to continue to Prince Edward Island. We forged on.

New Brunswick kept up with more little surprises. The University of New Brunswick in Fredericton was the first English-speaking university in Canada in 1785. And 90 years after that, in 1875, New Brunswicker Grace Lockhart got her degree in Science and English Literature at Mount Allison University, becoming the first woman not only in New Brunswick and the whole of Canada to receive a Bachelor's degree, but the first woman in the entire British Empire.

It was another scorcher of a day as we continued past Fredericton. My sunglasses were streaked from sweat. As we biked east, our arms and legs on the right-side of our bodies got most of the direct sun and needed most of our sunscreen attention. We were tempted to cool off in the Saint John River when we crossed over it for the last time near Foshay and Grand Lakes. But we held out and kept our focus on biking. At least until we could not resist a sign to turn-off for McCabes Ice Cream. The timing was perfect as we had begun to melt a bit out there on our bikes.

Janice McCabe let us know that if we continued on Highway 2, the Trans-Canada, we wouldn't find accommodation options until getting almost right into Moncton. We knew we couldn't make it all the way there with the amount of daylight we had, so we called an audible and rerouted ourselves south on Highway 10 towards Sussex and Four Corners. It was a big detour, but there were places to stay there within our reach. It did, however, add the challenge of a significant climb over New Brunswick's Kierstead mountain at the tail end of hot, long day of biking. Buddy managed it well and said that his knee wasn't feeling any worse. By the time we got to the Pine Cove Motel, we were back to biking in the dark. I felt bad that our riding had been creeping later into the evenings too often this year. By no means had it been by design, but each day had taken us longer than expected and dusk was sneaking up on us earlier being mid-September.

With a goal of keeping our biking inside of daylight hours, we aimed for an early start the next morning. Davis and Sarah, the owners of the motel, helped by offering to wake up early to pack continental breakfasts for us. When we were leaving and dropped off our keys at the office, there were two little to-go bags waiting for us with muffins, yogurts, bananas and juice boxes. It was a nice touch.

We rounded the northside of Moncton mid-day and as we approached Shediac we got our first glimpse of the Atlantic Ocean. We would have rejoiced but we were hit with big winds out of the northeast that had picked up, gusting to 60 kilometres/hour. We were being blasted. It was a tough ride until we hit the Atlantic shoreline and our route turned south. It put the winds in our favour. We pedalled fast as we pushed down the coast, looking out at swaying salt marshes and the high winds whipping the seas of the Northumberland Strait.

With a reputation of having some of the best fish cuisine in the region, we attempted to eat at the One Fish Bistro in Shemogue, but they were completely booked with reservations. We tried to talk our way into take-out, explaining how we were biking and this was our only chance to try their food, but they were not having any of it. We turned to dehydrated seafood chowder for dinner instead.

Our goal through the entire day had been to make it onto Prince Edward Island, but as we got closer to the Confederation Bridge, we were not exactly sure how we were going to accomplish that. Biking is not allowed on the bridge and much to our chagrin the shuttle they usually offered to cyclists had been shut down due to COVID-19 policies.

By happenstance, the minute we jumped off our bikes at our last stop before the bridge, an Islander named Shane pulled up in a 15-passenger van and volunteered to give us a ride. Timing is everything sometimes. We masked up, threw our bikes in the back, and had found our way to the island. I snapped a few pics of Buddy loading the back of the van. One, to record our luck of finding our way to PEI. Two, it was a full moon and I playfully mentioned to Buddy that a guy volunteering to give a couple of cyclists a ride across the bridge in a van on a full moon is just like something loup-garou would do.

When the Confederation Bridge opened in 1997 it became the longest bridge in the world crossing seasonal ice-covered waters. At a cost of $1.3 billion, it spans an amazing 12.9 kilometres between mainland Canada and Prince Edward Island. The two-lane, eleven-metre-wide toll bridge took four years to build on a total of 61 piers each anchored to the floor of the Northumberland Strait. Most of the bridge sits 40 metres above the water, but there is one higher portion at 60 metres for ship traffic. Shane told us the bridge was designed with a slight curve after studies suggested it would help drivers pay more attention. The crossing takes approximately twelve minutes. Locals, including Shane, say it is exciting the first time, but despite the curve the drive becomes monotonous when you do it all the time. The side walls of the bridge are high enough that it blocks the view for many cars, and it becomes kind of like driving in an open-air tunnel.

As our luck continued, Shane's van rode high enough for Buddy and me to see over the concrete sides of the bridge. We couldn't have had better timing for our crossing. The full moon was rising up and sparkling off the Northumberland Strait.

In order to enter Prince Edward Island, during COVID-19 protocols, Buddy and I had to have pre-arranged special PEI Passes after proving that we were vaccinated and clean. When we approached the point where the Confederation Bridge connected to the island, we could see that the old terminal and vehicle staging area for the out of service ferry had been repurposed into a COVID-19 checkpoint. There was a line of pop-up market tents set up to examine documents of incoming travellers and conduct nasal swab tests on new people entering the island. Inspectors scurried from tent to tent in protective medical gear, giving the scene an eerie military feel like we were in an apocalyptic movie. A fully gowned, gloved, and face-shielded medical official greeted us at the window of the van, and proceeded to mark away on her clipboard as we showed our PEI Passes, answered a series of probing questions, and had our snot sampled. Buddy and I could only imagine the amount of dust and gunk that must have been in there after us being on the road for days. We were confident we would test clear on the COVID-19 front, but who knew what else might have made its way up our noses.

We passed the tests and were granted passage. I'm sure our chauffeur Shane was relieved, or that would have been the last time he picked up a couple of wayward cyclists before crossing the bridge.

I promised Buddy this would be my last one. "Unless of course it was all part of a well-designed werewolf plan, with the checkpoints serving as a handy government funded way to pre-check how pure and safe we were."

We were officially on Prince Edward Island, our eighth province! Yay! And we were ending our day in the dark again. Boo! After unloading our bikes and thanking Shane, Buddy and

I had a short ride to the Carlton Motel where we gladly crashed for the night.

To drive a vehicle from tip-to-tip on Prince Edward Island reportedly takes about three hours. For us, we had a pleasant half day ride with 50 or so kilometres left to make it to Charlottetown.

There is a palpable serenity being on PEI. Maybe no one has captured the feeling better than Lucy Maud Montgomery of *Anne of Green Gables* fame.

> *You never know what peace is until you walk on the shores or in the fields along the winding red roads of Prince Edward Island in a summer twilight when the dew is falling and the old stars are peeping out and the sea keeps its might tryst with the little land it loves.*

Those words set the tone for our casual approach to our last day of riding for the year.

Potato farmers on PEI don't seem to adhere to that approach. PEI grows more potatoes each year than not only neighbouring New "McCain" Brunswick, but every other province in Canada as well. Quite the feat considering the island is less than one per cent of the land size of the second highest producing potato province, Alberta. Nearly 90,000 acres of potatoes are grown on Prince Edward Island, with over a hundred different varieties that are then shipped to over 20 different countries around the world. We had to figure that some of those potatoes were undoubtedly making their way back to the Potato King.

After an easy-paced early morning ride that got us nearly halfway to Charlottetown, we stopped at the Bakin' Express in Crapaud for bacon and eggs, and fried potatoes of course.

We then rolled into the PEI Capital at midday.

Our first stop was to see Danny MacQueen at MacQueen's bike shop, who set us up with a couple of free oversized boxes to pack our bikes in for our plane rides home. Next, we settled ourselves into the big comfy chairs of the Gahan House for a celebration of making it to our eighth province—flights of local beer and a platter of PEI oysters on the half shell. The oysters we sampled were classified by which part of the island they came from, and surprisingly how each were quite different in taste and appearance. The famous Malpeque oysters remain the most popular, but Buddy and I took a liking to the green tinted ones from Colville Bay.

We had the rest of our afternoon and evening to explore Charlottetown harbour, known as the Birthplace of Confederation. We went on a hunt for a famous PEI lobster roll and checked that off in a big way when we found a place that had been featured on The Food Network, The Chip Shack in Peakes Quay Marina. We sat in the sun at one of their marina-side picnic tables, under a yellow umbrella, tucked into our lobster rolls, and watched the harbour traffic go by.

We later had a memorable evening at Buddy's choice of Slaymaker & Nichols. The restaurant had been named after the Slaymaker & Nichols Olympic Circus, which some say played a major hand in the birth of our nation. In 1864, the electric atmosphere of the circus created an environment that was rumoured to break the ice of a gathering between the Maritime

Colonies and a Confederation contingent that included John A. Macdonald. The meetings became known as the Charlottetown Conference with the *Fathers of Confederation* socializing into the wee hours of the morning and mapping out the plans for a union that would become the Dominion of Canada. As they say at the restaurant, "if it wasn't for Slaymaker & Nichols, the nation may never have been born."

The circus, however, did not survive and disbanded shortly thereafter. Fortunately for Charlottetown diners though, Slaymaker & Nichols was reborn a century and a half later as a sublime addition to the cuisine scene on Spud Island. Everything our server Lindsey meticulously described sounded delicious, so Buddy and I ordered a variety of dishes to share. Two of the most memorable were their seared scallops and their Lost in Translation dish featuring tuna, avocado, and quinoa. A high-flying act to be sure.

Our night out in Charlottetown topped off a magnificent year for us. It felt amazing to have reconvened our annual biking, but it was admittedly bittersweet for me to be thinking that the following year could very well complete our Cycle of Life. But a new treasure had emerged to look forward to – a possible follow-up adventure was in discussion.

Year Fourteen Completed

Kms 5642 to 6626
Days 56 to 63

Québec City to Charlottetown

YEAR FIFTEEN - Buddy 26 Years Old

BRING ON THE SCREECH - THE WRAP UP TO AN INCREDIBLE JOURNEY

Onward from Spud Island. Organizing for our trip started earlier than any previous year. A few friends and family were aiming to join us on the east coast at the end of our cross-country adventure, so that put an additional wrinkle into the planning.

Buddy's knee was feeling good, but he injured his hamstring skateboarding a few months prior to our trip. Thankfully it wasn't serious and he was alright by the time we left to get back to Prince Edward Island. I was healthy going into our trip too. If I started to feel older, I quickly reminded myself of baseball great Satchel Paige who defied how old he was with his pitching and answered questions of his age with, "How old would you be if you didn't know how old you are?" Great words to live by

I arranged flights for Buddy and me to connect in Montréal so we could travel together into Charlottetown. We unboxed our bikes at the airport, relieved to see them undamaged, but discovered I had a different surprise in store for myself.

"Somehow in the last flurry of packing and heading to the airport," I said to Buddy, "I left my shoes in the car, and I only have my backup sandals that I wore on the plane."

"Not sure if you should be embarrassed that you forgot your shoes or the fact you wore those sandals on the plane," Buddy said. "Are those things older than I am?"

It wasn't going to be ideal, but I decided to Satchel Paige it with my sandals. I stubbornly took it as a challenge to bike in that footwear. My Scottish heritage's grip on my purse strings probably had a bit to do with it too.

We biked away from the airport and made our way to a room I had rented for us in the dorms at Holland College near the city centre. Our late afternoon arrival gave us the chance to enjoy one more evening in PEI's capital before we picked up our biking trail.

Leading up to our departure, the entire east coast had been experiencing weeks of heat warnings. It was so warm on the evening of our arrival that my shirt clung to my back while we walked around Charlottetown. The hot streak ended the next morning with a heavy downpour just as we were getting back on our bikes. In addition to full rain gear and in an attempt to keep his toes dry, I watched as Buddy wrapped his feet in clear plastic garbage bags before putting on his shoes. He then taped his rain pants over the bags. I had decided to go with a rain poncho over shorts and bare legs but followed his lead with putting bags over my socks, taped around my ankles, before stuffing my feet into my sandals. It may not have been pretty, but the bags seemed to help when we first set out.

"You know it's raining hard when you get hit by waves from cars coming in the opposite direction," I said.

There was so much heat built up in the pavement from the recent heatwave that the splashes were surprisingly warm.

After an hour of getting drenched, we stopped for a break and got a big laugh at the plastic bag on my left foot. It had filled with so much rain running down my leg that it ballooned out the side of my sandal to look like a goldfish bag coming out of a pet store. Any notions I had about keeping my feet dry were long gone.

Buddy and I were in great spirits. Once we came to terms with taking on the elements, our ride was remarkably enjoyable. As we moved further southeast down the island on Highway 1, the rain didn't let up, but no wind and it was pleasantly warm out. The rain even deepened the colour of the red sandy beaches we were biking past and that Prince Edward Island is famous for.

By the time we reached the ferry terminal at Wood Islands, I was dripping head to toe. Buddy's weather gear had served him better, but the rain had not spared him completely either.

We couldn't have timed our arrival for the ferry better. We had just enough time to grab a couple of lobster rolls at Treena's Take-out beside the ferry ramp right before we were ushered onto the boat for our crossing to Nova Scotia. The only hiccup was watching my sunglasses fall to their demise under the vehicle ramp as we walked our bikes aboard.

We scanned the horizon for the legendary ghost ship that has regularly been sighted on the Northumberland Strait, but the closest thing we saw to the famed fiery three-mast schooner was the charred ferry docked directly beside us in the terminal. It had been towed there two weeks earlier after a fire broke out in their engine room and they had been forced to evacuate over 200 passengers mid-crossing.

The ferry ride was 75 minutes which was enough time to get a bit comfortable, but not long enough to dry anything much. We disembarked at Caribou and biked into the ninth province of our journey, Nova Scotia. The pirate province. There is no shortage of stories about pirates and buried treasure in this part of Canada. Perhaps none as infamous as the attention-grabbing mysteries surrounding Oak Island. Ever since 1795, when teenager Daniel McGinnis stumbled upon a circular depression under an oak tree scarred by what many thought to have been made by a rope and tackle winch mechanism, treasure hunters from all over have sought to uncover unimaginable fortunes on Oak Island. High profile treasure seekers too, including the likes of Errol Flynn, John Wayne, and Franklin D. Roosevelt. When flagstones were discovered four feet under the depression, and then log pillars, and then what seemed to be broken wooden platforms every ten feet as they excavated further down, the furor over what would be found reached new heights. Little clues fueled speculation that it was the hush-hush location of Captain Kidd's treasure trove or Blackbeard's final bounty. And after the discovery of some Templar symbolism, some were even convinced it was the Templar Knights' hiding spot for the Holy Grail and the Ark of the Covenant. The mystery magnified when the excavation shaft reached a hundred feet and it suddenly flooded with seawater and explorations have been plagued with problems ever since. Many believe that it was a sea-tunnel-booby-trap made by pirates. The kind that perhaps inspired stories like *The Goonies*, a classic which Buddy still considers the best kids' movie ever made. Nonetheless, the dig site on Oak Island became infamously known as *The Money Pit* and the treasures have remained secret to Nova Scotia to this day.

I'm not sure if it was due to our long day of biking in the rain, but during our short ride to Pictou after the ferry, I had to chuckle at myself when I noticed I was biking in spurts and then coasting for periods. It took me back to the way Buddy rode on Vancouver Island when he was a little guy at the start of our adventure. Full circle, I thought. Now he was having to deal with his dad riding sporadically.

Then the rain picked up again. Soaked and in need of a good drying out we got a room at the old three-storey Braeside Inn overlooking historic Pictou Harbour. It was so wet out that the owner Linda invited us to bring our bikes inside and store them overnight in their well-appointed sitting room.

Much to my heart's delight, Buddy renewed his talk about the two of us continuing our yearly get togethers after our bike trip was over. After mulling it over for a year, he was still keen on the idea of a food and craft brewery type of adventure. I liked the idea too, so as a potential precursor to what that might be, I arranged for us to leave our bikes in New Glasgow the next morning and rent a car for a detoured overnight break to Halifax—on a beer quest. Having the most bars and pubs per capita of anywhere in Canada, I figured the Nova Scotian capital an apt place to test our prospective next father and son adventure.

It hadn't taken us long to get into full bike mode. Being in a car felt unusually fast to us both. When we got to the Angus Macdonald Bridge to cross into downtown Halifax, the toll caught us off guard too. Buddy had to scramble into the back seats and cobble together $1.25 in coins from our bike panniers.

Our afternoon was a wonderful taste of what our yearly tours might become. We sampled at Unfiltered Brewing, the Propeller Brewing Co., and then treated ourselves to a delectable tapas assortment of scallops crudo, oysters and caviar, and steak flank at the 50-seat Highwayman restaurant. In between it all, we even worked in a rock-climbing session at Seven Bays Bouldering for Buddy's extra satisfaction. It turned out to be a special impromptu day, plopped into the middle of our bike journey.

We stayed that night at the Nelson House B&B and started off our next day with Linda's signature tart-hollandaise-sauced eggs benny. Before heading back to New Glasgow, we decided on one more sidetrack since we were so close to the Bay of Fundy. At the mouth of the Shubenacadie River, the massive tides create a natural phenomenon ominously referred to as the Tidal Bore. That sounded too irresistible not to check out, especially when we heard that on that particular day it was going to be an extreme tidal change of a jaw-dropping 27 feet! We hopped on a Zodiac at Fundy Tidal Bore Adventures, and our big, shirtless, red-bearded raft guide Chris, zoomed us down the river to meet the

Tidal Bore. At the river's mouth we could see the visible, slow-moving wall of wavefront moving towards us. It is an amazing phenomenon. The incoming tide slowly moved over the sandbars that were exposed just moments before, pushing against the outflowing forces of the river, and magically converted the flat river water into mesmerizing sets of six-foot standing waves. Huge stationary rollers. We ripped and roller-coasted back and forth over the sets of waves, repeatedly swamping our Zodiac. The swells were so high we could not see over the crests when we were between waves. We broadsided one so hard that it nearly knocked Buddy into the river off the front of our raft. The incredibly unique experience lasted for almost an hour and then the river simply settled back down to its serenely flowing normal self as if nothing had happened. Buddy and I beamed for the entirety of while we were out there.

The crazy tides also produce steep slopes of mud on the banks of the Shubenacadie. Chris took us to a spot where we could slide down the mud into the river. After a few slides on our backs and bellies, we turned into mud monsters, completely caked from head to toe. It was an invigorating reminder of how good it is to feel like an eight-year-old once in awhile. I harkened back to riding on a GT Racer on the mountain. *How old would you be if you didn't know how old you are?*

The whole Tidal Bore experience was a first for both of us. Could we have done that anywhere else in Canada? In the world?

Back at the river's base camp, we got introduced to Washer Toss. A maritime classic backyard game where you toss metal washers into a cup that sits inside a wooden box. The cup had broken away from the box though, so it was virtually impossible to get the washer in. We made a house rule that if someone got a once-in-a-lifetime shot that stayed in the cup and the cup stayed in place, we would celebrate it like Nova Scotia's Sydney Crosby's golden goal and the game would be immediately over. No one got a Crosby.

After lengthy outdoor showers to try to rid ourselves of all the mud, and drive back to New Glasgow, Buddy and I were finally ready and raring to get back to biking. We got going quickly and headed out of town on Mountain Road.

"It's Nova Scotia, how mountain can it be?" I said.

But it turned out to be appropriately named. It was steep and it got our lungs working hard right away. Buddy heard my panting and halfway up took the opportunity to enlighten me that horses do not actually breathe by expanding and contracting their chest when they run or gallop.

"They don't breathe like us in that moment, all the air flow for them is naturally generated by the movement of their legs and diaphragm," he said.

I did not think this revelation was going to help me get up the hill.

"I think it has turned out to be you who knows a good deal of random, extremely odd pieces of information," I said, gasping and pumping my pedals.

Buddy agreed. I think he was proud of that. I think he figured it was one of his important roles as my adult son. Ahh, The Cycle of Life.

Our reward at the top was a panorama of the entire area. 200 degrees of deep green forested hills, contrasted against 160 degrees of striking bright blue ocean and an unencumbered view back towards the Northumberland Strait and Prince Edward Island.

As we continued towards Cape Breton, it became evident how our break from biking in Halifax and the Bay of Fundy had left Buddy extra energized. He was geared up for our riding that afternoon. I watched him cruise past me and surge ahead. It was challenging to keep pace, but I put my head down and pedalled as hard as I could—it was too early in our travels for the year to set a precedent of falling too far behind. I figured I had to keep Buddy at least thinking I could still come close to keeping up with him.

The Cycle Of Life

I gasped a sigh of relief when we finally did stop, in Antigonish, for groceries and to ask for directions to our campground.

While I grabbed supplies, Buddy found himself in a chit-chat with an older fellow from Cape Breton, with a heavy accent. He was enchanted by our coast-to-coast adventure, which he said made us rich. "Creatin' yer own energy is yer way to being *billonaires*," he said with a big grin.

We think we got the gist of what he was getting at. The encounter made us look forward to the quirkiness of Cape Breton ahead.

Buddy and I pitched our tent at the Oasis Campground. The owner Al put us right beside a handy shelter, complete with a fireplace, patio lanterns, and dartboard. We were the only tent in the campground that was otherwise full of motorhomes and trailers. A young neighbouring kid, Jackson from Canso, who was camping with his grandparents in a big trailer, came to chat with us while we got ourselves organized. He asked us where we were sleeping and when we pointed to our little two-person tent, he said, "Oh, that's sad." He had a different idea as to what camping was.

Buddy and I had a light breakfast in the morning while we packed up but made up for that and more when we got to Big Mamma's Triple S restaurant in Monastery. They weren't even open yet for the day, but Big Mamma herself gave us a warm welcome and took care of our appetites with two of her *regular* (gigantic) East Coast Donairs. Nova Scotians have an odd love affair with donairs. Halifax made claims to be the street food's birthplace, a twist on the gyro, and even made donairs the official food of their city in 2015. Big Mamma's *regular* version was so big we couldn't finish them. Even Buddy with his superhero eating capabilities was stuffed. It made it hard to fathom what Big Mamma's *large* $27 donairs must look like.

At Aulds Cove there is a 1.3-kilometre causeway across the Canso Strait that connects Cape Breton Island to the rest of

Nova Scotia. It is the deepest causeway in the world, with over 10 million tonnes of rock used to fill the 65 metres depths. Google Maps didn't like something about the causeway for bikes and repeatedly suggested a 2970 kilometre back-tracking route to the Gaspé Peninsula in Québec and then involving ferries to and from Newfoundland. A lot of people seem to follow Google Maps blindly these days. We decided to bike the 1.3 kilometres.

Our first stop on Cape Breton was at the Lockmaster's Pub in the Bras d'Or Lakes Inn in Saint Peters. It was very Cape Breton. Ice-cold Island Time Lager from Breton Brewing Co., live music of Cape Bretoner Duane Nardocchio, and a pot of fresh mussels.

Bras d'Or is an impressive, large estuary running through the middle of Cape Breton with both fresh and salt water supply. When we left the pub, we walked our bikes across a boat lock that connects Bras d'Or Lake to the ocean and then made our way into Battery Provincial Park where we secured one of the nicest tenting spots of our entire trip. The view from the opening of our tent was down to the deep blue waters of St. Peters Bay and the Jerome Point Lighthouse. The Atlantic Ocean stretched out to the south on the same longitude towards St. Lucia or Barbados. We noted that we were a good deal closer to Cuba than we were to Thunder Bay in Northern Ontario, let alone all the way back to the west coast of Canada. There was some sense as to why Nova Scotia became a secret spot for pirates to hide their treasure.

The lighthouse was one of 150 in Nova Scotia, the most lighthouses in any province. With all of its oceans and lakes, Canada has more shores to light up than any other country in the world. A whopping 750 lighthouses dot Canada's coastlines in total. Some of the navigational lights along the south shore of Cape Breton are the most famous and photographed in the country or anywhere in the world for that matter.

There was something about Saint Peters, I got a great vibe. Some places seem to have an ease and comfort about them, and Saint Peters was that for me. My feelings solidified further the next morning at the Cosy Corner restaurant when a couple at the next table, who had overheard about our biking adventure, anonymously bought our breakfast. We hadn't said a word to them, and they left before we knew what they had done or had a chance to thank them.

Our whole day of riding on Highway 4 followed the southern edge of Bras d'Or dotted with islands and a meandering shoreline. Looking out over the lake from a Nova Scotia Picnic Park spot, it made no wonder to me that Alexander Graham Bell fell in love with the area and built his summer home, Beinn Bhreagh (*beautiful mountain* in Scottish Gaelic), on a peninsula jutting out into the lake. As Bell said, "I have travelled around the globe. I have seen the Canadian and American Rockies, the Andes, the Alps and the Highlands of Scotland, but for simple beauty, Cape Breton outrival them all!"

I Google mapped on my phone to see just where Beinn Bhreagh was in relation to our biking. I don't think Bell could have imagined that I would have been able to do that when he changed the world and first invented the telephone.

It was a hot, sunny, humid day and I had constant sweat dripping down my nose. I watched the drops hit the road under me as I biked. Buddy and I were both running low on water by the time we rolled into the village of Big Pond. It was a Saturday, but there was a vehicle outside of the Volunteer Fire Hall so we pulled in to see if we could get a water refill. We were graciously welcomed by firefighter Paul, who was getting the place ready for a community open house. He happily filled up our bottles and gave us a tour of the hall to boot.

As we continued towards Sydney, we biked directly alongside the summer-greened runs of Ben Eoin Ski Area that rise over East Bay of Bras d'Or. Nova Scotia and PEI were the only provinces

I had not yet skied in, so I made a note for a hopeful return one day. Maybe I was already searching for any excuse to come back to enchanting Cape Breton.

"We should look for a good place to pull over for a bite to eat," Buddy had just finished saying when we found ourselves beside a roadside stand, Chippin' Dale's.

We had made good time through the day so decided we weren't in any rush. We parked our bikes by a picnic table in the shade of a big trembling aspen, ordered some of Dale's famous fried cod and Buddy spurred us into an extensive conversation on free choice. Not a back and forth easily captured in a few sentences. It became our in-depth topic du jour and continued while we got back on our bikes and headed down the highway. We kept on it for most of the afternoon. It made me reflect on how our biking chats had evolved over the course of all our years of biking. And also how they had *not* changed as we later diverged into the heavier topic of how the superheroes Deadpool and Wolverine were Canadian. Both conversations gave me dad smiles.

Our journey through Cape Breton felt like it went by too fast. Before I knew it, we were pedalling into Sydney. Fortunately, we had one more night and a half day to doodle around the former capital of Cape Breton Island before our ferry to Newfoundland was scheduled to depart. Sydney was the capital city up to 1820 when the island united with the rest of Nova Scotia. We biked along the waterfront where even Sydneyites proved they couldn't resist the temptations of getting on the long list of Canada's world's largest attractions. A 60-foot-tall fiddle, the world's largest, stands in the harbour where the ships come in.

We had sunglasses on all morning in Sydney. Including while we enjoyed an eggs benny poutine Sunday brunch overlooking the ocean from the roof top deck of the Governor's Pub & Eatery. The sun kept shining right up until we headed out for our 20-kilometre ride around the Y-shaped harbour to get to the Marine Atlantic ferry terminal. It was as if the skies had been waiting for us to get back on our bikes to lay down a flash flood. It came fast and hard. So fast it formed puddles across the entire road. For the first few I picked my feet up as I floated through the little lakes on my bike, but eventually I conceded to the reality that I could not avoid getting completely soaked. Our hope was that it would at least finally wash out the last of the silt from the Bay of Fundy that we were somehow still finding in our ears.

Nine provinces and 15 years earlier, Buddy and I rode up to our first ferry, in the west coast's Sidney on the opposite side of the country. That one had taken us from Vancouver Island to the mainland. We were now readying ourselves to take the last ferry of our journey, from east coast's Sydney, to overnight us into Newfoundland. How could we not be proud that we had biked 7000 kilometres between the two? When we got to the west coast ferry we had been ushered right on board. This time, however, we arrived to news at the terminal that operational issues were going to delay our much-anticipated ferry ride for five hours.

With unexpected time on our hands, we jumped back on our bikes to search out distractions in North Sydney. Being a Sunday, other than Tim Hortons, most places around the terminal were closed. But hospitable Kyle of the untypical basement bar The Cellar, saw the potential business of a bunch of idle ferry goers. We sat at the bar and Kyle told us a bit about growing up in the area while we sampled Breton ales. Other delayed Newfoundland bound passengers found his place too. The place filled up around us and Kyle got busy.

When Buddy and I returned to the terminal, there was a lot of car confusion being worked out by the ferry workers. The delayed departure time for our ferry had coincided with their other ferry's departure and resulted in the lanes getting all the vehicles mixed together. We watched as all the drivers were beckoned back to their vehicles to comically get it sorted just in time to hear that our ferry was going to be delayed another few hours.

This time Buddy and I decided to hang out at the terminal. We roamed around, did some journaling, and I decided to tell Buddy the last of my annual stories. Being the last year of our journey, I thought it apt that the story I had in mind for Buddy was about a biking adventure—one that likely had influence on my initial thoughts to do a cross-Canada trip with him. I felt it also maybe embodied an ethos to embrace adventure at all stages in life. Which for sure had been a key driving force behind how our *Cycle of Life* came to be. Afterall, *how old would you be if you didn't know how old you were?* The story also made me laugh. That is always something good to share. I figured especially on year fifteen of a one-on-one trip with my son.

How to Face a Gun-wielding Cuban Soldier When You're Turning 40

Again, great friends have a way of making everything in life better. I've had the good fortune of having some life-long friends that I consider close enough to call family. When I turned 40, three of those friends took me on a surprise birthday trip. One of the many out-of-the-ordinary adventures I shared with Wendell, Tor, and Mike—but this one was extraordinary.

I was put on an airplane to Toronto. I had no idea where I was going until I met up with those guys and the four of us boarded our next plane to Cuba. Wendell filled me in on the details—two nights in the Cuban capital of Havana, then a multi-day bike ride through the western portion of the island. Happy birthday to me!

No matter how far apart the four of us lived from each other or how long had passed since last getting together, we could always instinctively pick up as if we had never missed a single beat. A special feeling came over me when I was with those guys, equanimity, where everything was going to have a way of turning out right when we were all together. I looked at those three guys wearing corny fake moustaches on the plane, and I felt that was going to be the case again.

Considering our packed agenda, we talked about taking it easy on our first night. No one told Havana though. We had a delicious *arroz con pollo* dinner in Old Havana and were walking back to our rented apartment. We nonchalantly stopped at a restaurant to quickly use their washroom. The place was closing, but we were reluctantly directed to their facilities in the back near a picturesque little outdoor courtyard. There were overhanging balconies lining the square with green vines draping down all around. Tucked in the corner was a small stage with a piano. For the briefest of moments, I sat down to play a tune.

The owner came marching briskly towards the stage, I was sure to shoo us out. But he was all smiles. He asked me to play another song. I could have easily said 'no' but what a mistake that would have been. Out of nowhere, a guy with a guitar pulled up a chair beside me. He made us sound brilliant. The owner summoned a round of Cuba Libres and some cigars appeared. A girl came down from one of the overlooking balconies and started to sing—and wow, this girl could sing. Wendell, Mike, Tor, and the owner were all on the little stage too, singing away.

One song led to another, which led to another, which led to another. More people started to show up. One round of Cuba Libres led to another, and another. Cigars led to more cigars. You get the idea.

By sunrise, we had fallen in love with Cuba. Ahhh, Havana!

Only Mike and I got up before noon the next morning and decided to go for a walk along the Havana seawall. We hadn't made it far when two Cuban guys came running up to us, pointing enthusiastically to my old Alberta baseball jersey I was wearing. At first I thought the guy wanted to buy it. But it turned out he was an infielder for the Industriales baseball team (los Leone Azules – "the Blue Lions"). He was excited to talk baseball. He lived close by and wanted to show us his los Leone Azules jersey.

To put this in perspective, some of the best baseball players in the world have played in the Cuban league, and the Industriales were the New York Yankees of that league. It was like a crazy scenario where Derek Jeter saw a couple of hungover guys strolling around New York and joyfully invited them over to his place.

And that is how by one o'clock in the afternoon, Mike and I ended up in a little Havana bar playing the drinking game "Quarters" with a world class baseball player. It was immediately obvious that baseball was not the only thing our newfound Cuban pal was incredibly good at. Non-stop quarters were sunk and a host of new goofy rules got added to the sequence of the game. And that is how by three o'clock in the afternoon, Mike and I found ourselves standing on the bar, kissing our waitress on the cheek, and singing the first lines of the Cuban national anthem. And that is also how at four o'clock in the afternoon, Mike and I found ourselves giggling down the streets of Havana to meet Wendell and Tor for a night out at the Tropicana es Cuba Club. It was Havana after all.

The following day the four of us were off to Pinar del Rio and the start our multi-day bike trip. Our first night after a day of biking was in Puerto Esperanza, a small fishing village on the southwest coastline. Our hosts needed to split the four of us up to stay in two separate *casa particulares*, residences with permission from the Cuban government to run B&B style operations. Strict governing rules would not allow for all of us, even a group of four, to stay in the same *casa particulares*. Additionally, breakfasts were allowed to be part of the package, but dinners were a no-no. Despite this, many of the families offered dinners as an under the table way to make additional money. The four of us were enjoying a 'secret' fresh seafood fest at the place Mike and Tor were staying at, when word came that a communist watchdog was making rounds and about to drop in for a random check. Wendell and I were quickly ushered into a darkened side patio room and asked to hide behind a pony wall. They cleared plates and food. Tor and Mike were sitting at the table having a drink (allowed) when the inspector arrived. Wendell and I could hear the whole conversation from our crouched hiding spot (not allowed). As soon as the inspector departed, Wendell and I were rushed back to our own place through a backyard shortcut so that we would be there for the inspector. We arrived through the backdoor when he was coming through the front. It felt like we were Fred and Barney in *The Flintstones*, trying to be in two places at the same time.

  The next morning, after our dodge and shell game with the authorities in Puerto Esperanza, we biked further down the coast to a gorgeous National Park area on the Cayo Jutias peninsula, a visually stunning jut of land with white sandy beaches, crystal blue waters, palm trees, and a small, simple beach patio restaurant. We had heard rumours that they might have camping gear for rent, but our inquiries were mostly greeted with blank stares. However, one of the staff thought maybe he had seen a couple of old tents in the back of the restaurant's storage room. He scampered off to check and sure enough, he found two old tents that he even set up for us on the beach.

The chef grilled us some fish they had caught that afternoon and served it with rice and fresh steamed vegetables to us as he was, literally, walking on his way to a bus that had pulled up to take everyone home from their workday. Every single park employee packed up and jumped on the bus to leave. We were happy that we were told we could stay, thrilled to have our fresh made supper, surprised that we had tents, and shocked that everyone else was leaving.

We were sitting on a patio on a world class beach in a remote stretch of Cuba, our two tents on a sandbar, with what seemed to be no one around for as far as we could imagine. We happily dug into our dinners and Wendell pulled out a bottle of port and a bottle of rum that he had been carting around and saving for a moment such as this. We dealt out some playing cards for a game of Hearts with the sun setting over the Caribbean.

Then suddenly, a guy in army fatigues walked out of the dusk and plopped himself down at the table directly next to us on the patio. We hoped that he understood that we had been told it was okay for us to be there. We nodded to him. He didn't even acknowledge us. He took out two guns and proceeded to fervently clean them right on his table beside us, in plain view to make sure we could see. Moments later, his patrol partner showed up to join him and the two of them took turns holding their guns up and checking the sights. It wasn't clear to us if they were guarding the beach for people coming or people trying to leave Cuba. Nonetheless, if they had been thinking their actions were intimidating, they were correct.

After close to an hour, the two soldiers got up and stood over our table to watch us play cards, with their arms crossed and stern faces. I don't imagine the pressure at a World Series of Poker is any greater. I didn't want to lose a hand in case they

The Cycle Of Life

were deciding on who to test their newly cleaned guns. Mike attempted a greeting, in Spanish, but that fell flat.

And then – equanimity – I thought what the hell and did a magic card trick. It was the ice breaker we needed. A big smile appeared on the lead soldier's face.

"Magic Man," he said slowly as he patted me on the shoulder.

They pulled up chairs and Wendell offered them a drink. They weren't interested in the port, but they had big eyes for the rum. We played cards, drank rum, smoked big Cuban cigars, occasionally glanced at their ever-present guns, and had an unforgettable night.

The fact that Mike and I knew the first line of their national anthem helped us even further.

At one point, one of our soldier pals jumped up and ran off to chase a suspected defector or someone down the beach. The rest of us hadn't noticed anything, but he had taken the event seriously, with guns at his ready.

As our port and rum ran out, we got ready to head to our camping spots on the sandbar, realizing that we were becoming the only 'moving targets' for a couple of gun-toting, recently sauced-up, Cuban army guys. We didn't have time to dwell on it though as we were furiously distracted by swarms of night bugs as soon as we left the patio and went out on the beach. Our tents, which had been stuffed in the rear of the storage room for an undetermined length of time, sported tears and unzippable zippers. It was a good thing we were Canadians on a bike trip. We weren't packing guns, but we had Duct tape. By headlamp, we taped every possible opening or tear in the old tents and escaped inside for the night.

The rest of our trip remains forever rememberable. Biking through the Vinales mountain range with lush mysterious hills looking like they had been plucked out of a James Bond movie. Exploring the stalactite filled caves, Cueva de Santo Tomás. A bonus scuba dive on a pristine coral reef at Maria la Gorda. Happy Birthday to me indeed!

We spent our last night in Cuba at a hotel in the more touristy Veradero beach region. It seemed out of place after what we had experienced, and now appreciated, about Cuba. It impressed on us how sometimes you have to get off the beaten path to know you've really been somewhere. And when and if you find yourself there with life-long friends, sometimes it is magical, and you stumble onto a little equanimity.

I had a nostalgic glaze plastered on my face when I finished telling my fortieth birthday tale to Buddy. Having the joy of sharing stories with someone you care about is one thing, but having someone who cares enough about you to be interested in hearing those stories is quite another. It was perhaps a good thing as Buddy and I knew I was likely to keep spewing out stories long after our bicycle journey was over. Each year I had realized more and more about the value of connection through sharing stories, parent to child. Maybe some of my stories were quirky, but each, in their own way had something I felt worthwhile to pass on. I would encourage it to any parent. Why hold back?

There was something else to my stories, but for my own benefit. I was cherishing all the things that I was learning from Buddy on our trips, but I was also inspirited to be discovering how I was learning from (and about) myself, too. Revisiting my past was part of that. The process of telling my stories had been cathartic. It reaffirmed to me on a general level of how some of my happiest times correlated with simply being open to adventures. It renewed and stoked a passion within to do more of that, and maybe create chances for a little more equanimity too.

The Cycle Of Life

As the end of our 15-year journey came nearer—my stories, Buddy's reactions, our biking pace, our conversations, our side adventures—it all started to come together and underscore how long and rich a journey it had been. A lot had happened since we first set out on our bike adventure. Could I be a more lucky dad?

When it finally was time to leave the Sydney terminal and ride our bikes onto the MV Atlantic Vision for our cruise to Newfoundland, I felt more nostalgic twinges. It brought back fond memories of Buddy and I proudly taking our bikes onto the B.C. ferry, father and son, all those years ago on our first leg.

One element of this year's pre-trip planning paid off particularly well and resulted in us having one of the otherwise completely booked-out cabins. With our delayed boarding that pushed our travel late into the night, it was a bonus to have a good place to sleep and a chance to recuperate for our last days of biking. The gentle rocking from the waves quickly lulled us off to dreamland.

It was incredulous to think that one of the ferries between Nova Scotia and Newfoundland, the S.S. Caribou, had been torpedoed and sunk by a German U-boat in 1942. There were an unimaginable 136 casualties in the tragedy. Known as the Battle of the St. Lawrence, German U-Boats sank over 20 vessels in the Gulf of St. Lawrence until Canadian forces managed to get the upper hand and put an end to their activity. Ferrying over those same waters with Buddy hit home to how close the fighting in World War II was to North America. We have a lot of brave Canadians to thank for what we have.

In the morning, a stroll through the various decks of the boat emphasized how packed the vessel had been. The overflow from people trying to find places to sleep was everywhere. No ball pits I noticed though, unlike my Finnish voyage all those years ago.

Buddy and I took all the advantage we could of the on-board breakfast buffet before we arrived at Placentia Bay. He refilled his plate three times before he was ready to head down to the vehicle deck and load up our bikes.

As we rode off the ferry and entered the Rock, our tenth and final province of our coast-to-coast journey, I gleefully pointed out that we were closer to Rome than we were to Victoria and the dock where we started 15 years prior. It had been a long journey to get to Newfoundland. My emotions were building about entering the last stretches of our adventure, and I sensed Buddy's were too.

As the last of the ferry traffic slowly passed us and drove away, Buddy and I were left with the Cape Shore Highway almost all to ourselves. Mother nature must have known that this was our final year and wanted to reward us. The sun came out and on cue, the wind graciously swept up from behind to help us cruise along at over a 20 kilometres per hour clip. It was our fastest section of biking of the year.

If we thought the moose warnings all across the country were notable, the one we wheeled past that morning took it to a whole new level. It was billboard sized, displaying an illustration of a moose hitting a car and alerting all on-coming traffic that there had been 660 moose collisions over the past year. The number seemed unimaginable. It meant an average nearing two per day!

"I guess we better be extra careful of moose," I called out to Buddy. "That's a heck of a lot of moose hitting cars!"

"Maybe we should be extra careful of Newfoundland drivers," Buddy said. "That's a heck of a lot of drivers all willy nilly going about hitting moose!"

He had a good point.

We continued under cloudless blue skies past ponds, brooks, muskeg fields, rocky outcrops, and short, thickly-forested landscapes. Postcard after postcard views of wild, natural beauty greeted us around every turn in the road. Sunshine continued to be our friend all day long. That said, one valley we rode through was filled with such thick fog it served as a good hint as to how so many moose got hit.

The Cycle Of Life

Our biking joined back up with the Trans Canada a few kilometres south of Dildo, where Jimmy Kimmel famously became the mayor for awhile. St. John's was within a day of biking distance when we neared Gushue Pond Park where Buddy and I connected with family and friends who had flown to Newfoundland to help us celebrate getting to our final destination. We first met up with Pam and Hali, and then my dad David (Buddy's Grandfather), and my sister Cindy. My sister ended up having to rent a U-Haul van for her and our nearly 89-year old dad, because of Newfoundland's annual shortage of summer rental cars. Hugs and update stories followed. It seemed a bit surreal for them all to be there. It also underlined how close we were getting to our journey's end.

Our group had arranged to detour up the east coast together, and before Buddy and I completed our last day of biking. Not exactly sure why I homed in on it, but a few years prior I had circled the quaint little coastal town of Twillingate on my map. I had timed it all to line up perfectly with Buddy's actual birthday. I wanted to celebrate it in full Newfoundland style and Twillingate became the target. We pre-arranged to meet family friends Lucci and Banks there too, who had flown in from B.C. The concept of our adventure had been put in motion on Buddy's tenth birthday, and we got underway on his eleventh—being able to ring in this one, all these years later, on this the final year of our biking trips, on the edge of the Atlantic Ocean in a little Newfoundland fishing village, seemed about as suitable as it could get.

Our entourage gathered at the bright blue Captain's Pub and grabbed a long table across from the stage. ~~I stole~~ Lucci gave me a pair of shoes to replace my well-worn sandals. Buddy and I toasted his day with two blue-bottled Iceberg Lagers, touted as being brewed with *"25,000 year old iceberg water harvested from Newfoundland's awe-inspiring icebergs which offer some of the purest water on earth."* Sounded like a worthy birthday beer and we raised our glasses just like we had raised our water bottles each time we had crossed into a new province.

Our party had just finished singing happy birthday and tucking into a local partridge berry birthday pie (of course) for Buddy, when Jordan Harnum climbed on stage to get the place hopping.

"Lord Tunderin' Jeezuz, these two guys down there rode all the way here from the west coast!" exclaimed Jordan after his first song.

"The west coast of Canada! That's the Pacific Coast that is. And rode, not rowed, like with oars, which is more what you'd think from around here. We best be *Screeching* them in as honourary Newfoundlanders."

Jordan, a cheerfully proclaimed born and raised Newfoundlander, a *bayman* from New Harbour on Trinity Bay, proceeded to get our whole crew up as he guided us through the grand traditional *Screeching-in* ceremony that equally pokes fun at, and welcomes, 'come from away'er mainlanders' to the 'true east coast' of North America. Bright yellow sou'wester rain hats were plopped on our heads and a few music-making *ugly sticks*—old broom and mop handles adorned with beer caps, tin cans, a rubber boot as its base, and a sock head—were passed around. We were then faced by the bushy bearded Jordan, looking like a captain off the fishing boats, who playfully challenged us with his raspy query, "So you wanna become Newfoundlanders, do ya?"

He had coached us well to answer affirmatively, "Deed Oi is, mee-all cahk! An' lahng may-yer big jib-jrah."

Perhaps it was our questioning—if this was in fact English—that led Jordan to give us a much-needed loose translation, "Indeed my old friend, and may your sails always catch wind."

The salty way Newfoundlanders belt out the phrase makes it far more dramatic. I think Buddy's grampa thought he was saying something naughty.

As everyone took turns replying with the correct phrase to our ceremonial leader, who allowed for more than a few stumbles and slightly slurred words, the crowd in the room cheered with approval. When Buddy was presented his big ol' shot of Screech, the whole pub was especially supportive and the room echoed with the rattling of ugly sticks. Screech, by the by, being a potent Newfoundland concoction that came about long ago by locals who distilled it with a touch of molasses to loosely imitate Jamaican Rum.

I felt as if my grin could have reached from the Pacific to the Atlantic oceans to match our journey.

"Did they do okay?" Jordan yelled to the crowd.

"Yes b'y!" the room roared.

Bright spirited people filled the room. And I'm pretty sure they wanted to get back to their own drinking and more music. Jordan obliged and got the crowd up with a fun-loving set of songs about cod fishin', St. John's town, and sweet forgot-me-nots.

It was a fitting birthday benchmark for Buddy on our adventure.

Between sets, Jordan came over to our table to secretly invite us to an after-hours Newfoundland shed party. More east coast music and a few more Newfoundland cold beers to boot, tough to say no. It was hosted in a little studio with an open garage door that looked out on a harbour famous for iceberg sightings.

Later, when we got to the party, we walked in while Jordan and his good friend Nick Earle, a talented up and coming musician from St. John's, broke into a song Nick had just recorded weeks earlier named Born to Lose. The impromptu mini-jam session put a cap on a not-to-be-forgotten evening.

News travels fast in little coastal towns like Twillingate. At Annie's Harbour Restaurant for breakfast the following morning, several people stopped by to congratulate us on becoming honourary Newfoundlanders and to ask about what we thought of the Screech.

We had one more detour to take before we got back to our biking. We had been invited to get in on a boundless fresh cod fish fry and kitchen party on the northern edge of the Eastport Peninsula. Lucci's brother Joals and his partner Roon, welcomed us to their oceanside summer place in Burnside, a settlement that got its name after a devastating forest fire tore through the area in the early 20th century. The island-dotted rocky coastline was spectacular, and their place looked like a beautiful little ship that had been perfectly plunked on the shoreline. We were taken in like family and felt privileged to be part of the night's festivities.

After the feast, their neighbour, Scott, ran out to get his guitar and we all got back into music again. I'm not sure it is possible to have a get-together of any sort in Newfoundland without music to get your feet moving. We searched through kitchen drawers to find whatever we could to join in on the playing. Lucci on the salt and pepper shakers was particularly impressive. I went to bed humming *Home Is Wherever I'm With You* after a winsome duet by Scott and my daughter Hali. Rhythmic echoes of homemade ugly sticks drummed me off to slumberland.

With fully rested bike legs from our detour, Buddy and I got dropped off back near Gushue Pond Park so we could reconvene our biking. We were about to undertake our very last day of our coast-to-coast, cross-country trek.

I felt I had been holding myself mostly in check, but I underestimated how emotionally stirring our last day of riding would be. I think Buddy was feeling it too. I had imagined how proud I would be to complete our whole journey together but that was joined by a host of other mixed sentiments as our kilometres wound down. My feelings ranged from the joy of what we were accomplishing, to the sadness of it being our last day on our bikes, and everything in between.

Not surprisingly, Buddy and I still managed to get into some weighty conversations while we rode our final stretches. We talked about a bevy of emotions that had built for each of us over the prior few days, complicated with sharing the last moments of our journey with others. Our moments put an exclamation point for me on the bond Buddy and I had developed.

As we rolled past St. John's welcome signs, we found out that they are placed well outside the actual city, which is a teaser when you're on a bike. After shouting out when we saw the first of those signs, we still had quite a lot of riding to do before we reached the real city. It didn't bother me though as I wasn't in any major rush to finish.

Mike Rossiter and Danny Arsenault of CBC had expressed interest in meeting up with Buddy and me for our arrival into St. John's. They wanted to capture the end of our journey. One of the deep back-and-forths Buddy and I had that day was his uncomfortableness with sharing our moment so widely. I didn't see it the same way but could understand part of where he was coming from when I considered how the foundation of our adventure had always been based on our one-on-one time. After years in that mode, we had already taken in a lot of change in the days prior with friends and family joining us. Buddy felt that having media at our final stage was taking it a step too far. Right up to our last day on our 15-year, cross country journey, we were finding opportunities to gain deeper understandings about each other and what made each of us tick. It was another moment that contributed to how our adventure had become so meaningful.

We talked it through and together opted to finish off our Cycle of Life in a more low-key style. Our aim was to end our biking on a little inlet on the northside of St. John's, Quidi Vidi, as our final destination. The colourful little historic harbour, surrounded with dramatic hills that peered out on the Atlantic Ocean, seemed an idyllic spot for us to conclude our journey.

With sunshine warming our backs, Buddy and I slowly rode our last few kilometres toward Quidi Vidi. In a moment all to ourselves, we bumped fists as we biked through one last narrow street, lined with multi-coloured east coast houses. We coasted around our last corner of our journey and saw our spot, the brilliant yellow Quidi Vidi Village Artist Studios, sandwiched on both sides by boat ramps leading down to the sea.

Our family and friends were there waiting for us.

Buddy and I were quiet while we walked our bikes down the concrete boat launch, our tires softly thudding over each rill in the ramp. Old lobster traps were piled up all around us. We paused for a moment with our front wheels inches from the water, our eyes met, we bumped fists one last time and dipped our tires into the ocean. From the Pacific Ocean to the Atlantic Ocean, we had biked all the way across the most magnificent country, Canada.

"I'm officially retiring my bike," I immediately told Buddy, smiling.

I had nostalgically decided that I wasn't going to get back on it ever again, not even to ride around the harbour.

"I thought you might dump it in the ocean," Buddy said, as he smiled back.

A little less nostalgically, the thought had crossed my mind a few times, especially on some of our more demanding climbs, but I figured maybe I owed my old Motobecane a place on a wall somewhere.

Buddy and I didn't really say much else in the moment ... but after 15 years, 7131 kilometres, ten provinces, tiny bikes, ferry rides, scenic mountain passes, locked fences, deserts and desserts, bear chasings, bicycling snow-outs, ghost towns, fruit stands, abandoned railways, back-country trails, washed-out bridges, first girlfriends, prairie winds, five and half time zones, drunk inn keepers, bee stings, chocolate chip and no raisin cookies, Halloween costumes, big cities, graduations, Great Lakes, plumps of geese, roadside diners, snapping turtles, flat tires, frigid tent nights, sunburned arms and noses, tick bites, poutine feeds, Sasquatches and Loup-Garou, pandemics, plenty of pies, tidal bores, cod frys, Screech-ins, deep conversations, and a whole cycle of life full of love—what was there to say? We were a dad and his son finishing off a bike ride around their neighbourhood, albeit a large neighbourhood.

If there was a mantra that I've always thought worth striving for and always tried to espouse to my kids, it was *bloom where you're planted*. It was particularly gratifying for me to think how our Cycle of Life had been so in tune with that sentiment.

Buddy and I walked back up the ramp and pushed our bikes towards the bright green Quidi Vidi Brewing building on the other side of the inlet, where they brewed Iceberg Lager in those luminous blue bottles. There was a beer garden in the bay in full swing and I could hear Great Big Sea's *Ordinary Day* over their speakers. What could be better than having *just an ordinary day* with my son? It was extraordinary.

And I say way-hey-hey…

Year Fifteen Completed

Kms 6626 to 7131
Days 64 to 70

Charlottetown to Quidi Vidi

Fifteen Years Completed
Kms 0 to 7131 - Days 1 to 70
Victoria, BRITISH COLUMBIA to St. John's, NEWFOUNDLAND

A BRIEF FINAL NOTE

I will forever be glad I gave Buddy his eleventh birthday present. I also think it was one of the greatest gifts I could have ever given myself. I love my son. I love our time together. One-on-one time with a child is a remarkable, wonderful, worthwhile endeavour. I convey that story to anyone who will listen.

I have also been incredibly fortunate with a one-on-one adventure with my daughter, too. Each year since my daughter Hali turned eleven, the two of us have chosen a different place to visit, along with a local cause, and have ventured out to play music together, busking in the community for that chosen cause, Hali on the fiddle, me on the guitar. We originally dubbed our trips Playing for Change, championing the notion that small change can make a big difference. The two of us have a special bond from our experiences. Our efforts have snowballed over the years into its own special story, where we have raised funds and awareness for some amazing causes led by incredible people.

Our undertaking blossomed into the creation of the Tidbits of Change Foundation, a not-for-profit entity that encourages and helps young people, parents, and mentors to collaborate in the adventure of bringing their own passion projects or community building, charitable, and inspiring initiatives to fruition. Learn more at www.tidbitsofchange.org. Part of the proceeds from this book, *The Cycle of Life*, will help support the youth bursaries and education programs of the Foundation.

Tidbits of Change Foundation

Small change can make a big difference

Buddy and I are still doing a bike trip once a year, too. On the first anniversary of getting to Quidi Vidi and the Atlantic Ocean, Buddy arranged for us to pedal around Calgary on a two-day, ten-stop micro brewery tour. He even had a bike at the ready for me as my Motobecane remains retired. I got misty-eyed on our first stop when he pulled out two little notepads for each of us to jot down our comments and take notes on a project idea he had for us to work on. It made me feel like the luckiest dad all over again. I'm looking forward to next year already, as I wonder where he'll have us go. Cycle of Life.

Thank you for being Canadian

Wendell Zerb, Edmonton, Alberta, page vii
Wayne Gretzky, Brantford, Ontario, page ix
Pamela Anderson, Ladysmith, B.C., page 5
Jim Carrey, Newmarket, Ontario, page 6
Bruno Gerussi, Medicine Hat, Alberta, page 6
Robert Clothier, North Vancouver, B.C., page 6
Ryan Reynolds, Vancouver, B.C., page 13
Michael Bublé, Burnaby, B.C., page 13
Dave Thomas, St. Catherines, Ontario, page 14
Daniel Powter, Vernon, B.C., page 15
Bruce Greenwood, Rouyn-Noranda, Québec, page 22
Andrew McCollough, Lanark County, Ontario, page 23
Rocket Robin Hood, Toronto, Ontario, page 25
Captain Kirk, Montréal, Québec, page 27
David Suzuki, Vancouver, B.C., page 36
Lorne Greene, Ottawa, Ontario, page 40
Randy Bachman, Winnipeg, Manitoba, page 40
Fred Turner, Winnipeg, Manitoba, page 40
Terry Jacks, Winnipeg, Manitoba, page 41
Billy Van, Toronto, Ontario, page 43
Larry Walker, Maple Ridge, B.C., page 51
Jeff Francis, Vancouver, B.C., page 51
Steve Smith (Red Green), Toronto, Ontario, page 53
Wally Huser, Salmo, B.C., page 59
Sharon, Lois, & Bram, Toronto, Ontario, page 67
Fred Penner, Winnipeg, Manitoba, page 67
Leslie Feist, Amherst, Nova Scotia, page 67
Tom Cochrane, Lynn Lake, Manitoba, page 71
Felix Belczyk, Calgary, Alberta, page 74
Renate Belczyk, Castlegar, B.C. (via Germany), page 74
Ted Allsopp, Edmonton, Alberta, page 77
Rick Moranis, Toronto, Ontario, page 78
Donovan Bailey, Oakville, Ontario (via Jamaica), page 79
Jason Kwasny, Lethbridge, Alberta, page 80
Tom and Emmy Droog, Bow Island, Alberta (via Netherlands) page 86
Gordie Johnson, Winnipeg, Manitoba, page 87
Brent Butt, Tisdale, Saskatchewan, page 95
Arrogant Worms, Kingston, Ontario, page 95
Gainer the Gopher, Parkbeg, Saskatchewan, page 97
Ann Hui, Vancouver, B.C., page 103
Leslie Neilson, Regina, Saskatchewan, page 105
Mark McMorris, Regina, Saskatchewan, page 105
Jon Montgomery, Russell, Manitoba, page 111
Paul Henderson, Kincardine, Ontario, page 113
Bobby Clarke, Flin Flon, Manitoba, page 115
Gord Downie, Amherstview, Ontario, page 120
Bobby Hull, Point Anne, Ontario, page 121
Cindy Klassen, Winnipeg, Manitoba, page 124
Mike Reno, New Westminster, B.C., page 128
Mike Myers, Scarborough, Ontario, page 129, page 165
Barenaked Ladies, Scarborough, Ontario, page 135
Princess Green Mantle, Kaministiquia River, page 137
Ryan Gosling, London, Ontario, page 139
Terry Fox, Winnipeg, Manitoba, page 143
Corey Hart, Montréal, Québec. page 145
Michael J. Fox, Edmonton, Alberta, page 146
Winnie-the-Pooh, White River, Ontario, page 148

Ken Daneyko, Windsor, Ontario, page 152
Pat Verbeek, Sarnia, Ontario, page 154
Group of Seven, page 156
Paul Shaffer, Thunder Bay, Ontario, page 159
Connor McDavid, Richmond Hill, Ontario, page 163
Jake Muzzin, Woodstock, Ontario, page 163
Mishebeshu, The Great Lakes, page 165
Bobby Orr, Parry Sound, Ontario, page 167
Gus Agioritus, Edmonton, Alberta (via Greece), page 167
April Wine, Halifax, Nova Scotia, page 169
Giles Blunt, Windsor, Ontario, page 175
Marc Garneau, Québec City, Québec, page 179
Dan Aykroyd, Ottawa, Ontario, page 179
Hayden Christensen, Vancouver, B.C., page 180
Five Man Electrical Band, Ottawa, Ontario, page 181
Mike Lake, New Westminster, B.C., page 181
Margaret Webb, Barrie, Ontario, page 181
Fernand Lachance, Warwick, Québec, page 184
Rick Mercer, St. John's, Newfoundland, page 184
Jean Crétien, Shawinigan, Québec, page 185
Alwyn Morris, Kahnawake, page 187
John Humphrey, Hampton, New Brunswick, page 188
William Shatner, Montréal, Québec, page 188
Trivial Pursuit, Montréal, Québec, page 188
Leonard Cohen, Montréal, Québec, page 189
Daniel Lavallée, Montréal, Québec, page 189
Oscar Peterson, Montréal, Québec, page 189
Steve Podborski, Toronto, Ontario, page 190
Ken Read, Calgary, Alberta, page 190
Dave Irwin, Thunder Bay, Ontario, page 190
Todd Brooker, Waterloo, Ontario, page 190

Rob Boyd, Vernon, B.C., page 190
54-40, Tswassen, B.C., page 191
Jean Drapeau, Montréal, Québec, page 193
Gilles Villeneuve, Saint-Jean-sur-Richelieu, Québec, page 193
Flora Marie-Lily White, Contrecœur, Québec, page 194
Louise Penny, Toronto, Ontario, page 196
Pierre Trudeau, Montréal, Québec, page 197
Guy Laliberté, Québec City, Québec, page 199
Gilles Ste-Croix, La Sarre, Québec, page 199
Arcade Fire, Montréal, Québec, page 201
Jean-Michel Blais, Montréal, Québec, page 207
Bourgault Brothers, Saint-Jean-Port-Joli, Québec, page 209
Andrew Bonar Law, Rexton, New Brunswick, page 214
Allison and Clare McCain, Florenceville, New Brunswick, page 223
Alden Nowlan, Stanley, Nova Scotia, page 223
Grace Lockhart, Saint John, New Brunswick, page 225
Lucy Maud Montgomery, New London, PEI, page 229
John A. Macdonald, Kingston, Ontario (via Scotland) page 231
Daniel McGinnis, Oak Island, Nova Scotia, page 234
Sydney Crosby, Cole Harbour, Nova Scotia, page 237
Duane Nardocchio, Sydney, Nova Scotia, page 240
Alexander Graham Bell, Cape Breton (via Scotland), page 241
Deadpool, Regina, Saskatchewan, page 242
Wolverine, Cold Lake, Alberta, page 242
Jordan Harnum, New Harbour, Newfoundland, page 254
Nick Earle, St. John's, Newfoundland, page 256
Mike Rossiter, Danny Arsenault, St. John's, Newfoundland, page 257
Great Big Sea, St. John's, Newfoundland, page 260

ABOUT THE AUTHOR

Greg Scott is a dad. He is thrilled to have cycled with his son all the way across Canada over fifteen years. He is an author, speaker, lecturer, and entrepreneur with a multifarious background in business development, restaurants, the ski industry, board games, and tiny houses. He has lived and worked on projects in beautiful places in Europe and North America, but he and his wife proudly call Western Canada home. Greg and his daughter co-founded the Tidbits of Change Foundation to encourage youths to take on passion projects in collaboration with a parent or mentor. While visiting schools in British Columbia to introduce students to the bursaries available through the Foundation, he and his daughter became the first to ski all the lift-serviced ski areas in the province in one single winter – 44 ski areas in 44 dayswinter - 44 ski areas in 44 days - @tidbitsofchange. Fifty percent of the time Greg throws rock in Rock, Paper, Scissors. He has been told that he sometimes wears dad socks on bike trips.

More at thecycleoflife.ca